PRAISE FOR STEPHEN GRACE

Under Cottonwoods

"In his first novel, Grace writes with a lyrical power, celebrating the healing power of the human spirit set free in the wilds."
Los Angeles Times

"A humane and hopeful story that will engage both nature lovers and champions of the human spirit."
Wally Lamb
Bestselling author of *She's Come Undone*
and *I Know This Much Is True*

"Inspiring without being maudlin, exciting but not contrived…a must read. It has my highest recommendation."
Midwest Book Review

It Happened in Denver

"By the evidence of this excitement-packed narrative history, Denver has been simply bubbling with major events."
Barnes & Noble

"You'll never see the city in the same way again."
"Between the Covers"
Tattered Cover Book Blog

Shanghai: Life, Love and Infrastructure in China's City of the Future

"Stephen Grace has a love affair with Shanghai, and he portrays it wonderfully."
Mel Gurtov
Editor-in-Chief, *Asian Perspective*

"Grace understands his place in the story and his are the novelist's sensibilities; his observations and scenes are in turn horrifying and hilarious…."
Jon Billman
Author of *When We Were Wolves*

PRAISE FOR *GROW*

"*Grow* is gorgeously written and a true pleasure to read. Grace is a lovely writer and here he puts his mastery to the highest purpose—changing the way we live so that we can take care of our planet."

Helen Thorpe
Author, *Just Like Us* and *Soldier Girls*

"If you are a person who eats food, this is a book you need to read. Stephen Grace has written with passion, wisdom, and—yes—grace about the backstory of the food on our plates, and about the people in Denver who are working to bring that story closer to home. Ultimately, *Grow* opens the possibility that simply asking about the story of our food can be a catalyst for saving us from ourselves, and that's a story we need to hear."

Nick Arvin
Author, *The Reconstructionist*
and *Articles of War*

"A captivating and original book. While it offers a serious look into the urban food movement, the stories here are funny, inspiring, and, above all else, offer unique and doable solutions. *Grow* is the rarest of gems: Grace gives us the stories of those on the ground and in the dirt and thereby gives us all hope and know-how. I absolutely loved this book. A must-read—for everyone."

Laura Pritchett
Editor of *Going Green*
Author, *Stars Go Blue*

"This book is full of gems mined from the...wait a minute: Can a book about urban farming have gems and mining? Oh, yes, and Stephen Grace shows us how. One of my favorites is, 'Beware the everyday brutality of the averted gaze,' from the folks at SAME Café, where diners pay what they can afford. This book is the opposite of an averted gaze. It is a highly engaged and engaging conversation, a compassionate conversation, with the foragers, restaurateurs, vintners, waste farmers and community gardeners who are building the soil of a restorative economy."

Woody Tasch
Founder and Chairman of Slow Money

"Years from now, people will read this book by Stephen Grace and think, 'That's how we did it! That's how people in cities figured out how to feed themselves instead of relying on food trucked in from thousands of miles away!' In *Grow: Stories from the Urban Food Movement*, Grace introduces us to the intrepid visionaries in Denver who are wielding the nuts and bolts of this transition. His book shows the obstacles, certainly, but also the hope that drives this movement, as well as suggesting ways the reader can participate."

Kristin Ohlson
Author, *The Soil Will Save Us*

"In *Grow*, Stephen Grace serves up generous helpings of nutrient-dense stories of farmers and farming in the gritty urban tangle of a sprawling metropolis, revealing a hidden revolution with the power to quietly heal lives and communities. Drawn by a common urge to rebuild food security and sovereignty, the unsung pioneers that Grace discovers arise from broken communities to forge a regenerative local economy that is steadily and unexpectedly transforming fractured landscapes. The book emerged from Grace's attempt to find the bounty available in his own backyard ('so many tasty foods, so many fascinating people'). As writing it did for the author, reading *Grow* fires our imagination, inspires hope, and compels us to join the local food revolution and experience the joys of 'living deeply' in our cities."

Michael Brownlee
Publisher, *Local Food Shift* magazine

GROW
Stories from the Urban Food Movement

Stephen Grace

Bangtail
Press

Published in the United States by

Bangtail Press
P. O. Box 11262
Bozeman, MT 59719
www.bangtailpress.com

BP

*This book is dedicated to everyone who is
strengthening the soil and rebuilding the world
one meal at a time.*

No species but man, so far as is known, unaided by circumstance or climatic change, has ever extinguished another, and certainly no species has ever devoured itself, an accomplishment of which man appears quite capable.

PETER MATTHIESSEN
Wildlife in America

Ask not what you can do for your country. Ask what's for lunch.

ORSON WELLES

Contents

Chapter One
Saffron for Laughing

Aron navigated Big Bertha across the intersecting streets and through the alleyways of downtown Denver—a moment's inattention and the repurposed garbage truck could knock down a streetlight, crumple a car, or pancake a pedestrian. I worked as Aron's wingman. My job was to push bins into the mechanical embrace of the truck's hydraulic arms, which lifted the bins above the truck and emptied compostable waste into its cavernous maw. Relying on my rusty rock-climbing skills, I scaled Big Bertha's sides to gain its summit. Once atop the truck, I used a power hose to scour out the inside of the bins.

"Careful on that metal ladder," Aron yelled to me as I climbed. "It gets slippery when your hands and feet are wet. And really get those bins clean, bro. Don't make me come up there and do it myself!"

As Aron stepped down from the truck's cab onto the street, I aimed the water cannon at him; he fled from the spray, taking cover behind a dumpster.

After I finished blasting the bins, I waved flies away from my face and tried to ignore the stench wafting from several tons of rancid meat and rotting produce. I took a moment to check out the view from the top of Big Bertha. The Rockies shimmered behind Union Station. The streets of Lower Downtown Denver, or LoDo, were crowded with people checking their smartphones, scurrying between handsome brick buildings, and packing themselves into trendy cafés. Putrid food collected from the alleyways behind those cafés was dripping down my coveralls.

I had signed on as a wingman with Waste Farmers, a sustainable agriculture start-up, partly because I needed a job and wasn't qualified to do anything except write books. But I also wanted to figure out why my friends who'd purchased Big Bertha were determined to be part of a revolution that would change the way we eat, and perhaps more important, change the way we live. This made no sense to me, but after my friend Mostafa died, nothing else seemed to make any sense either. I decided to go along for the ride.

"What's Mostafa's last name?" my wife asked me as she walked inside from the garden and picked up the local newspaper. The panic in her voice when she said Mostafa's name made me fear the worst: Amy had learned to keep herself steady when dealing with trauma in an emergency room. Rarely had I seen her so rattled. As the newspaper slipped from her hands, I thought, *Oh shit, Mostafa finally wrecked his SUV.*

Mostafa, an engineer from Iran living in Colorado, was one of the worst drivers I have ever had the misfortune to accompany. "I don't have to stop, right?" he had once said to me as he accelerated toward a flashing red light, a car on a cross-street speeding toward a flashing yellow light. Shrieking brakes, screeching rubber: A road trip without a near-death experience meant Mostafa wasn't behind the wheel.

But at the end of those harrowing drives awaited some of

the best meals of my life—as memorable for the stories Mostafa told me as for the food he shared. During one dinner, as he served me soup made from a roasted white pumpkin, he told me that Iraqi forces had once bombed a pumpkin patch in Iran near where he'd grown up. War planes had dropped bombs on the pale and furrowed gourds, mistaking them for the heads of turbaned mullahs praying in a field. "The Iraq government said it had made a great victory and killed many mullahs. But the Iranian farmer who owned the field was so confused." Mostafa's big belly wobbled as he laughed. "The farmer, he wanted to know who would pay for his pumpkins!"

On our first of many camping trips, Mostafa breathed deeply, inhaling the scent of the pine forest. "I'm addicted to that smell," he said. Then he surprised me by pouring tea from a porcelain pot that he had wrapped in a towel to withstand the bumpy drive in his SUV. He handed me a cup of tea he'd prepared with a blend of cardamom and honey and spiked with scarlet threads of saffron. "In Iran we say that if you have too much saffron you will not stop laughing."

"Is saffron like a drug?" I asked as I inhaled the peppery cardamom rising from my cup. "Like an antidepressant?"

"If you are sad and you have a little saffron tea, you will feel better. But if you drink too much, there will be so much laughing." Mostafa unpacked a picnic basket, and after we built a campfire, he proceeded to prepare a feast: shish kebabs with skewered cubes of steak flavored with Persian spices, chunks of pepper branded with char marks from the grill, sweetcorn roasted over red coals, wedges of cantaloupe for dessert. When I thought the meal was finished, he reached into the basket and produced a small block of Dubliner cheese. As he drizzled a slice with honey, he told me he'd bought the cheese after hearing me talk about how my wife and I had enjoyed traveling in Ireland. I was surprised that he remembered this detail, and I was grateful for his friendship as well as for the delicious meal.

Throughout most of my life I had gorged myself on storyless food. I had peeled back the foil from TV dinners, had collected bags of burgers from drive-thrus, had slapped gelatinous cold cuts on pale squares of bread. I had no more idea where my meals came from or what they meant than I could comprehend a sentence in Farsi, which, incidentally, I had been trying to learn by bumbling my way through language CDs. Mostafa and I had made plans for me to accompany him to Iran as soon as the political situation settled down (or we would figure out a way to sneak me in—*Argo* in reverse).

Mostafa explained that the Persian Empire had introduced to the world not just kebabs but ice cream. In the heat of summer, ancient Persians had dished up fruit concentrates cooled with snow carried down from mountaintops. These chilled treats, flavored with saffron, were served to kings. Mostafa told me we would harvest saffron from the crocuses that bloomed around his family's farm, which was watered by underground canals designed by Persian engineers more than three thousand years ago. This water sustained Mostafa's family's grapes, once used to make wine. "Now it is illegal in Iran to drink wine but I do it anyway when I go there. There are private gardens where we can drink wine and no one will bother us." While buzzed on Malbec one evening, Mostafa and I plotted our trip to Iran, where we would eat kebabs and ice cream flavored with rosewater, saffron, and according to a traditional Iranian recipe, meal ground from the roots of Old World orchids.

Through Mostafa's friendship I began to see food as a series of stories. The dream of traveling to his homeland to gather tales of Persian food culture gave me a reason to get out of bed when the middle-age blues made me want to pull the covers over my head. I was determined to help him get in better shape so we could hike together in the hills above his family's farm. His belly had grown so large it was starting to strain against his shirts. After living in the U.S. for fifteen years, he was falling victim to the American plague.

Sometimes when we hiked mountains together, Mostafa couldn't summit a peak. His face would turn pale while sweat beaded on his brow. The sound of his labored breathing unsettled me, but when I expressed my concern he'd wave me on. Later, after I returned from the summit and rejoined him, we would head back down the trail together. He'd stop and tip back his round and balding head, a fringe of black hair springing from the sides. He'd grin and say he was happy just to be in the mountains where he could smell the pines.

Mostafa had decided in 1996 to attend the University of Colorado in Boulder after completing a degree in Iran. He wanted to enroll in a graduate program but had no idea what school he should choose. While flipping through university catalogs, he came across one that featured a photo of mountains skirted by pine forests.

"That's why you decided to study in Boulder?"

"If I couldn't find a place to live in the city I thought I could camp in the mountains with the trees. They smell so good!"

Though Mostafa and I spent many hours sharing tea and food, rarely did he reveal personal information other than details from his family's farm, where dates dropped from the trees, sweet water flowed from the wells, and saffron crocuses bloomed. But sometimes he'd let a shadowy story slip.

One afternoon in late May, while resting on the summit of a small mountain after Mostafa had managed to wheeze his way to the top, I opened a bag of figs and offered him a handful, but he waved them away. As I bit into their chewy flesh, he warned me, "You must be very careful they were not grown in Iran." He explained that Iranian fig trees had been poisoned during the war between Iraq and Iran. His lips trembling, he told me he'd been drafted and had gone to the front lines, where Saddam Hussein had committed chemical warfare. He had watched people choke to death on poison gas. In the Islamic Revolution and the war with Iraq, more than a million of Mostafa's generation had been killed, including his brother.

"Why didn't you tell me any of this before?" I asked.

"I didn't want you to feel sad," he said. "You already seem so sad."

"Really?" I sat up straight and stared at him.

"I think you have enough problems and you don't need to hear bad things that happened to Mostafa. It is better to smell the pine trees."

My own problems, of course, instantly seemed minuscule, and I was embarrassed by my petty ennui. My life had been orders of magnitude easier than Mostafa's. When I managed to look past myself, I realized that beneath the surface of Mostafa's relentless cheer dwelled a vast pain. I couldn't imagine this magnanimous Iranian surrounded by the carnage of war. I closed the bag of figs and stashed them in my pack. We sat without speaking for several minutes, wind battering the boulders at our backs. To this day I can't chew a fig without remembering Mostafa and his stories.

IN THE EARLY SUMMER of 2011, when the bulk of winter snow had melted from the mountains, Mostafa and I hiked together several times each week to help him shed some weight. We made plans to climb Quandary Peak, a mountain that rises above fourteen thousand feet outside the town of Breckenridge. After I had to change my plans, Mostafa enlisted another friend to hike with him. Two days later, the local newspaper slipped from Amy's hands as she read his name, and I learned the awful news: he'd had a heart attack near the summit, and the emergency medical crew that had been helicoptered in couldn't save him.

I found some solace in knowing that in his final moments, on the high slopes of Quandary Peak, Mostafa had most likely seen the pine forests that spread across the mountain's lower flanks. Of course I wish I could drink one more cup of saffron tea with him, share one more meal. And I wish I could ask him why he wasn't honest with me about his health.

While reading the coroner's statement in the newspaper, I learned that Mostafa had a history of serious health problems. Then a mutual friend told me that Mostafa had regularly checked his blood sugar levels and had injected himself with insulin. He'd worked hard to hide his disease from me. Not once had I suspected he was diabetic. He'd kept it from me in the same way he'd hidden his dark history of war.

ARON ROSENTHAL, MY trash-truck-driving buddy, had had a rough reentry to the United States after leaving Guatemala. This was not entirely unexpected. The Peace Corps has a program in place to reacclimatize volunteers who, after spending two years surrounded by starving citizens, come back home to see Americans scarfing down supersized fries and triple cheeseburgers.

One afternoon when Aron and I were hanging around my condo reading the newspaper and listening to NPR, we gleaned the following three truths about our nation: The Centers for Disease Control and Prevention was predicting that, in the coming decades, as many as one-third of Americans would develop diabetes due to obesity; *Jackass 3D* was the number-one movie in America; and political commentators were declaring that, thanks in large part to Sarah Palin, anti-intellectualism had become a goal to which many Americans were aspiring. Later in the day, when Aron sat down with me to watch *Idiocracy* he wasn't laughing.

I decided that what ailed Aron could be cured by a good dose of Mostafa. When I brought the two men together for one of Mostafa's Iranian meals, I saw a smile form on Aron's face for the first time since he'd returned from Guatemala. Over the next few months Mostafa welcomed Aron into his home, sharing stories and meals, and he laced Aron's tea with saffron for laughing.

One evening, when Aron and I were walking home from Mostafa's apartment, Aron said, "When Mostafa tells stories about Iran I remember my Guatemalan neighbors patting tortillas in their homes. When I look at him, I remember the way the Mayan people smile when they give thanks for the corn that keeps their families alive. They worship the crop as the source of life. We put it in the processed food that kills people."

A few days after Aron and I learned of Mostafa's death, we decided to hike Quandary Peak in his memory. Rare for the high mountains of Colorado, there was no wind, and the weather forecast called for no chance of afternoon thunderstorms. A clean blue expanse of sky stretched to the edge of space. We climbed through pine forests toward the upper slopes. The summit, hidden behind a shoulder of the mountain, was near. We found the approximate place where Mostafa's large heart had given out, and in the Iranian tradition—according to his relatives' wishes—placed gladiolus blossoms at the site. We also scattered a few pinches of saffron across the rocky soil.

"Mostafa saved me," Aron said.

I asked him what he meant.

"A man can have the biggest mansion—he can have cars, money, whatever. But if he doesn't have loved ones to share a good meal and laughter with, then he's poor. Really poor. In the Peace Corps I was surrounded by so much poverty. But in Guatemala, when we killed a chicken or pig and feasted together—those were some of the best experiences of my life. I didn't have that kind of community after I came back to the U.S. And I was surrounded by so much false wealth. I totally fell apart. Mostafa helped me find that sense of community again by sharing his meals with me."

IN AUGUST OF 2011, A FEW weeks after Mostafa died, Aron maneuvered Big Bertha down a blocked alley behind City O' City Restaurant at 13th and Sherman. He leaned out of the cab to stare down the driver of a Mini Cooper, and said, "I'm going to need you to move your car *right now.*" Aron gave the man a scowl that made him immediately move his car. "No one ever argues with me," Aron explained. "I mean, think about it. A guy with a tattooed arm and a shaved head driving a trash truck? No one wants to get on the wrong side of a man they're pretty sure has done time in the state penitentiary." His forearm bore a tattoo of a French horn with a hand reaching out of it, the signature illustration of one of Aron's intellectual heroes, Eduardo Galeano, a Uruguayan-journalist-turned-Argentine-dissident. On our lunch break, Aron reread passages from *Open Veins of Latin America.* Then he wiped his grimy hands across his coveralls and lit a professorial pipe packed with tobacco.

During Aron's two-year stint in the Peace Corps in Guatemala, he had been tasked with increasing citizen participation in local government. But the people he'd worked with were citizens of a country that had been shoved by American diplomacy into a thirty-six-year-long civil war. "Most of the Guatemalans I worked with were on the edge of survival—one bad harvest and they'd starve. I didn't get very far explaining the principle of government transparency." But then he switched from assisting with a political decentralization plan to helping people heal the soil. After inheriting a worm box from another Peace Corps volunteer who was leaving the country, he began the work of spreading earthworms among the villagers. "Basically I went ag on them. I realized that the single most important resource in the world is healthy soil."

"The dirt under our feet is the most important resource? Seriously?"

As Aron maneuvered Big Bertha past a panel van and made a tight turn behind Chipotle, he delivered a quick "Worms 101" lesson. Earthworms eat organic matter and eliminate their waste in fertile castings, enriching the thin layer of living soil atop the sterile stone of our planet. Worm burrows form passageways through which oxygen, water, and roots move. And these industrious creatures mix organic material from the top of the soil down to its deepest layers—"ploughs of the earth," Charles Darwin called them. Darwin had studied earthworms with the same diligence he'd applied to his survey of finches in the Galapagos, and he wrote about earthworms with as much eloquence as when he'd made his case for natural selection as the driver of evolution.

"Worms are like hordes of little workers under our feet," Aron shouted over the pneumatic hiss of the truck's hydraulic arms. "If they stop turning dead plants and animals into compost, then we have a problem." According to Aron, the path to political stability begins with a stable food supply. And a stable food supply depends directly on the health of the soil.

As I climbed the ladder up the side of Big Bertha, Aron quoted soil scholar Dr. William Albrecht: "Food is fabricated soil fertility." When I reached the top of the truck, Aron yelled up, "Albrecht also says, 'It is food that must win the war and write the peace.'"

Aron explained that during his stay in Guatemala "democracy was done 'Chicago style.'" Corrupt politicians bought the vote by purchasing fertilizers from their cronies in petrochemical companies and distributing the product free to peasants so they could apply it to their fields to provide a quick fix of fertility. But the chemical-laced soil washed down steep hillsides peeled bare of plants, poisoning rivers and streams, sickening residents. "I helped farmers fight back with worms," Aron said. Red wiggler worms are known in Guatemala as *la coqueta roja*, meaning "the red flirt" because, according to Aron, "When you touch them, they shake their little moneymakers like they're flirting with you." Aron's red wigglers caught on across the highlands. Indigenous Mayan farmers started making their own vermicompost to feed the soil, which nourished the crops that fed their families.

At age thirty-five, Aron, a guy who'd been raised in a remote mining town in Arizona and had, as an adult, grown addicted to global affairs, came to the conclusion, while surrounded by the denuded hills of Guatemala, that to be a steward of the world's soil was as high a calling as he would ever find. "When my time in the Peace Corps ended, I left a country that needed a lot of help and returned to a country that needed even more help."

"We need more help than Guatemala?"

As Aron maneuvered Big Bertha through a labyrinth of side streets, he said, "Soil is like an inheritance that builds up over centuries. In America we're spending our soil inheritance in less than a single human lifetime. I've read that a hundred empires could rise and fall in the time it takes for a foot of fertile topsoil to form. And just—" Before he could complete that thought he cranked up the volume of Neil Young's "Like a Hurricane" and honked Big Bertha's horn.

"If you're going to drive a trash truck, you might as well have some fun."

I stopped laughing and started gagging after I opened the lid of a bin filled with particularly foul contents. Maggots writhed on heaps of decaying meat. I wrapped a bandana across my mouth, train-robber style, to filter the stench, and I tried not to stare at that rotting mass. Aron yelled over the rumble of the truck's engine, "You want some salad with that, bro? Our next stop usually has lettuce."

As I ungloved my hands and soaked them in sanitizer, I said, "Remind me how you talked me into working on a trash truck?"

"It's not a trash truck, amigo—it's a compost collection machine. All that ugliness we're gathering is going to make beautiful soil. And that soil is going to be used in urban farms to grow great food. And that food is going to change everything. You'll see. You just keep emptying those bins."

Three needs kept me showing up for the job: my need for a paycheck, my need to do something more constructive than lying in bed all day bummed out that Mostafa was dead, and my need to answer some questions. Why did an erudite Peace Corps volunteer choose to haul rotting leftovers through bumper-to-bumper traffic in downtown Denver? Is our food system really that broken? And what on earth is urban farming? Is it just a fashionable oxymoron? Or was Aron right? Was urban farming part of a movement that could change the way we eat and the way we interact with one other? Could it stop the plague of poor health that had killed Mostafa and was threatening so many other people?

Chapter 2
Farming Waste, Growing Soil

While working as Aron's wingman on Big Bertha, I learned some important lessons.

I learned to duck under low-hanging power lines when I climbed on top of the truck. Rumor has it you can touch power lines and nothing will happen—as long as you aren't touching anything else. Birds sit on them, right? Squirrels run across them. I was told that you can grab onto a power line and dangle from it with your feet kicking the air and you'll be fine. But if your feet touch something solid, you'll be barbecued by a bolt of electricity.

From Aron's soil lessons that he delivered as he drove, I learned that every atom in my body was born in the fiery core of an exploding star, and almost every one of those atoms had at some point passed through the gut of an earthworm.

I learned that the amount of perfectly edible food that Waste Farmers, the company that employed Aron and me, collected from alleyways could have fed a village in Guatemala—or at the very least could have supplied the homeless shelters in the surrounding streets with countless meals. When I took a look at a landfill piled with food, I started to get a sense of the staggering scale of our wastefulness. Don't think piles of unused food—think Great Sand Dunes National Park, think of entire landscapes made of things people could eat. Forty percent of food in the United States is thrown away and ends up rotting in landfills. This is not a fact that sits well with Aron, or with John-Paul Maxfield, the founder and CEO of Waste Farmers.

WEARING RUNNING SHOES AND coveralls, John-Paul paces the floor of his closet-sized office, ping-ponging between the walls. Unkempt hair escapes from beneath his ball cap, which sports the Waste Farmers signature pitchfork—an implement passed down to him from his forbearers. John-Paul's great-grandfather ran one of the largest sheep operations in the nation, his grandfather was nominated one of Wyoming's Agricultural Citizens of the Century, and some of John-Paul's uncles carried the farming legacy forward. "I've always been proud of my family's role in helping scale up production and drive down food prices," says John-Paul. "They were well-intentioned pioneers. They made food affordable for everyone. But I worry about the costs."

John-Paul explains that what began as a laudable dream to liberate humanity from hunger has turned into an escalating race. More chemicals and more machinery are used to force tapped-out topsoil to produce more crops, which fattens the profits of agribusiness corporations, allowing them to purchase more machinery and more chemicals to cultivate more food to feed more people. "It's like the Seinfeld joke about the racehorses," says John-Paul. "At the end of the race, they wonder why they had to run so fast just to get back to the place where they started."

John-Paul, his eyes bloodshot from lack of sleep and the constant stress of figuring out how to keep the company afloat, tells me that he launched Waste Farmers after losing his job at a private equity firm in 2008. He cashed out his IRA, traded his family's grocery-getter for a pickup and started collecting recyclables and compostable waste. His dream has always been to build Waste Farmers into a sustainable agriculture company so powerful that it disrupts the industrial food system. He's convinced we need to find a better way to feed ourselves.

"America is the most food-insecure country in the world," a farmer from Africa once told John-Paul. "If the truck doesn't make it over the hill, you have no food." At his village in Kenya, everyone had a garden and everyone knew how to grow food.

Is America food insecure? That's hard for me to understand given all the bloated waistlines and the supermarket shelves crammed full of edible substances. John-Paul points out that our cities only have enough food on hand to feed their populations for three days. He insists that the people who really need the help of NGOs are not the rural poor in faraway countries who subsist by farming. "The people who need the most help are Americans in suburbs and cities. They're only one interruption in the oil supply away from hunger." According to John-Paul, that's not going to change until the stranglehold that a few corporations have on our food supply is released and a decentralized system of locally produced food emerges.

Where will all that food come from if it isn't transported from far-flung places by ship, train, truck, and plane? John-Paul answers with one word: "Lawns."

Forty million acres of our nation are covered in lawns, making turf grass America's largest irrigated crop. Pushing mowers around in circles on Saturdays to farm the color green is a ritual John-Paul is desperate to stop. He wants people in cities to grow food instead of grass. John-Paul is convinced that the next great American lifestyle brand will help people exercise and interact with nature not by kayaking rivers and climbing cliffs in a distant wilderness but by planting and harvesting food around their homes. He envisions a day when a healthy gardening lifestyle will replace a stale gym culture. He explains that some ten thousand years ago agriculture separated us from natural processes. As we settled in communities based around farming, we stopped wandering the landscape hunting and gathering, and our lives began to be shaped by culture more than nature. John-Paul says, "Agriculture, ironically, can help us reconnect with nature. When we cultivate our gardens and work with the soil to grow our food, we also reconnect with a part of ourselves that's been neglected for too long. We were all farmers once." In this ever-crowded world, the way of the hunter-gatherer is gone forever for the vast majority of humanity, but the way of the farmer is an option open to us all, whether we live in the countryside or in a city.

When John-Paul launched Waste Farmers in 2008, he began by climbing into dumpsters so he could see what was being thrown away. When confronted by heaping piles of biomass that restaurants, schools, and supermarkets were discarding, he imagined this waste being broken down into its components and spread across gardens and fields, replenishing nutrients to help rebuild soil that could grow crops.

He started gathering putrid food, plant matter, even paper products—anything that could be put back into the soil instead of piled in landfills. He delivered the waste to a company that converted it into the black gold of compost. John-Paul explains that none of that biodegradable material should be rotting in landfills where it leaks methane gas into the atmosphere and leaches nitrates into groundwater; it should be turned into clean compost to nourish the earth. When organic matter is mixed back into the soil, it is transformed from reeking waste to a rich biological resource.

How did Waste Farmers scale up compost collection from a pickup truck to Big Bertha, and then pivot into producing soil products for farmers of the twenty-first century? Enter Matt Celesta.

MATT CELESTA IS CURRENTLY in the Year of the Bookworm. He has vowed to read one book a month for a year, a surprisingly modest goal for a guy who finds ways to weave mentions of Maslow's hierarchy of needs into casual conversation; a guy who uses words like *zeitgeist* when overseeing the soil operations at Waste Farmers; a guy who, while unbuckling the straps of his overalls at the end of a long day of driving trucks and moving pallets with forklifts, will let loose a sentence that goes something like this: "I'd rather see the world after it's been washed in salt than after it's been covered in sugar."

Matt has just finished working thirteen straight hours ankle-deep in soil inside a building filled with black dust. Delirious from fatigue, clad in grungy Carhartts and wearing a raccoon mask of dirt after taking off his goggles, he tugs on his shaggy goatee. Part of the Year of the Bookworm, along with forming a book club and reading and discussing one novel a month, is a vow to not trim his goatee, to let it grow so that his fingers can twirl it in meditative thought as he digests the endless pages of books.

Before the Year of the Bookworm, there were other themed years. During the Year of the Pirate, Matt didn't cut his hair for the entire twelve months; at the end of 365 hirsute days, he shaved his head and donated a plump bag of his locks to charity. He lived in his van, which he dubbed his "land vessel." He sucked a lot of lemons and limes, not because scurvy posed a danger but because it was part of being a pirate. He concocted his own grog recipe. He tried to pay for everything in coins.

Then the pirate became a shaman. Matt is a card-carrying member of Michael Harner's Core Shamanism, which he earned during a stint at the Esalen Institute in Big Sur. A class called "Shamanism" had some openings, so he decided to give that a try. He signed on as a work-scholar and cleaned the bathhouse in exchange for room, board, and tuition. "All of the classes at Esalen were experiential," notes Matt. If you want to be a shaman then you're going to have to go into trances; and to get yourself into trances, that's going to take beating on drums. "Basically, we beat on drums a lot."

After leaving Esalen as a certified shaman in search of a purpose, Matt came back home and reconnected with John-Paul. A few years earlier the two men had hiked the Colorado

Trail together, five hundred miles from Denver to Durango, to increase awareness about MS and raise money for a cure after one of their childhood friends was diagnosed with the disease. "John-Paul and I argued the entire time we were on the trail," Matt says. "But I was all about John-Paul's vision to build living soil. I was instantly hooked."

Matt had grown up surrounded by roots, stems, and leaves, and the plants of his childhood had left lasting impressions. He had kneeled next to his mother, a talented horticulturalist, to tamp seeds into the earth. Together they had watched shoots pushing through soil, and they had witnessed the wonder of crinkled leaves unrolling and smoothing themselves in the sun. When Matt finished high school, he traveled with his mom to university campuses to find the right fit. As soon as he saw the on-campus organic farm at UC Santa Cruz, he knew that's where he'd study. He eventually became caretaker of the campus farm and earned a bachelor's degree in sustainable agriculture.

So what drives a man with shamanic training to work for a company like Waste Farmers?

"Maggots, man—I fuckin' loved 'em back in the days when we were collecting compost. They reminded me that I was alive. It's like the Buddha, man. You gotta get outside the palace walls, gotta get away from everything that's easy and safe, and you gotta take a good hard look at the real world. That's how you get enlightened. Not by sitting your soft ass on the sofa."

Matt had earned a commercial driver's license in order to operate buses for a wilderness leadership school, so he was qualified to take the helm of Big Bertha. More important, his brain was wired to solve each piece of the compostable waste collection puzzle. His first challenge was to develop a system that made composting hygienic. Restaurant owners want to do the right thing—they want to compost. But they can't have breeding grounds for bacteria fouling their waste bins. How do you make composting clean and convenient on a commercial scale? The answer wasn't covered in Matt's coursework at

Santa Cruz. He was forced to figure it out for himself.

Matt found mechanics that could help him MacGyver Big Bertha with water tanks and a high-pressure water cannon to blast clean the composting bins. Then he moved on to new challenges. "I loved the complexity of the composting route," he says. The traffic patterns of the one-way streets, the maze of alleyways, the collection schedules: everything about it intrigued him. He mastered each challenge of putting this puzzle together, making sure each piece fit precisely in place. Purchasing, maintaining, and tricking out a $150,000 truck, organizing 120 man-hours of collection scheduling per week: he got all of it dialed in. But once he had come up with a solution to each problem and everything was running smoothly, he faced his biggest problem of all: boredom.

"Things were really stalled for me," says Matt. He explains that the adventure of creating a system to collect compostable biomass and divert it from landfills eventually degenerated into a dull routine—up at 5:00 a.m., drive to the office, inspect Big Bertha, fire her up, grit your teeth and power through the dawn, then drag your sorry ass through the rest of the day.

"I'm a goal-driven motherfucker," says Matt, explaining why one day he decided to take a very long break from Waste Farmers. "John-Paul and I were starting to mix soil, but that wasn't the focus of the company yet. I needed something else to fill the void." And so began the Year of the Monk (also sometimes referred to as the Year of the Ascetic). He shaved his head and face, and he tried to wear only blue clothes so he'd blend in with backgrounds and not stand out.

Before setting out on an around-the-world pilgrimage to immerse himself in the spiritual practices of four continents, Matt hired Aron, who'd just returned from his Peace Corps service in Guatemala. Aron took over the wheel of Big Bertha while Matt sought enlightenment.

Matt explains that while he was circling the planet, Aron was not only piloting Big Bertha, he was also helping John-Paul shift the company from compost collection to making products for urban pioneers to empower them to grow their own food. "When I got back to Colorado, I heard Waste Farmers had sold the collection route to another company and we were finally ready to help everyone be a farmer. I got excited. Really excited. We were going to help everyone grow food to harvest and eat—I was hooked all over again."

Matt pauses to reach into a sack and grab a handful of soil. "You can make honey taste a certain way by growing a certain plant near bees. With agriculture we can tell a story while we are eating and living. I want to tell the story of the beet I'm eating just like the hunter tells the story of the elk. I want my food to be sacred. We can't just live on bread alone—we need the celebration, too. The celebration gives us sustenance for our souls."

Soil trickles through Matt's fingers. He says, "Agriculture is intention applied to food. When you get into the garden, you interact with nature by working with it and making it work for you. So many people feel physically, mentally, and spiritually whole when they are working in the dirt. That's what Waste Farmers wanted to help people do. We started saying, 'What we walk on is what we stand for.'"

After returning from his spiritual pilgrimage, Matt had vowed to master the new challenge of crafting healthy soil. No small task: Seven billion microorganisms, as many as the number of people on the planet, can inhabit a single tablespoon of soil. Within this teeming zoo, microscopic creatures compete and collaborate, the waste of one organism is fuel for another, and energy cascades through complex systems. Soil scientists devote lifetimes to understanding the connections.

BACK IN THE EARLY DAYS of Waste Farmers, it was based in the gritty industrial center of Commerce City, a northern suburb of Denver. The company's headquarters was tucked between parking lots filled with giant trucks and guarded by chain-link fences. But it had what a real estate agent would call a "mountain view." Which would be accurate—except for leaving out the part about the oil refinery that rose up right in the middle of that postcard-worthy vista of the Rockies. "We like the view," Matt said one day, a pitchfork resting on his shoulder as he looked off into the distance. "It keeps things real. It reminds us why we do what we do."

Within view of the refinery, Matt established a laboratory of sorts in a wooden shed. Strange bubbling sounds escaped the windows and doors. Sunlight sliced through gaps in the walls, and the air smelled of feather meal and biochar dust. In this shed, Matt dabbled and dreamed, tweaking blends of fertile compost tea, which he brewed in a contraption rigged out of fish aquariums, pickle buckets, and spare plumbing parts wrapped in duct tape. Sometimes I'd find him talking on the phone with his horticultural mentor, his mother, asking her advice about a soil recipe. Sometimes I'd find him deep in thought as he studied fungi, algae, and worms.

Why such diligent study? Isn't all dirt pretty much the same? Not so, insist soil scientists, also known as pedologists. From *pedon*, the Greek word for soil, the pedosphere is the zone beneath our feet—the unseen realm where the planet's lithosphere, atmosphere, hydrosphere, and biosphere interact. Aron had made me aware of the multitudes of worms plowing the earth under my shoes; Matt was now focusing my attention on both the biological and structural diversity necessary to create good soil. Cuts in the earth reveal up to six distinct horizons ranging from a top layer of humus (decomposed organic matter) to unbroken bedrock down below. Soils vary in color, texture, and mineral content, and they are classified into twelve main types, with numberless variations shading across the orders.

Saying "dirt is dirt" to Matt would be like telling a sommelier that all wines taste alike. Soil connoisseurs discuss the crumb and tilth of soil samples as wine specialists speak of the acid and bouquet of vintages. And the features that make each wine unique are linked directly to the terroir that gives rise to the grapes. From *terre*, the French word for land, terroir is the sum of local characteristics, such as soil quality, that produce a particular wine. Matt was as focused as a vintner on crafting distinctive batches of dirt. He aimed to create the Bordeaux of potting soil, the Chianti of planting mix, the Champagne of soil conditioner.

One afternoon as I watched Matt don a pair of safety glasses and blend some mycelium and bone meal into a soil amendment that he had formulated for Colorado's dry climate, he told me, "It's all about biology. Life builds life." The life-forms that inhabit the soil food web include the simplest single-celled bacteria, fungi, and protozoa; the more complex nematodes and microarthropods; the earthworms, spiders, voles, and mice; the mycorrhizal fungi that colonize roots, forming a biological link between plants and the soil; and on and on. Matt said, "The fact is, *all* life is sacred. Soil shouldn't be sterilized to kill its biology. And plants shouldn't be drenched in synthetic fertilizers and forced to live in organized rows—that's not a good life."

While mixing his organic ingredients, Matt talked to me about the Faustian bargain at the heart of industrial agriculture. Monsanto's patented seeds are genetically modified to survive applications of Roundup, the company's weed killer and a major money maker. Farmers can saturate their fields with Monsanto's herbicide while corn and soybeans keep right on growing. Matt said, "But do you really think that's the end of the weeds?" Weeds have now mutated to become "Roundup Ready." Farmers are fighting back with stronger herbicides to combat the strengthened weeds, which will further evolve to resist the stronger herbicides. And so on. "The chemists and biotechnologists at Monsanto are engaged in an evolutionary arms race," said Matt. "Scientists in white lab coats can win battles, but nature wins the war. It's time to declare a truce. It's time to learn to live with nature instead of killing the soil with chemicals. I want to put an end to this war."

There's a war taking place among microbes in the soil—which is a good thing, Matt explained. "Soil is no utopia. It's more like Game of Thrones. Entire populations of microbes are constantly rising and falling. It's like human empires that dominate and then deteriorate—but within hours instead of centuries because microbial life mutates and adapts really fast. Through all this devastation and change in the soil, homeostasis emerges. That balance builds healthy soil. When we upset that balance by blasting soil with chemicals that kill the microbes, the protozoa, the springtails, the mites, the earthworms, then the soil stops functioning like a living system. It stops rebuilding itself. And when the soil stops growing, so do the plants nourished by the soil. And so do we."

Sir Albert Howard, a British agronomist who popularized organic farming in the 1940s, and inspired modern agricultural luminaries like Wendell Berry and Michael Pollan, was driven to treat "the whole problem of health in soil, plant, animal and man as one great subject." This is the subject with which Matt will never grow bored. He was a monk for a year but he'll remain a soil shaman for life.

"Soil is the stomach of the Earth," Matt told me. "It consumes and digests the dead, recycling the nutrients that life needs to survive. Without it, we have no chance for a future. Who should care about the health of the soil? Everyone who eats food, that's who."

WASTE FARMERS IS NOW located in Arvada, a twenty-minute drive from downtown Denver. That ramshackle shed in Commerce City has probably since been bulldozed into a pile of boards. Big Bertha has been passed on to another company. Matt, sporting a black leather vest, gives me a tour of the new facility, a sprawling operation that is part science, part factory floor, part just plain figuring-shit-out and making-stuff-up-as-they-go-along. Matt has repurposed greenhouse spaces in order to increase production of the company's line of soil products. Between putting out a fire here and fielding a few phone calls there, he squeezes in the time to take me on a tour.

Matt points out piles of compost and mounds of perlite and pumice, volcanic rocks with the airiness of Styrofoam that enhance the aeration and drainage of potting soil. He shows me stacked bricks of coco coir, the hairy fiber that covers the

husks of coconuts. Coir, a waste byproduct of commercial coconut production, rises in mountainous piles on the shores
of Sri Lanka. The coir takes the place of peat in potting soil
by improving structure and absorbing water, eliminating the
need to mine peat bogs, which are storehouses of biological
diversity and sequester vast amounts of carbon.

In a building as big as an airplane hangar, Matt mixes soil
ingredients together. Selecting components and then com-
bining them in the perfect proportions and with the correct
amount of aging to create stable and effective soil products
takes a lot of science and no small amount of art. Matt says,
"Some vintners swear that the wine they produce tastes like
strawberry because the grapes were grown in the same soil
where the berries grew. What's happening under our feet is so
intricate, so immense, we'll never really understand it. Soil is
the history of all past life and the source of all new life. It's like
the planet's over-soul. Soil is the unity of all life."

Matt stops talking to me for a few moments so he can shout
directions to workers on the production line. The soil products
that Waste Farmers sells as its Maxfield's brand are mixed and
bagged with machinery so complicated it could have been created by Rube Goldberg. Does nostalgia for the good old days of
turning soil by hand linger at Waste Farmers? Does Matt miss
cranking cylindrical drums of dirt in endless circles? Crafting
cheese or caramels by hand makes a certain amount of sense.
But soil is bulky and heavy, and to blend soil ingredients in a
hand-cranked tumbler seems not so much cleverly artisanal as
it does absurdly medieval. A mechanized production line can
be a magnificent thing. And each batch still receives obsessive
attention from Matt. He tests and tweaks just as he has always
done. He samples and inspects. Atop his workbench are bea-
kers and vials and tools for measuring pH levels. In a greenhouse next door, seedlings sprout from soil samples concocted
in the fertile laboratory of Matt's mind.

One of Matt's inventions is "Batch: 64," a growing medium used by the commercial cannabis industry. Before vot-
ers in Colorado passed Amendment 64 in 2012, legalizing

recreational marijuana use and ushering in a gold rush of cannabis commerce, John-Paul saw an opportunity to help the company grow. Waste Farmers formulated products specifically to retain water and nutrients, allowing cannabis growers to use less fertilizer and water. In the arid West, reducing water use is critically important.

But how does Waste Farmers move from selling bags of organic soil and environmentally responsible products for cannabis cultivation to helping advance a farming revolution? John-Paul argues that because our culture trains citizens to be consumers, selling bags of healthy soil is a small but necessary first step in empowering people to start growing their own food. One of the core values of Waste Farmers is "civil disobedience through self-reliance." John-Paul's hope is that urban pioneers will become so adept at making use of what they have on hand that they won't have to be sold bags of soil, or any other tools, in order to grow bounteous harvests in their backyards. But this post-consumer utopia of self-reliance is still off on the horizon. For the time being, Matt is mixing locally sourced ingredients, fine-tuning recipes, testing the tender roots of seedlings in each iteration of product he conceives.

Matt walks me through the ingredients he uses: compost and pine bark, biochar and rice hulls, organic fertilizer and fungi. These substances enrich the soil and improve the quality of our food, Matt explains. Nutrients in the soil, after dissolving in water, are taken up by the roots of plants and then enter us through the food we eat. From soil, the Earth's stomach, nutrients pass into our stomachs. In previous decades, fruits and vegetables were much richer in vitamins and minerals than the produce sold in supermarkets today. The culprit? Soil depletion. Industrial agriculture strips nutrients from the soil, sacrificing substances essential for our health—phosphorous, riboflavin, calcium, iron, vitamin C—for the higher yields that allow our population to increase. When we consume soil fertility without replenishing it, we put ourselves and every other species on the planet at risk.

I scoop some dark crumbs of potting soil into my cupped palms and lift them toward my nose. When I breathe the aroma in, I smell the life and death and life again that cycles through the ages, piling millimeter upon millimeter into the precious skin of our planet. Each nutrient absorbed by the plants we ingest and the animals we eat circulates through our blood to become the stuff of our heart and muscles and lungs, the substance of our bones. Food is fabricated soil fertility, and so are we. This is what Aron, John-Paul, and Matt had been telling me all along.

They were by no means the only soil stewards telling this story. Ian Davidson, the agronomy manager at Hāna Ranch in Maui, told me, "Right now we're living in the middle of the greatest story in the history of agriculture, and of humanity actually, which is the rediscovery and modernization of agricultural practices that regenerate soil health."

And this story was being told in Uganda, I learned. After working for several months with Waste Farmers, I took a page from Matt Celesta's book: I temporarily ditched my job to go questing in Africa, where I volunteered in a medical tent putting bandages on wounds in the Ugandan city of Kampala. Surrounded by crowds of starved children, I nearly gave in to despair. But at a farm on the outskirts of the city, I saw regeneration. At the end of a road with ruts so deep they threatened to snap truck axles, a man named Joshua walked among his tended crops, green hills rising in the distance and birds calling from the trees. With Joshua I stooped to pull weeds. We laid these plants on the ground so their decomposing bulk could become part of a mulch blanket to retain moisture, creating a healthy environment for organisms in the soil. Dead corn stalks also formed part of this blanket—a new technique in Uganda, where farmers in the past had burned their stalks, leaving bare ground vulnerable to erosion. While Joshua worked among his peppers and carrots, he spoke to me of farming in harmony with the earth. He said, "When we learn the language of soil and speak it with each other, we talk about what we have in common. All of us must eat. All of us must take care of the soil."

From Guatemala to Maui, from Uganda to Denver, citizens of the world were speaking this language of soil.

WHEN I RETURNED TO Colorado, I went back to work with Waste Farmers in a windowed room flooded with light, where I tested the fertility of the soil I helped mix. As plants threaded their roots through loam and tilted their leaves toward the light, I touched this new growth, testing the stiffness of the stems, the resilience of the leaves. After the death of Mostafa had unmoored me, the work of collecting compostable waste and creating healthy soil had anchored me with purpose. John-Paul, ever the trailblazer, was talking about getting out of the soil business and starting to manufacture foods made from amaranth and nutrition bars prepared from insect protein. The determination of Aron, Matt, and John-Paul to battle industrial agriculture by rolling up their sleeves and getting their hands dirty had planted a seed in me.

Back in the days when I was working as wingman, one afternoon I had climbed to the top of Big Bertha. After ducking past a power line, I dabbed some menthol rub under my nose to combat the stench of rotting food. Aron climbed up and joined me on top of the truck. As we looked out over the alleyways of LoDo, he said, "It wasn't long ago that Denver was a dusty little town supplying the gold mines, amigo. Denver was isolated on the plains—it was totally cut off from the nation's economy. But in the 1860s, some citizens who were looking to the future built a rail line to connect Denver to the transcontinental railroad. That link saved the city. The new pioneers are trying to save us from another kind of isolation. They're building a lifeline back to the soil."

And so began my search for pioneers who are improving the way we eat and educators who are teaching the next generation of farmers how to grow food in the city. I would collect their stories—not unlike how I had planned to gather tales of ancient foodways in Iran with Mostafa. After working as wingman on Big Bertha, I decided to do something that was really a stretch for me, something to get me completely out of my comfort zone. My next challenge: hip-hop.

Chapter 3
Going Green, Living Bling

etef Vita, who goes by "DJ Cavem" when performing hip-hop, pedaled his lowrider, blinged-out bicycle onto the stage at the Ellie Caulkins Opera House at the Denver Center for the Performing Arts. Sporting a brown fedora and a baggy t-shirt emblazoned with a world map, a braided silver chain dangling from his neck, Ietef (EE-teff) parked his bike and summoned the audience at this TEDxMileHigh youth event to rise up and wave their arms. This was not your average TED Talk. Nor was this your average hip-hop performance. Ietef began, "We have to remember to recycle, reduce, reuse—and remember to stay fresh and fly." He turned toward a blender on a table, grabbed handfuls of greens and wheatgrass, and proceeded to juice these veggies. Then the Denver Public Schools Honors Choir ran onto the stage and joined Ietef in singing his signature song "Wheatgrass." "You must cultivate the earth…You reap what you sow / You only eat what you grow." In the audience, hundreds of students from Denver Public Schools opened their palms and put their hands in the air as Ietef's rhymes about sustainability reverberated through the room.

When Ietef teaches kids about hip-hop history, he tells them that hip-hop stands for "higher inner peace, helping other people." And his lyrics, like these from his song "Let it Grow," walk the talk: "I see the god in you and me, that's what I aim for / So all my little OGs, just grow more / And if you freeze and save your seeds you can plant more."

For someone with a voice that filled the Ellie Caulkins Opera House, Ietef speaks with surprising softness when we meet at a coffee shop in Denver's Five Points neighborhood. I have to lean forward to listen as he tells me that he drifted into the gangster lifestyle like so many other young men in Five Points.

The posturing of his rap performances is absent as we find a table and sit down. He moves like a yogi, fluid and calm. "I realized I wanted my life to be about more than money, power, and respect," he tells me. "I wanted the true wealth of good health, you know what I'm sayin'." So he'd picked up a shovel instead of a gun and changed his status of OG (Original Gangster) to Organic Gardener.

"But so much rap music is about gang violence, right? Why are you rapping about brown rice and broccoli?"

Ietef rolls his eyes. "You gotta get educated, man."

Ietef gets me up to speed on hip-hop history, and I do some research after we talk. Hip-hop began in the South Bronx in the early 1970s. But hip-hop culture is rooted in influences that range from the music of James Brown to the speeches of Dr. Martin Luther King, Jr. Ethnomusicologists trace hip-hop all the way back to the dances, drums, and songs of West African storytellers. Rapper's Delight by the Sugarhill Gang, released in 1979, really got the party started. The innocence of those old-school lyrics is endearing when held up against the rawness of the rants of Tupac Shakur.

After hip-hop caught on, corporations got in on the act. Some rappers sold out and played the role of violent thugs because that's what Americans seemed to want to buy. Thus the multi-billion-dollar business of gangsta rap was born. But many rappers have maintained their independence from big labels that mint money by shilling the gangster lifestyle to suburban youth, and these independent hip-hop artists, such as KRS-One, have been spitting rhymes for decades about staying in school, staying healthy, valuing family and friends. KRS-One, a legendary MC and a chronicler of hip-hop history, explains that rap is what you do; but you live hip-hop, which is an attitude, a stance, a style. Under the umbrella of hip-hop culture is rap, along with DJing, graffiti writing, and b-boying (breaking or breakdancing—though don't ever call it breakdancing to someone who's down with hip-hop).

I've been schooled: Ice-T is no more representative of the hip-hop lifestyle than Rush Limbaugh is characteristic of American culture.

Ietef speaks with a rhythm that makes me think he might start rapping his answers to my questions. He tells me, "If you want kids to read your book, you gotta use some of that street art style, man." The cadence of his words is soothing, and his laughter puts me at ease. I'm clearly in over my head when it comes to hip-hop culture, but Ietef is a patient teacher, a generous guide. "I'll find you some graffiti artists, man. They can help you with your book." His hard stare softens into a smile. I appreciate his taking on the challenge of helping me be cool—as difficult as getting gang members into gardens.

Ietef tells me that one of the urban farms he started is connected to Denver's Prodigal Son Initiative, an anti-gang youth program in Northeast Park Hill founded by a guy who'd called the shots for the Park Hill Bloods. One day when Ietef was working in the garden, a young gang member approached him. He told Ietef that he'd seen someone helping himself to food. The garden was within the gang's territory, so the young man felt a sense of responsibility for watching over it. Ietef thanked the gang member for looking after the garden. Then he explained to the guy that it's not a problem for people to eat from the garden—that's what it's there for.

"I've learned to tap into that territoriality that's so important to young men in gangs, man. Their instinct to guard their area—you can turn that around, you know what I'm sayin'. That can be turned into pride in protecting their surroundings. Young people need an outlet." Ietef tilts toward me and stares me straight in the eye. This is clearly something he feels strongly about. He's been there. "They need to feel like they belong. They need to be a part of something. They need to have a role. You gotta channel their energy in constructive ways."

Ietef says he's gone to his gardens to water but found that the food had already been harvested. "It's hard, man," he says, laughing and sinking back into his chair. "It's hard to let all that beautiful produce go." But he likes that people are making use of the food. He hopes they come back to the garden to learn about planting, to help with the harvest. "I don't want their hunger to be shameful. I don't want them to feel like they have to sneak into the garden in the dark and steal." Ietef shakes his head. "That gang member who was watching the garden, man, he told me couldn't find a pepper anywhere in the 'hood."

Ietef led him into the garden and pulled a ripe pepper from a plant. He handed it to the young man: an offering from an organic grower to a gang member, a sign of life in a sterile land.

I'M SWILLING COFFEE BUT Ietef isn't drinking a thing. He sits low in his chair, speaking in a mellow voice. The public swagger of his hip-hop persona conceals a core of Zen-like calm. He says, "Young people in cities, man, they are stuck in a mindset to hustle or be hustled." Ietef has to shatter stereotypes on two fronts. Along with challenging mainstream culture's negative perceptions of hip-hop, he has to convince urban youth that farmers aren't poor and weak. Hip-hop is all about keeping it real, and what could be more real than growing the food that keeps us alive? But try telling that to a kid from the inner city.

Much of the knowledge that former generations of farmers accumulated has been lost, Ietef explains. Because of slavery's poisonous legacy, many African-American youth associate farming with being powerless and exploited. "I have to teach kids that people who earn their living from the land aren't peasants or slaves but are the ones who are really free."

Ietef has deep roots in agriculture and art. His great-grandfather was a sharecropper, and his grandfather, born on a plantation, is not only a master carpenter who builds Adirondack chairs from tree branches but also a sculptor with pieces in the Smithsonian. Ietef's mother, Ashara Ekundayo, a poet and serial social entrepreneur, helped develop a food justice movement in Denver and then in Oakland.

Ietef's father worked jobs like landscaping and playing an organ in church to supplement his income as a photographer and musician. He also put in hours at the Purina dog food plant, near where Ietef's family lived when he was growing up. Fumes from the plant contributed to Ietef's asthma, and there were few places in his neighborhood where he could find anything to eat other than greasy fast food and processed substances sealed in plastic. He shakes his head and says, "Man, the only fresh produce up in my 'hood was lemons sold in liquor stores." The Five Points area of Denver, once a cultural mecca, had become a food desert and a battleground for gangs.

From the 1930s until the 1950s, Five Points was known as the "Harlem of the West" for its predominantly African-American population and its burgeoning cultural scene. The musical venues of Five Points drew legendary performers such as Billie Holiday, Miles Davis, and Duke Ellington. The neighborhood's storied Rossonian Lounge now holds a prominent place in the history of American jazz. But beginning in the late 1950s, as residents moved out to the suburbs, Five Points suffered the same fate as so many other inner cities across America: urban decay.

Beverly Grant, who founded Mo' Betta Green farmers' market in Five Points where Ietef sometimes spits rhymes to help draw in the crowds, once told me that when she was growing up in nearby Park Hill she saw its downtown empty out and the grocery stores get boarded up. "It looked like a ghost town," she said.

Drugs and crime became scourges, and Five Points and surrounding neighborhoods were overrun with gangs, creating waves of violence that crested in the 1990s. Some of Ietef's friends were locked up in a youth penitentiary three blocks from his high school. Ietef tells me he was headed down that path. But his family's commitment to health and social justice helped him find his way through the cracks in the hard city streets. When he started sharing his enlightenment with others he adopted the MC handle "DJ Cavem," an acronym for "Communicating Awareness, Victoriously Educating the Masses."

Ietef wears a staggering number of hats, both literally and figuratively. I've seen him sporting fedoras, bowlers, and baseball caps that could only be described as seriously fly. He brings more style to bear in a single hat selection than I can muster in my entire wardrobe. On his business cards, he wears these hats: organic gardener, music producer, emcee, health and social awareness educator, festival creator, vegan chef, B-boy, midwife, Afro drummer, graffiti guru, hip-hop yogi, and award-winning activist.

Ietef and his wife, Neambe, who joins us in the coffee shop, created "The Produce Section," an environmental hip-hop album they recorded, and "Going Green, Living Bling," a curriculum they wrote. They created these materials for educators to use when trying to engage young people who roll their eyes at speeches about their carbon footprint, who don't think of hoes as something they use to dig with in a garden, who don't understand that cultivating greens can be about growing things to eat instead of smoke.

"So many kids don't have the slightest idea what a tree is," Neambe says, shaking her head. "They don't even know what is real." Neambe sports a distinctive Afro and wears traditional African dress. Like Ietef, she delivers her message with both street smarts and heart. She tells me that she and Ietef conduct tree-hugging workshops; they lead kids through parks where they are challenged to hug each tree that they see. She hopes that the young people she and Ietef teach will start to understand basic science principles like photosynthesis and will come to appreciate a tree—the shade and oxygen it provides, the structure of its roots.

When Neambe and Itetef teach at schools and lead summer workshops together, they bring along their two daughters so that the young audience can see the whole family. Ietef helped deliver both their children in natural births at home; this stirs conversation among curious kids. And Ietef's street cred at being born and raised in Five Points and having mad rhyming and b-boy skills makes teens more receptive to his message.

Ietef is confident and smooth. When he talks, kids listen. When he starts rapping, they move their feet to the beat. When he drops to the floor and busts out some dance moves, they nod their respect. When he breaks into a live cooking demonstration, he still has their attention. He definitely has my attention when he hands me headphones and cues up a couple of his tunes on his laptop. My appreciation of music in general is weak; my connection with rap was nonexistent until I heard Ietef's rhymes. Nature has cursed me with no sense of rhythm, and when I try to dance, my left foot has two left feet. But now I'm a full-fledged fan of DJ Cavem. I'm just hoping he doesn't try to teach me how to b-boy dance.

IETEF AND NEAMBE INFORM young people that they have tremendous power within themselves. "Everything around them in the city is designed to get them to buy into an unhealthy, unsustainable way of living," Neambe says, gesturing toward the window of the coffee shop and the streets outside. The surrounding neighborhoods are crowded with fast-food outlets. "But they can choose to ignore all that. They can become conscious consumers and conscious movers through the world." Neambe explains that we are taught to be the exact opposite, to simply consume whatever's put in front of us. "But we can be so much more," she says.

If this conversation about power and autonomy doesn't get a teenager's attention, some of them start to listen when they hear about the connection between food and health. Ietef says, "Man, I tell kids, 'Diabetes doesn't run in your family—the problem is, no one runs in your family.' They start laughing but it's not funny."

Neambe explains that so many of the youth they teach are surrounded by family members and neighbors who are sick with diabetes, heart disease, or cancer. Some of the most powerful economic interests in the nation want the residents of Five Points to put dangerous substances into their bodies. Neambe says, "When people in low-income neighborhoods with no access to real food start gardening, they stop being passive consumers." They begin to battle the scourge of diabetes—a condition from which industrial food corporations and pharmaceutical giants profit.

The real money's in sick people, comedian Bill Maher has tartly observed. Companies don't make money from healthy people; they can't profit from dead people. Keeping people sick enough so that they need medicine and constant healthcare is lucrative. Ietef and Neambe tell kids it doesn't have to be like that. "Food can be your medicine," is the mantra they share with young people in Five Points. McDonald's appropriates hip-hop to push Big Macs and fries; Ietef fights back by using hip-hop to make kale cool.

When kids learn of the damage that fast food and junk food sold in convenience stores are causing to themselves and their families, some stop laughing at Ietef's vegan diet and start listening to the lyrics of his songs. Neambe says, "When kids drink the fresh juice we make, some of them decide it tastes a lot better than the meals they'll be eating in hospitals if they keep eating junk food. And when they remember wheezing the last time they played outside, some of them start paying attention to what we're telling them about riding bikes and walking instead of driving. We try to teach them that everything is connected."

Not all of the kids get it, or care, of course. But enough of them do to keep Ietef and Neambe taking on the task of changing minds and lives in Five Points.

LIKE SO MANY OTHER American inner cities, Five Points is in a state of transition. Developers have descended on distressed properties in the neighborhood, and gentrification is underway. As run-down houses are renovated in Five Points and abandoned buildings are converted into upscale restaurants and shops selling kombucha and artisanal cheeses, the rents and taxes rise, forcing residents born and raised in the neighborhood to pack up and find more affordable housing.

Ietef and Neambe insist that the urban food movement isn't just about filling food deserts with fresh produce; it's about making healthful food affordable and accessible for people of all income levels. If families are pushed out of Five Points by urban homesteaders, they won't benefit from the trendy new corner market selling locally farmed tomatoes; they will consume chips and soda in another food desert where they are displaced. Neambe says, "True food justice begins with educating youth and empowering them to take charge of their health."

Ietef explains that once young people get the hang of urban farming, they can become financially self-sufficient doing something healthy and legal. He says, "They learn that growing food is like printing money."

To generate green jobs, Ietef and Neambe established two community gardens where kids can grow food to sell. Neambe explains that their second garden was funded by Urban Farming out of Detroit, an organization seeded with Motown money that has spread community gardens to distressed inner cities across the nation.

Ietef grins and says, "This one fifteen-year-old I mentored, man, he's in college now, and he started his own business tearing up lawns and turning them into gardens. That's real, man."

LATER IN THE DAY, AFTER Ietef and Neambe head off to another meeting, I set out on foot through Five Points. Young men with baseball caps slanting sideways lounge in the shadows on a stoop. I walk by the youth detention center down the block from where Ietef grew up, and I check out some bodegas. Ietef's right: they only stock plastic-wrapped food. The shelves are crammed with chips and candy, the refrigerators are stacked with soda. There's not an apple in sight. I buy a Snickers bar because I need some energy; I bite into the bar as I walk, sugar speeding through my blood. I swallow a few mouthfuls and then toss the bar in a trashcan. When I see a tree marooned on a small island of soil, I take a page out of Neambe's book and give that tree a hug. Then I jump on a bus and head to Ietef and Neambe's garden in the Northeast Park Hill neighborhood.

When I enter the growing space at 33rd and Elm, the rich aroma of dirt replaces the smell of hot asphalt. Sunflowers rise as high as the tree I hugged, and stalks of organic corn spear upward from the soil. Pepper plants pop with color. The air vibrates with bees, and butterflies dart among the blooms. A young man stands up straight and wipes his brow with the back of his hand. We exchange nods. Then he goes back to working the dirt with his hoe.

On my iPod I cue up "Let it Grow."

"I see the god in you and me, that's what I aim for / So all my little OGs, just grow more."

Chapter 4
The American Way

While listening to Ietef's rhymes, I thought that the worth of what he does—spreading love across a concrete wasteland, showing kids it's cool to carry a watering can—makes him one of the wealthiest people in Denver. Yet I kept wondering if anyone was making serious money growing food in the city.

I MEET UP WITH URBAN farming entrepreneur Nick Gruber at Sustainability Park, a block of more than two-and-a-half acres at 25th and Lawrence. The park's urban farms and green building demonstration site are surrounded by a mix of dilapidated row houses and gentrified dwellings in Denver's Five Points neighborhood, not far from where Ietef and Neambe do their work. Like Ietef, Nick wears a baseball cap, but the bill of Nick's cap is curved, and points forward instead of slanting to the side. Nick is as soft-spoken as Ietef. But in the uncluttered field of Sustainability Park, protected from the din of the city by this swath of open space, Nick's words are clear—and so is the tension in his voice when he speaks about the obstacles that block his path in his quest to grow produce on a commercial scale in the city.

As Nick gives me a tour of Sustainability Park, he explains that as part of a study called "Gardens for Growing Healthy Communities" he interviewed nearly nine hundred Denver residents. He tells me, "In all income levels and in all neighborhoods, most people were interested in growing and eating their own vegetables. But they were blocked by physical barriers like not having the space to build a garden, and mental barriers like not knowing how to grow plants."

Nick, along with one of his study partners on the interview project, James Hale, decided to get rid of those barriers. They launched a company called Produce Denver. A friend gave them $1,000; they bought a truck and tools and went to work scouting locations to grow food. In four neighborhoods they established gardens in people's backyards.

Nick takes off his hat and rubs his head. With his balding pate laid bare to the sun, he suddenly looks much older than a guy who talks about a study he did in college as if it were recent history. He runs his fingers down one of his long sideburns and sighs. "Produce Denver made $87 its first year. And that was without me and James paying ourselves a salary." Urban farming seems one of the few professions that pay worse than writing. As we walk among Nick's raised beds, I ask him why he didn't just start a nonprofit and try to find grant money.

He stops walking and looks into the distance, where the sky is tainted with a yellowish hue. "We founded Produce Denver as a for-profit company because we didn't want to wait for 501(c)(3) status. And we didn't want to overlap with all the nonprofits working on urban ag, sustainable ag, local food, food education, food justice. We wanted to do something, anything—we wanted to be part of the solution as fast as possible. And building a business based around neighborhood agriculture seemed like the best way to do it."

Nick found gigs moonlighting as a sous chef to make ends meet. He had a cool connection at Mercury Café, where he worked as a cook. He would harvest vegetables at Moondog Farms (one of Produce Denver's urban gardens). Then he'd walk over to Mercury Café and use the fresh produce in the meals he made. The lucky recipients of this arrangement would dine on greens, radishes, and other veggies that an hour earlier had been rooted in soil—produce that had been planted, tended, harvested, washed, and prepared for their plates by a single person.

Nick's partner, James, after a year with Produce Denver, began focusing most of his time on developing Sprout City Farms, a nonprofit that aims to put community farms on public land such as the property of Denver Public Schools. Nick continued to lead Produce Denver's edible landscaping and urban agriculture efforts. Nick paid himself a salary last year. He wants to make a living by growing food for local restaurants on underutilized land in the city and by building edible gardens for people. He tells me, "My goal is to figure out a way to not lose money farming in the city."

"That's about as low as a bar could be set."

Nick doesn't laugh. He explains in a tired voice that the limited amount of farmable land in cities, coupled with the high cost of labor, makes growing food profitably in an urban environment extremely difficult. He turns in a circle and gestures at this changing neighborhood, where trendy lofts rise from the ruins of crumbled brick buildings. "I don't know how long Produce Denver will be able to stay here. Sustainability Park will disappear when all this is developed."

"That doesn't sound very sustainable."

He nods without smiling.

As we walk through Nick's farm, I wonder if his raised garden beds are a serious means of feeding people or merely a hobby. A basketful of heirloom tomatoes gathered from an urban farm that may soon be bulldozed strikes me as a bit precious when held up against a mountain of corn harvested by a combine and processed into countless consumable substances sold in supermarkets across the country. "Why bother?" I wonder aloud as we trudge through the slush of the sun-warmed soil. The remains of a snowstorm are vanishing around our feet. "Can urban agriculture really make a difference?"

Nick puts his hat back on and reaches down to touch the soil. "It has to," he says. "It's about so much more than just the food."

WHEN STEVE JOBS LAUNCHED Apple he aspired to put a computer in every home. It seemed a pretty wacky idea at the time. Computers required enormous space and were only used by specialists. Urban agriculture entrepreneurs like Nick have the audacious dream of putting a farm in every yard.

Nick's dream is not without precedent, nor does it lack for contemporary examples. People I met in the urban food movement were quick to point out that when a Victory Garden campaign swept across America during World War II, up to 40 percent of the produce consumed in the United States was harvested from gardens in backyards, on rooftops, and in vacant lots. The nation's food supply was bolstered without using massive tracts of land for agricultural production, without consuming great quantities of fuel for transportation, and without the aid of synthetic fertilizers, pesticides, and herbicides. In short, citizens on the home front became de facto organic farmers, and much of the food consumed around America's tables was nutrient-rich produce grown in urban and suburban backyard gardens and in public parks.

European cities such as Paris and Berlin have been growing significant amounts of food within their urban confines for a century and a half. London, the city where the Industrial Revolution began, now stands at the leading edge of a revolution to move agriculture from the countryside to the city: In time for the 2012 Olympics, London established 2,012 new urban gardens. Detroit, known for its bankruptcy, has also been making headlines for its proliferation of farms. In the city that gave birth to car culture, a local food movement is rising from the rust.

And the entire nation of Cuba offers proof of concept. When the country's supplies of petrochemicals and crops were cut off because the Soviet Union collapsed and the United States imposed a strict trade embargo, from one end of the island to the other Cubans rallied to grow food locally and make their cities self-sufficient; urban organic gardens are now ubiquitous in Havana and other major cities in Cuba.

As Nick and I step from the cold Colorado air into the tropical heat of a greenhouse on the grounds of Sustainability Park, he explains that he's a huge fan of John Jeavons. For more than forty years, Jeavons, a California-based agricultural innovator, has been developing "biointensive" farming methods that produce a staggering amount of food in improbably small growing spaces. The crux of Jeavons's philosophy is a focus on building healthy soil. Nick explains that industrial agricultural practices have depleted topsoil by exposing it to wind and water erosion, and we've replaced the nitrogen and other nutrients we've exhausted by saturating the soil with chemicals. Jeavons insists that we should be replenishing soil biology each time we grow and harvest crops.

Jeavons teaches gardeners to grow the topsoil that nourishes plants by composting items raised in the garden. A plant that absorbs nutrients from the soil will release them back into the earth as the plant is broken down through composting. By feeding the soil a steady diet of compost, a sustainable system is created. More organic matter in the soil lessens the need for watering—a critical issue in the drought-prone West. With Jeavons's system, the victory garden movement meets modern soil science in a promising paradigm for the future, not just for America but for the planet: Jeavons's methods have been used to produce balanced diets on small plots of land in 143 countries and in virtually every type of environment in which food can grow.

Nick tells me, "The greatest danger to food security in the future is the loss of farming knowledge." From a plastic bin he grabs some radishes and rolls them around in his hands, inspecting them with the scrutiny of a jeweler studying gemstones. "Another challenge is that food will become more expensive as fossil fuels run out and the cost of oil rises. Produce transported from California and Mexico will go up in cost. Which isn't necessarily a bad thing. It's an opportunity."

"An opportunity?"

"It's a chance for people to learn how to grow their own food."

When he talks about teaching people to garden, the weariness that weighs down his voice lightens. "I like teaching people how to grow food for themselves," he says. "I like helping folks get started. It's amazing to see their progress." He hands me a few small red globes—the radishes are smooth and cool in my hands and smell cleanly of dirt.

Nick explains that after he puts newbies on the path of urban farming, they often charge ahead on their own. He goes to their houses and offers free consultation. He talks with them about wind and sunlight and the optimal location for their gardens. "Sometimes I get the job of building them an edible garden, sometimes I don't. But I like talking with people about that kind of stuff."

When youth affiliated with a local organization called GreenLeaf show up at Denver's Sustainability Park, Nick mentors them. "If I see a harlequin bug on the plants the kids are growing, I'll let them know it'll eat all of their cabbage. Then I'll help them find a way to deal with the problem without resorting to chemicals." Removing weeds that attract harlequin bugs is one potential solution. Another is planting wildflowers and herbs that attract parasitic wasps that prey on pests. "I talk with them about all the different options," Nick says.

He explains that when kids work in a garden, they learn about the natural world. Children who think all spiders are bad discover nocturnal spiders that hunt insects in the dark. They see a dragonfly's metallic blue body and its glinting wings as it chases mosquitoes. With the tips of sticks they nudge different species of beetles and learn that some of them benefit the plants they are growing. "They giggle when they hear that many kinds of bugs are their partners in farming," Nick says.

When he introduces kids to his beehives, their screams of fright turn to squeals of delight. They learn the difference between dangerous wasps and friendly honeybees that signal, in a dance, the direction and distance of pollen and nectar. Children whose notions of royalty have come from Disney movies hear stories of the queen and the worker bees that clean her and feed her and attend to her every need. They learn about the guard bees standing watch at the door, the drones that emerge from their cells to mate with the queen and then die, and the foragers who gather nectar to make the golden fluid that burns sweetly on their tongues. It is rare that a child learns these kinds of lessons in a classroom. In the gardens Nick tends, ecological education happens every day.

When Nick talks about teaching people how to garden, his hands, which have remained quiet while giving a grim litany of the all the hurdles he faces, mime digging the soil and pulling up carrots. "Most of the kids I work with don't know that beans come from a bush, not a can. They have no idea that a French fry begins as a potato in the ground." He once watched the eyes of a child grow large as she saw a potato being pried from the soil. No television program she ever sat through, no advertisement she ever saw, had prepared her to witness food being dug from the earth. As Nick talks about what children learn in gardens, his determination to keep building a business that earned $87 its first year starts to make sense to me.

Nick speaks of the education he does in gardens not in terms of teaching people new concepts so much as erasing preconceived notions. He explains that because we've been conditioned by supermarkets to expect produce to be perfectly formed and flawlessly colored, our sense of aesthetics is challenged by the sight of a purple potato or a crooked carrot. He once harvested a crop of carrots that were contorted due to the soil compaction. He used the crooked carrots as a teaching tool. "I let their bent shape tell a story about the soil. When people work in a garden, they see what plants look like in nature instead of what they look like at Safeway. And they learn that food tastes different when it's freshly harvested." He feeds organic cherry tomatoes and sungolds he picks from the vine to kids. "They tell me the tomatoes are sweet as candy."

I came to Sustainability Park expecting to hear from Nick about business plans and profit margins, but what he really wants to talk about is teaching. Because of the work he does with Produce Denver, community members receive not just fresh food but education—and not the kind of education that comes from sitting in classrooms. They feel the taproots of carrots slip from the loose grip of the soil when they grab their green tops and pull. They kneel among plants to cup in their hands plump eggplants. They taste the juice of tomatoes plucked from vines. They feel the slippery resistance of fresh zucchinis yield beneath their knives as they prepare dinner for their families.

"Every day I see kids enjoying themselves in gardens," Nick says. "I think they like growing so much because they feel connected to the food. The plants they grow become a part of them."

In 2013 Nick followed the lead of Sprout City Farms, the nonprofit founded by his former Produce Denver partner, to help introduce farming on the grounds of Denver Public Schools. Sprout City Farms and other organizations had worked with Denver Public Schools to eliminate the red tape that prevents the school system from developing a farm-to-cafeteria model. Everyone agrees that boosting children's health with fresh food and enhancing their knowledge of nutrition are worthwhile goals. But getting permission to farm produce for kids in American schoolyards, it turns out, can be about as straightforward as filling out a tax return.

There have been innumerable meetings and many long discussions about legal barriers. For example, crops cannot be grown taller than a certain height because they pose the danger that students might hide in them. Orchards are a potential hazard because kids could choke on apples.

What? I ask Nick how he manages to stay sane.

His brow furrows. "The thing is, I have to remind myself that the people who come up with these rules are doing their best to protect the school system from getting sued."

Though I'm struggling to process the idea of kids slurping soda while being kept safe from the dangers of produce, he does have a point: The source of this strangeness lies less with the school district than it does our litigious society. And despite the red tape, Denver Public Schools has made remarkable progress with a garden-to-cafeteria program.

From 2001-2012, a culinary visionary named Andrew Nowak grew Slow Food Denver's "Seed to Table" program from four school gardens to more than sixty. Thanks to Andrew's efforts, the kitchen staff in Denver Public Schools now cooks largely from scratch, and salad bars are found in cafeterias throughout the district. Lunches that once consisted almost solely of processed substances from cans are now focused on whole foods sourced locally. Andrew developed food safety protocols that allow students to grow produce for the school lunch program. Kids who spend time in school gardens learn that food comes from the soil and doesn't just appear on plates in a cafeteria. For a child who grows up in a food desert, this is no small discovery. Andrew, now serving as director of Slow Food USA's National School Garden Program, is replicating the success he achieved in Denver across the nation.

Nick and I take a break from discussing school gardens and farms as we check out an aquaponics system in a Sustainability Park greenhouse. Aquaponics combines two food-growing methods: aquaculture (raising aquatic animals like fish) and hydroponics (cultivating plants in nutrient-rich water). The fish excrete waste that is broken down by bacteria to become food for edible plants, and the plants clean the water that circulates through the fish tanks. I watch schools of tilapia fingerlings swim beneath a miniature forest of tasty-looking greenery as Nick explains this clever design. And Nick, it turns out, has created something of a symbiosis with Denver Public Schools.

"I think it could be a real game-changer," he says of his new partnership with the school system. "We're scaling up from gardens to farms." We step outside the steamy greenhouse, and as we walk, Nick reminds me that land and labor are the major challenges that confront every urban farming enterprise. Denver Public Schools owns a lot of property in the city, and they have selected Produce Denver to farm one and a half acres. Nick grows vegetables on school grounds, harvests and packages the produce, and then transports it to a warehouse where school officials inspect the food and send it to school cafeterias throughout the city. The school system owns the produce and provides the land, water, storage, and distribution; it pays Produce Denver to grow fresh food to support the school menus. The first year, this pilot project produced a whopping thirteen thousand pounds of vegetables.

NICK'S LAND PROBLEM HAS been solved by farming school grounds. The labor part of Nick's puzzle is being cracked by Groundwork Denver, a nonprofit organization that is using grant money to subsidize the cost of its Green Team to grow food on Nick's farms.

Groundwork Denver's Green Team program pays low-income students in their teens and early twenties to work on environmentally focused service projects. Many of the Green Team members have extraordinary stories. For example, Silivere Kamanzi Bakomeza, two years old when his family fled a civil war, arrived at a refugee camp in Rwanda; he was sixteen and a half when the UN relocated him to Denver. His stomach had ached with hunger for fourteen and a half years. And he'd been surrounded by malnourished kids with kwashiorkor—a debilitating disease caused by protein deficiency.

After his first summer working for Groundwork Denver, Silivere wired some of his earnings to an uncle still living in the refugee camp. Silivere encouraged his uncle to walk to a farm in the hills outside the refugee camp to buy cows and then sell the milk at a price everyone in the camp could afford. "I did it because I understand what it feels like to be hungry," he says. And now this refugee philanthropist is expanding his microbusiness: Silivere is having his uncle search for fields in Rwanda where Silivere can fund the growing of crops like cassava and potatoes.

"Some people think we work with at-risk kids," says Shane Wright of Groundwork Denver. "I say absolutely—these kids are at risk of taking over the world."

UNTIL I STARTED WORKING for Waste Farmers and meeting urban farmers like Nick, growing food in the city had seemed as strange to me as building a ski resort on a beach. My suburban upbringing had conditioned me to believe that there are cities and there are farms, and never the twain shall meet—with sprawling subdivisions buffering these disparate worlds. But the closer I looked at our current food system, the more urban farming started to make sense—and the more I started to get that growing food in cities is, as Nick insists, something we *must* do.

Industrial agriculture began with a dream of abundance. From the 1940s to the late 1960s, innovations such as hybrid seeds and synthetic fertilizers went a long way toward achieving that dream. This technological revolution saved more than a billion people from starvation—certainly one of humanity's great achievements. But Nick and many other urban farmers are quick to point out the costs.

In the wake of World War II, bomb-making factories were reconfigured to manufacture synthetic fertilizer, chemical warfare agents were tweaked to kill insects, and the mechanization that built tanks was retooled to churn out tractors. With industrial food, we waged war on nature. And from thirty thousand feet, gazing out an airplane window onto the tidy grids of cornfields that have replaced wild forests and prairie, it would appear we've won. Down on the ground, surrounded by corn stalks that have grown as tall as trees after having their roots drenched in nitrogen fertilizer, you might conclude that all is well. But if you happen to be the parent of an infant who stops breathing because nitrates have seeped from the soil into the well that supplies your drinking water, your perspective could be decidedly different.

Industrial agriculture may have succeeded in separating us from nature's cycles of sunlight and rain, but it hasn't excused us from the law of unintended consequences. Critics of our current food system point out that the way we feed ourselves contributes more greenhouse gases to the atmosphere than anything else we do. Producing our food depletes and pollutes rivers and aquifers. At our present pace of land abuse, the last of the world's topsoil could be washed away in our children's lifetime. Perhaps most important, the United Nations has estimated that to keep pace with the growth in human population—which was made possible by industrial agriculture— more food will have to be produced over the next half century than has been produced during the past ten thousand years combined.

One-half of the planet's population now lives in cities; by midcentury this percentage will increase to three-quarters. And the fossil fuels used to transport food from the countryside to the city are finite. Growing food in cities is more than a fad, many urban farming proponents insist. It is a matter of survival.

Recent federal farm bills, despite including some funding for local food initiatives, reflect an attitude of business as usual. According to U.S. PIRG, a consumer group that takes on powerful interests that threaten public health and safety, agribusiness spent $200 million in a single year, 2008, on lobbying and campaign contributions. Agribusiness has deep pockets to fund armies of lobbyists, ensuring that Congress continues to provide taxpayer-financed subsidies for corporations that create a glut of commodities such as corn and soy, which the food industry turns into substances ultimately sickening the entire population. Our federal farm policy benefits large, highly profitable farm businesses, some of the most successful corporations in the country, while virtually ignoring small-scale growers struggling to make a living by putting real food on the plates of people in their communities.

The true beneficiaries of Produce Denver farming on the grounds of the Denver Public School system are, of course, children. Many students help plant and harvest the school farms during volunteer days, and most of the Green Team members who work with Nick attend Denver Public Schools, or have in the past. The fresh produce that's harvested is delivered to school cafeterias where young bodies are nurtured and malleable minds form lifelong eating habits.

The crisis of childhood obesity is caused by what's known as "overnutrition"—a form of malnutrition in which more nutrients are supplied than are required for normal growth and development. And overnutrition is caused, at least in part, by subsidies that make processed foods cost far less than they would in a free market. There are good reasons for the government to support agriculture to stabilize the nation's food supply. But if agricultural subsidies are to continue, why not build a system that encourages the production of *real* food that reduces the burden of spiraling healthcare costs due to lifestyle diseases such as diabetes, heart disease, stroke, and many cancers? Why not remove some of the subsidies from agricultural corporations and distribute that funding among the Nick Grubers of the cities? The beneficiaries of our tax dollars would not then be shareholders in multibillion-dollar corporations but schoolchildren who have never seen a carrot pulled from the ground, boys and girls who think bees are enemies, kids who drink soda for breakfast but have never tasted a fresh peach.

"The latest farm bill was a joke," says Nick. "Small family farmers can't afford to lobby Congress." But Nick doesn't have time to be outraged. He's too busy trying to run a business.

Nick can't afford to pay lobbyists to influence Congress. But he can keep working the soil and finding innovative ways to make a living farming in the city. There is no place Nick would rather be than in a garden, teaching people how to grow, giving them the tools to become the farmers of the future. I don't feel sorry for this businessman who is barely scraping by. Far from it. In fact, I'm jealous. I envy someone who has found his calling and knows exactly what he wants to do with his life—

especially when that calling has the potential to help so many people grow.

BLUE BEAR FARM, WITH MORE than five thousand square feet of growing space on the grounds of the Colorado Convention Center, is tended by Produce Denver. Nick's company designed and built this urban farm that boasts crops from basil to beans, parsnip to peppermint. Two beehives provide pollination for produce such as squash and peppers that fill forty-one raised beds. But Nick could work at this farm for an entire year cultivating fruit, vegetables, herbs, and honey and only harvest enough food to supply a single event at the convention center. For all the press that urban agriculture has recently received, for all the proliferation of farmers' markets and community supported agriculture, less than 1 percent of food sales in the United States are direct from farmer to consumer.

After Nick tells me about Blue Bear Farm, I spend some time checking out the farm and the surrounding neighborhood. At the bustling crossroads where Champa Street and Speer Boulevard converge, a light-rail hub deposits and collects passengers throughout each day and night. Across the street from the farm, the Auraria Campus of University of Colorado Denver, Community College of Denver, and Metropolitan State University of Denver stirs with student activity. A steady flow of pedestrians and cyclists slow down and turn their faces toward the garden as they pass on a bike path. I remember Nick's mention of a study he worked on when he was in college. The study demonstrated that just being near a community garden increases people's sense of wellbeing. To add some anecdotal evidence to that research: I feel pretty damn good myself looking at this garden oasis.

Nick fields phone calls from commuters who've seen Blue Bear Farm and then contacted him for help in starting gardens of their own. By having an urban farm within people's sight, gardening and food are on their minds. Candice Orlando, cofounder of UrbiCulture Community Farms, a Denver-based nonprofit that creates edible gardens in the city, tells me, "Backyard gardens are good, but front-yard gardens are even better." Candice explains that when people farm food in their front yards, neighbors can see what they're doing and be inspired to start cultivating their own edible gardens. "When people grow food in front of their homes, neighbors start talking to each other, and they start sharing gardening tips and recipes. They offer to watch each other's gardens, to water when needed, to lend a hand."

Nick sums it up in his succinct way: "Urban agriculture is about connecting people. Connecting them to nature, connecting them to farming and to food. Connecting them to each other."

As I hang around Blue Bear Farm people-watching and studying the edible landscape, I feel connected both to the diversity of the city and to the diversity of nature. And I realize that I am drawn to edible landscapes if for no other reason than they are more interesting than lawns. Why stare at the monotony of grass when your eyes can follow the creeping vines of a pumpkin plant or linger on the textures of leafy greens? Why smell chemical-soaked Kentucky bluegrass when you can sniff the perfume of lavender? Why listen to the silence of a sculpted hedge when you can hear bees buzzing around a shaggy growth of flowering shrubs?

AT SUSTAINABILITY PARK, I'm struck as much by the smells as by the sight of plants blooming in the heart of the city. Snow is melting, baring the dark soil beneath, releasing its rich scent. I recall days spent on a Wisconsin farm when I was a little boy. I grew up in suburban St. Louis, and our family's food came from a supermarket chain called Schnucks, but we vacationed in rural Wisconsin in the summers and became friends with a local farm family. Helping out on their farm when I was barely big enough to lift a hay bale taught me lessons that linger: Growing food takes a lot of time and makes for sore muscles, food tastes best when fresh, and people who share in the work of growing and harvesting the things they eat build bonds that aren't easily severed. All of this comes back to me as I inhale the aroma of Sustainability Park.

As Nick and I walk among his tended beds, it occurs to me that growing an organic plot in the city is like planting a flag in a barren landscape and declaring, "Here there will be life." Each edible garden is a victory for the values of self-reliance and community. Nick has begun the hard work of freeing children from the tyranny of industrial food. What if we had more Nicks, whole armies of them, working in every city in America? Like many farmers, Nick is a tenacious optimist. He sees farming on school property as the most effective way to get healthful food to nutrition-starved communities. "Schools— that's the answer," he says, squinting at the soil he has nurtured. "Everyone wants to make it happen. It needs to happen. I know I can make it work."

Chapter 5
Spiraling Upward

On the grounds of Waste Farmers I see a strange herb garden. Soil is held within a brick structure that spirals like a nautilus, rising to an apex three feet above the ground—a garden in three dimensions. As I pinch off a leaf of basil and crush it beneath my nose, Ash, the young woman who designed this garden, tells me, "Patterns in nature are based on waves and circles and spirals. There are no straight lines in nature."

"So the straight lines of garden beds are a problem?" I ask. "And the straight rows of crops?"

"Straight lines are everywhere in bad design," Ash says. "And bad design is what got us into this mess we're in right now. Permaculture can get us out of it."

AFTER MEETING WITH NICK, I knew that I needed to talk with Ash. Nick's emphasis on education was a theme I encountered repeatedly as I journeyed through the urban food movement. Teaching people about food is more important to entrepreneurs like Nick than making a profit—no one in their right mind would get into farming in the city thinking they'd earn a fortune. There has to be a larger purpose that leads them to the work. Something called "permaculture" seemed so filled with larger purpose I wasn't sure if it was a system for growing food or a philosophy. An awful lot of people involved with urban farming were into it. I kept hearing them talk about "stacking functions." What were these functions that needed stacking?

Ash would enlighten me. Not unlike religion and politics, food can inspire fervency in people. Each school of sustainable agriculture—biodynamics, biointensive, holistic management, permaculture—has its true believers. Of all the urban farmers I had met who were into permaculture, Ash stood out as the most enthusiastic evangelist for the movement.

WHILE ASH AND I WALK around her spiral herb garden, she puts on a large gardening hat to shield her pale cheeks from the sun. In her soil-darkened hands she holds a sheet of paper illustrating a permaculture diagram of interlocking circles, like a Celtic pattern. She explains that many people's first impulse when constructing a garden is to plot out a rectangular bed in two dimensions that will receive uniform amounts of water and sun—a miniature monoculture to grow rows of plants in stern uniformity. Ash's herb garden, in contrast, rises from the earth in a riotous spiral. She planted drought-tolerant herbs near the apex. Species that need more water she placed near the bottom, where the soil is most saturated. She also arranged the plants according to their need for sun throughout the many microclimates of light and shade produced by the winding design, creating a multitude of little growing spaces that overlap and merge.

"Edges are where the action is," Ash tells me. Where forest meets field, where water touches land, the greatest biodiversity and productivity can be found. Ecologists call these transition zones "ecotones." Along Colorado's Front Range, the grass sea of the Great Plains laps against timbered slopes of the Rocky Mountains. This mixing of biomes creates a large diversity of plants in a relatively small space: nature's permaculture garden.

When I ask Ash how she became interested in permaculture, she tells me about her experiences in Central America. At ages seventeen and eighteen, self-directed study in Mexico and Guatemala changed her. "I sat down to meals with families eating food they had grown in the same way for generations." Her speech quickens: "It was like a beam of light hit me straight in the face."

Back in Colorado, while picking up trash along the side of a highway for a service project, a fellow volunteer told Ash about permaculture. "It sounded a lot like what I'd learned from living with farmers in Central America." She smiles and shakes her head. "When I took a permaculture design course at the Colorado Rocky Mountain Permaculture Institute, I was instantly hooked."

Bill Mollison and David Holmgren, Australians who met at the University of Tasmania in the 1960s, started the movement by publishing *Permaculture One* in 1978. The term *permaculture* was originally coined as a portmanteau of *permanent* and *agriculture*—the term has since been expanded to also include *permanent culture*, reflecting the movement's holistic orientation. Permaculture is a branch of ecological design and ecological engineering that encompasses fields as diverse as horticulture and city planning. Mollison's moment of enlightenment came as he observed that plants tend to group themselves in mutually beneficial communities. This inspired him to develop an approach to agriculture and community design that places elements together so that they can support one another, creating systems that provide for their own needs and recycle their waste in closed loops. Permaculturists point out that there is no waste in nature. For example, leaves shed by trees decompose, providing nutrients that cycle through the soil to nourish plant growth—unless the leaves are taken in a straight line to a landfill.

After Ash got hooked, she started to crave a daily fix of ecological design. A stone wall stores sunlight and warms citrus trees on frosty nights. Dandelions punch their taproots through compacted soil to bring minerals toward the earth's surface. Diatomaceous earth—the fossilized remains of tiny marine creatures that crumble to a fine white powder—can be sprinkled on insects to kill them. "I couldn't get enough," says Ash. When she learned of an advanced permaculture course in Australia, she knew she had to make a pilgrimage to the country where Bill Mollison and David Holmgren had started the movement.

Deep immersion in permaculture Down Under further ignited Ash's interest. In an Australian landscape stripped of minerals through mismanagement, she watched permaculturists rejuvenate the pauperized soil. They brought in salt licks for livestock; then the animals absorbed the minerals in the salts, metabolized them, and excreted them into the landscape. And minerals crucial for animal health began to cycle through the soil as they had before the ecosystem was shoved out of balance by agricultural companies devoted to making money rather than mimicking nature's design.

"So permaculture is about more than designing gardens?" I ask Ash.

"Permaculture is about designing *everything*," she says. Rocket stoves, for example, are a mainstay of permaculture design. These small, efficient stoves can produce prodigious amounts of heat in homes by burning sticks no thicker than a person's thumb.

Ash says, "When I finished the course in Australia and came back to Colorado, I saw so much bad design. It was frightening." She points out that in America cows had once been kept on farms and their waste had been recycled as fertilizer for crops; now livestock stand crammed together on feedlots, and monocultures of plants are starved for nutrients. Synthetic fertilizer has to be trucked in to farms to replace the missing animal manure, which instead of being returned to the soil leaks out of fetid waste lagoons at feedlots, contaminating water supplies.

Ash says, "I wanted to start solving problems with permaculture. But so many people I tried to help were only focused on profit. They didn't care about basing design on natural systems." For example, when she consulted with the owners of a property in Arvada with a pond that was being treated with biological slurry to prevent algal blooms, she suggested instead planting cattails at the edges. This would create an ecosystem that could cleanse the water of the nitrates causing the algal blooms by using the natural filtration of plants, a self-sustaining system with no need for external inputs—good design to a permaculturist. "But the owners wouldn't do it," Ash continues, her voice rising. "They couldn't see the big picture."

While Ash and I walk to one of the spaces where she is designing permaculture gardens, she says, "I get frustrated. I want to help people understand that permaculture offers sustainable solutions in place of short-term fixes. When I can't convince them, I get upset. It takes a leap of faith to move from a conventional system to a permaculture system. And when people aren't willing to take that leap, it makes me crazy."

Waste Farmers, however, was willing to take the leap. Though still a small company struggling to meet payroll month to month, Waste Farmers had hired Ash to transform the grass and dirt of the grounds outside their buildings into an edible landscape to demonstrate the potential to grow large amounts of food in small spaces, and to help pass sustainability principles on to the next generation. Waste Farmers had also hired Groundwork Denver's Green Team. Some of the same youth who were helping Nick Gruber farm school grounds were also assisting Ash in building out this demonstration urban farm. Veggies from Ash's gardens were eaten by employees of Waste Farmers and donated to Denverites in need of nutritious food.

Ash leads me down a winding path among greens, tomatoes, zucchini, and sunchokes. She says, "I made this path wavy so there's more edge to plant along." She stoops down to inspect a garden bed, searching for plant life pushing up through the cover of straw. She explains that when our farm systems are unhealthy they need external inputs—chemical fertilizers and pesticides. When our bodies are unhealthy, we, too, need external inputs.

"Drugs?" I ask.

"We're all junkies. Whether it's heroin or diabetes pills, cocaine, donuts. Reality TV. Cars that make us go faster and faster." She grabs a handful of soil and squeezes. "We're so numb. Only huge doses of sugar wake us up. We're addicted to drugs that keep our food addictions from killing us. And all of us are hooked up to a petroleum drip." She throws the handful of dirt at the ground. "Oil is the worst drug of all. The *worst*. We have to stop using chemical fertilizers."

On this point she's preaching to the converted. I recall reading about an ammonium nitrate fertilizer factory just north of Waco, Texas, that exploded, demolishing a Texas farm town. Bodies of the dead were dragged from the rubble of houses as ribbons of burning debris rained down. Here's a rule of thumb: Don't grow food with substances that can blow a crater in the ground.

But chemical fertilizers have allowed farmers to produce enormous quantities of food. How do we replace these synthetic substances?

"Think about companion planting," Ash says. She explains that the classic example is the Native American "Three Sisters" technique of growing corn, beans, and squash. The cornstalk serves as a trellis for the beans to climb. The beans fix nitrogen in the soil, which then nourishes the corn and squash. The squash shades the ground, keeping it moist and preventing weeds from growing. And the three plants, when consumed together, provide a balanced diet. To a permaculturist, this is the kind of good design that is consciously created by studying nature's patterns. The permaculture practice of placing complementary plants together to facilitate pollination and pest control, to maximize productivity in small spaces, and to reduce water waste, strikes me as the opposite of conventional agriculture, with its monotonous rows of single crops, its degraded soil, its constant demand for chemical fertilizers and irrigation. Adherents of permaculture principles place their faith not in quick technological fixes but in slow knowledge—the kind of accumulated awareness that comes from interacting closely with the land. The kind of knowledge that vanishes in the cockpit of a combine. Ash tells me she is planning to camp on the grounds at Waste Farmers within the "food forest" she's designing—an edible garden based on a woodland ecosystem, with multiple layers of food produced by fruit and nut trees, shrubs, herbs, vines, and perennial vegetables. Among the carefully placed components of this edible forest, the flowers to attract pollinators and the ponds to provide water for them, Ash will pitch her tent. "I want to interact with my plants day and night. I want to feel the weather they feel." Ash's food forest is a long way from the homogeneous corn fields I remember from my childhood in the Midwest.

Biologists insist that strength in diversity is no mere platitude. Monocultures of crops are susceptible to being devastated by pests and pathogens. In the 1840s, blight attacked Ireland's potato crop, most of which was of a single variety, resulting in the Great Famine. Today, King Corn dominates the American farmscape. "The world's food supply hangs by a slender thread of biodiversity," evolutionary biologist Edward O. Wilson wrote in *The Future of Life*, published in 2002. That thread grows ever thinner.

"We've lost more than 90 percent of the seed varieties in America in the last hundred years," Ash tells me. "Corn, wheat, and rice make up most of the world's grain production—more than 40 percent of all the food that's eaten on the planet. Three annual crops. That's all that stands between us and starvation."

Ash explains that corn, wheat, and rice are annuals: they live for a year, produce seed, and then die. In contrast, perennials like fruits and nuts can live for many years, or even many centuries in the case of trees. Cultivating annuals necessitates yearly tilling, planting, and purchasing seed; perennials, by comparison, require much less work to maintain. Perennials also build topsoil more efficiently than annuals. "Most plants in natural systems are perennials," says Ash. "Perennials form biodiverse ecosystems that are stable and resilient. That's what permaculture is trying to mimic. Permaculture systems use annual grains but never rely on them exclusively. The focus is always on perennials. That's the kind of good design that can save us from starvation."

EACH SPECIES THAT EVOLVED on this planet, from the first microscopic prokaryotic cell to the blue whale, the largest animal to have ever existed on Earth, forms a branch of a story that has been told for some 3.8 billion years. When permaculturists create systems to grow food and foster communities, they place the tree of life at the center of design, and they build systems based on mimicry of the natural world and suited to local environments. "Keyhole gardens," for example, are ideal for Colorado's dry climate. A notch is cut in a round garden bed, allowing easy access to the center, where a mound of compost holds water like a sponge. A homestead designed on permaculture principles might be sited in a natural depression to shield it from wind, with fences and hedges added for further protection. A pond could be precisely located to reflect sunlight into the house to warm it. Kitchen waste could be composted to recycle nutrients back into the garden that grows the food prepared in the kitchen. Trees are terrific multitaskers: along with providing windbreak, shade, and food, a tree can prevent erosion and create structural support for other plants to climb.

The permaculture landscape is designed to be not only dense and diverse but also self-perpetuating. Bill Mollison has said that after the work of the original planting in a permaculture garden is done, "the designer turns into the recliner." All this bounty and we get to nap, too? How does that happen?

"Stack functions," permaculturists say, meaning that every design element should accomplish multiple goals. Consider backyard chickens. Chickens devour vegetable scraps from the garden fertilized with their nitrogen-rich manure; we eat their eggs and put the birds to work in the garden gobbling insects and slugs, eating weed seeds, and aerating the soil as they scratch at it with their claws. A greenhouse-henhouse combo has become something of a permaculture holy grail. During the day, the sun-warmed greenhouse heats the chicken coop; at night, the heat from the chickens keeps the greenhouse warm. The birds breathe oxygen provided by the plants and in turn nourish the plants with their carbon dioxide. Stack those functions!

Permaculture is in some ways simply the crystallization of common sense. It has been said that permaculture is what our grandparents knew and our parents forgot. Bill Mollison has stated, "Though the problems of the world are increasingly complex, the solutions remain embarrassingly simple."

Nothing could be simpler for maintaining our personal health than following Michael Pollan's advice: "Eat food, not too much, mostly plants." But we are becoming what Dr. Joel Fuhrman, the physician and bestselling author who specializes in nutrition-based treatments for obesity and disease, calls a "medical cripple society." Doctors who prescribe a nutritious diet to prevent and reverse disease are viewed as outliers, and a plant-based diet centered on fruits, vegetables, and whole grains is seen by many people as extreme. This is particularly striking when one also considers that it's routine for half a million Americans a year to undergo bypass surgery to repair the damage caused by poor nutrition. "Let food be thy medicine," wrote Hippocrates some 2,400 years ago. And more recently, comedian Bill Maher says, "The answer isn't another pill. The answer is spinach."

Embarrassingly simple, indeed. Permaculture principles are distilled in statements as simple and potent as prayers. *Care for the earth. Care for people. Share the surplus.* Rarely have I encountered a person involved in permaculture who has studied the peer-reviewed science that supports the conclusion of anthropogenic climate change or who has an extensive background in genetics. Yet every permaculturist I've met believes human-caused global warming is real and genetically modified foods endanger human health. Few scientific studies document the efficacy of permaculture. But adherents of this system of ecological design don't seem to worry much about this lack of empirical research. They know that the world is broken and they have faith that permaculture will heal it. Science, they believe, could only confirm what they already know. I've heard avid gardeners say that growing plants is part science, part intuition. One permaculturist put it to me this way, "If you don't think plants respond to love, you've never grown plants."

Surely science is the sharpest tool we have for interrogating reality and providing answers to our most pressing questions. The application of scientific discoveries to the betterment of our lives has brought us to where we are today—no small feat. Who among us really wants to chase game across the parched plains of the Kalahari or plant potatoes by hand in the thin air of the Andes? The industrial efficiency of modern agriculture has made the famines that hounded humanity for most of our history seem as far removed from our lives as cave paintings.

But then again, our technological advancements have led to the disappearance of seeds that sustained our species for millennia, to meat production that seems more like car manufacturing than managing animals, and to a diabetes crisis that threatens to bankrupt our healthcare system. Science can do so much, but it cannot transform us into compassionate human beings who are careful stewards of the resources that sustain us. Ash would have us believe that permaculture can.

BEFORE ASH AND I PART ways, we step across a small stream that flows past one of her gardens. I ask her what permaculture has to say about water management.

"Slow it, spread it, sink it."

I wait for her to elaborate... "That's it?"

"Think about it. If water is racing over the ground, it erodes the soil. Slow it down. If water is all in one place, it can hurt plants. Spread it. Plants need water underground so their roots can get it, not flowing across the surface. Sink it."

Permaculture   designers   harvest   water   by   forming terraces and building pools and ponds and infiltration swales—by working with the natural flow of water instead of against it. And by observing patterns in nature, permaculturists understand that not building houses in a river's floodplain is the most efficient flood control of all.

After talking with Ash about water, I read about the Los Angeles River. Linear concrete walls straightjacket the river channel and send stormwater speeding toward the sea, while the parched city survives on water diverted from rivers hundreds of miles away. I immediately thought: bad design! A few days later I came across an article about single-use shipping containers that are loaded with cargo one time, sent across the sea, and then pile up in mountainous stacks. No function stacking going on there. While immersing myself in the teachings of permaculture I started to see edges everywhere: in the riparian areas along riverbanks where birdlife is so abundant, in the zigzag pattern of a fence that makes it more resistant to wind.

That's the thing about permaculture: Lessons learned by growing in the soil soon spill into the larger world beyond the garden walls.

ONE SUNNY MORNING IN April, Ash gives a permaculture demonstration on the Waste Farmers grounds to a group of eager onlookers. She is teaching a kind of permaculture called Hügelkultur (Hoo-gull-culture). This technique with a fun-to-say name was popularized by Sepp Holzer, a farmer who figured out how to cultivate food high in the Alps. "He grows lemons in the mountains of Austria," Ash says. "In *winter*."

In the 1960s, Holzer developed techniques for creating warm microclimates in cold places by carefully arranging boulders, ponds, trees, and terraces. These cleverly designed structures allow crops not considered cold-tolerant to grow in the chilly weather of upper elevations. A sheltered area tilted southward becomes a sun trap in which spinach can thrive, while a few feet away a patch of north-facing ground blasted with wind remains frozen.

To develop Hügelkultur (a German word meaning "hill culture"), Holzer tapped into hundreds of years of accumulated agricultural wisdom in Germany and Eastern Europe. This technique of building raised garden beds has the unique twist of burying wood beneath hills of soil. Ash explains that the woody biomass that's buried sponges up water beneath the mounded earth, similar to the natural process that takes place in forests when trees fall down and decompose. "The roots of plants go down and get that water," Ash says. "And as the wood breaks down to create soil, it generates heat." The result: a warm, wet place where plants can grow—a natural greenhouse.

Ash orchestrates the construction of the Hügelkultur bed as volunteers stack branches and roll old stumps into a long pile that curves like a snake. It's a sinuous shape you'd find in nature, not in the drafting software of an engineer. When the pile is covered in soil and straw, Ash walks along its sides and broadcasts seeds by throwing fistfuls at the ground. She explains that carrots rooted on one side will have a different flavor from carrots grown on the other side because the shape of the winding mound creates many microclimates. By contrast, I remember when I was a boy walking through fields of corn with stalks as orderly as pixels on a computer screen. That matrix of aggressive uniformity formed a strange wilderness, a green desert devoid of life save stalks endlessly repeated by an algorithm. A few years back, in China I wandered the streets of megacities among towers so vast they seemed inhabited by mechanical giants. What would Iowa's farmscape or Shanghai's skyline look like if they were designed by permaculturists?

Perhaps permaculture is so addictive because it addresses one of the largest questions of all: How will we move forward, together, to survive a crowded, hungry future?

Adam Brock, a leading voice in Denver's permaculture movement, puts it this way: "We're so used to thinking that it's humans versus the environment, and that it's a zero-sum thing. But permaculture design shows us that it's possible to meet our needs as humans and thrive while actively *improving* ecosystem health. It doesn't matter whether you're talking about climate change, police brutality, our parasitic economy, or our broken food system—pretty much all of the grave challenges we face today can be traced back to that separation between humans and nature, and permaculture offers an elegant, powerful way to begin healing that wound."

Chapter 6
A Cure for Affluenza

sh made a strong case for working with nature to cultivate our little patch of the planet. But I wondered how
far this focus on reaping a harvest from our own backyards should be taken. I'd heard of a woman in Denver who
had vowed to eat only what grew within a local foodshed for
an entire year. Coffee bushes don't grow in the Rockies, so to
eat local in Denver and be pure about it, she had to quit java. A
year without coffee? I'd rather spend a year poking myself in
the eye with a toothpick.

I wondered what the point of this punishing stunt was. Why
this radical localism in a globalized world? What was this person trying to prove?

BEFORE LAUREN BLAIR MEETS me at Hooked on Colfax coffee
shop, she gets a barista on the phone and makes sure that locally sourced milk is available. When Lauren and I finally sit

down to talk, she drinks steamed milk sweetened with Colorado honey while I self-consciously drink coffee, the smell of roasted beans wafting from my steaming mug, caffeine quickening my blood.

Lauren sports the toned arms of a rock climber, and the bright bead of a nose piercing offsets an otherwise staid look. She explains that her plan to eat only locally sourced food for one year came to her while walking around her Capitol Hill neighborhood. The spring sky was an unblemished blue, and recent rains had painted the land several shades of green. Peach trees on the corner of 12th Avenue and Clarkson Street were scattered with bright explosions of blossoms, and in a few months' time, after the pink petals had fallen, the boughs would sag with fruit.

Lauren realized that there is a quiet abundance of foodstuffs in Colorado: not the cornucopia that locavores in California can choose from, but Colorado boasts Palisade peaches and Rocky Ford cantaloupes; apricots, chewy and sweet, and cherries that dribble dark juice down your chin; Olathe sweet corn and grass-fed beef; jars of amber honey.

"But why deprive yourself of coffee?" I ask as I sip from my steaming cup.

"Eating whatever we want whenever we want is not sustainable," Lauren says. "Something could happen politically in some other part of the world and suddenly we don't have an oil supply and food doesn't get here. Food should never be taken for granted."

An oft-cited statistic is that food travels an average of 1,500 miles from farm to fork in our grocery supply chain. Looked at one way, this is a triumph of free trade in a flat world—the glorious realization of an economic system that spans the planet, lifting people in developing countries out of poverty and reducing the likelihood of nations going to war because of their interdependence. Global economic connectedness will be our salvation, optimists contend. Peru, for example, exports asparagus because the country has an abundance of warm weather, loose soil, and cheap labor. People in Peru need jobs; we need asparagus. Everybody wins, right?

Not the local asparagus producers in the U.S. and Europe, who are being bankrupted by supermarket chains importing asparagus from as far away as six thousand miles. Even worse, this kind of global interconnectedness depends on massive consumption of cheap fossil fuels—which means our food chain stretches not just to Peru for asparagus but to the Persian Gulf for oil.

These kinds of concerns weighed heavily on Lauren as she contemplated the size of her foodshed: the entire planet.

But she wondered if a person could really shrink her foodshed down to a size that would allow her to eat locally for a year in Denver. What kind of planning would that require? What kind of deprivation would it entail? How would it affect her health? Would she be miserable without chocolate, without avocado, without coconut in its many tasty manifestations— oil, milk, water, and flakes? Could she sacrifice citrus fruits and bananas? Would life be worth living without olive oil and coffee? Would she be able to dine with friends at restaurants? How would she define "local?"

The details were hazy but the core concept was clear: She vowed to eat only local foods for one year. Yes, esteemed author Barbara Kingsolver had already eaten locally for a year on her farm in the southern Appalachians and had chronicled her experiences in a book, *Animal, Vegetable, Miracle*. And yes, locavores on the West Coast had drawn a circle with a one-hundred mile radius around their homes and dined only on food sourced within that area. A Canadian couple from Vancouver had written the very charming *The 100-Mile Diet: A Year of Local Eating*. But the geography and food culture of Colorado present unique challenges and opportunities.

Palisade, a farming town on the parched plateau country of the western part of the state, lies in a region that has been turned into an agricultural paradise by diverting water from the Colorado River to irrigate crops. Peaches that hang plump in the trees are crated, cobs of corn with candy-sweet kernels are packed in crushed ice, and this bounty of produce is sent to cities on Colorado's Front Range, more than two hundred miles away. For the past seven years, Lauren had made the trek to Ridgway, Colorado, in the late summer and fall for a harvest weekend with her father and stepmother. "We'd stop in Palisade when we were passing through to load up on boxes of peaches. We'd pick apples and make them into gallons of applesauce."

Lauren explains that a one-hundred-mile radius is a nice round number that works well in San Francisco or Vancouver; in Denver it precludes a locavore from eating fruit and veggies sourced from western Colorado. And going a hundred miles north of Denver onto the high plains of Wyoming doesn't add anything to the menu that can't be found within the state of Colorado. So Lauren traded the symmetry of a circle for the rectangular confines of her home state, settling on anything grown or raised in Colorado as her definition of "local."

Lauren decided to start on her birthday, May 24, allowing plenty of time—and the full growing season—to put food away for the winter months. Before the year of austerity commenced, she celebrated a Last Supper. She invited friends over for a smorgasbord of nonlocal delicacies: chips and guacamole, Thai curry, shrimp and grits, polenta with porcini mushroom sauce, cheeses and baguettes, chocolate bourbon pecan pie. All manner of tasty items from beyond Colorado's borders were consumed in copious quantities. Then the adventure began.

IF YOU WANT TO EAT LOCALLY for a year in Denver, you can't find instructions on eHow. Not yet, anyway. There may come a day when it's so trendy that apps will guide you through the process. But Lauren had to blaze her own trail across the Colorado food frontier. She was no stranger to harvesting, preserving, and storing food: she had canned her own fruit and veggies, had made preserves, jams, and jellies. But when you're putting up food to get you through an entire winter, you're more pioneer confined to a sod house than urbanite with easy access to meals. "All of the preparation made me think about what previous generations went through to feed themselves," Lauren says.

The only way to figure out what to do was to just jump in and do it. Soon she was too busy eating locally to finish reading Barbara Kingsolver's book about eating locally. She sketched out the amounts of food she'd need for weeks and months in a notebook and made lists of all the vegetables she'd have to preserve; then she began the long, slow trudge of preparing and storing a year's worth of food.

She worked part-time at a bakery and did some other odd jobs to pay the bills. "Basically every spare moment I had was consumed by the demand of putting up food for the winter," she tells me. She tucks her long brown hair back behind her ear and delves into details. "In the summer I went to local farmers' markets and on road trips to the Western Slope of Colorado. When foods were in season, I bought them by the case." On the Western Slope she purchased three cases of peaches, which she froze and dehydrated; apples, which she canned and dehydrated; and cherries, plums, and apricots. From farmers' markets and Front Range farms she bought kale, chard, spinach, corn, peas, bell peppers, chiles, celery, and carrots. "And *lots* of tomatoes," Lauren adds. She mostly canned the tomatoes. To preserve the rest of this vegetable plethora for winter use she dehydrated small portions, but the bulk of it she froze.

In September and October, most nights Lauren was in her kitchen until 2:00 a.m. She insists that she's not a morning person and time management is not her forte; but she got up early nearly every day to go to work harvesting, preparing, storing. "There was so much to do all the time, I hardly ever slept." When she talks about the amount of work that went into preparing for her yearlong experiment, she uses words like *ridiculous* and *absurd*—even *loathsome*. "Blanching greens was a most loathsome task," she says. Then she lays out why: *Step one*: Wash greens. *Step two*: Chop greens. *Step three*: Blanch greens. *Step four*: Put greens in ice bath to cool them. *Step five*: Put greens in freezer bags. *Step six*: Seal freezer bags.

Whew. I'm worn out just thinking about it. It seems like an

awful lot of work when dinners can be prepared by pressing a few buttons on a microwave. The more time I save preparing my meals, the more time I have to read or go skiing. Blanching massive quantities of greens is not high on my list of leisure activities I would like to pursue.

Lauren says, "When the water was boiling and the kitchen was sweltering and filled with steam, there were too many things going on at the same time. I needed people to pitch in assembly-line style. I came to appreciate how much sense it makes for communities to come together and pool their resources—for them to work together to feed themselves." People gathered at a pea shelling party in her third-floor condo. Friends who stopped by for a chat would find themselves canning tomatoes or processing bunches of chard by the caseload. "Any friends who happened to be available—I got them into my kitchen and put them to work."

I'm fascinated by the planning and preparation. As someone who considers recipes with more than six steps only slightly less complicated than the launch protocol at NASA, I have an abiding respect for wizardry in the kitchen. I ask Lauren how she managed to store all her preserved food.

Neighbors in her condo complex agreed to let her put a chest freezer in a common storage area. "The freezer was key," says Lauren. She rationed out all of her frozen food stores into seven large bags—one for each of seven months when the growing season in Colorado is at a standstill. After the chest freezer at her condo was stuffed to the lid, Lauren enlisted her sister's freezer at her house in Fort Collins in the cause. "I way overshot on food storage," she says, laughing. "I put away enough food for a family of four."

Besides the hundreds of pounds of produce she bought by the case, Lauren obtained some of her food from as local a source as you can get: her own garden. Her condo neighbors had pitched in when she'd built raised garden beds in the past, and together they enjoyed harvests from the fruit trees and herbs Lauren had planted. But that yield was dwarfed by the amount of food grown in her mother's yard in Littleton, which was a cooperative effort: Lauren planted, weeded, and harvested; her mom watered.

Her mom had also allowed South Metro Urban Farmers, a community-supported agriculture (CSA) business, to cultivate part of her property. (People who join a CSA buy shares of food that a local farm will produce throughout a growing season. With this up-front purchase, CSA members then share in the risk and reward of the farm, receiving a portion of the harvest from week to week.) The owner of the CSA was impressed by Lauren's plan and pledged to donate a share of produce for the summer to support her cause; he also let her make use of any surplus produce he had on hand.

"When I was growing up in Littleton it was much more rural than it is now," Lauren tells me. She watched the fields fill in with houses until the horse pastures and open spaces of her childhood became suburbs. But as the surrounding farms shrank, her mother's gardens grew, until her yard was busy with chickens and bursting with food.

Lauren isn't shy about saying what she thinks is wrong with the way we grow food and communities. But like so many other people I've met in this movement, she seems more excited to pursue solutions than to point out problems. The tribe of which she is a part seems to believe that what has been paved over they can replant, and what has been taken from them they can reclaim by growing themselves.

As with all journeys into the unknown, Lauren's yearlong project involved a lot of guesswork, a lot of trial and error. Lauren explains that local meat wasn't a problem. Locally raised lamb, beef, and pork were available at the Whole Foods in Lauren's neighborhood, and Marczyk Fine Foods, a locally owned full-service grocery, stocked local chicken.

Early on in her yearlong venture Lauren decided to buy some fresh tilapia from an aquaponics operation she discovered at a farmers' market. She laughs and says, "They gave me the fish live. That wasn't part of my plan. The fish were splashing around in water in a Rubbermaid bin in my car." On the way home, Lauren stopped to get her eyebrows waxed. She shrugs and says, "I had already scheduled the appointment. And it was on the same side of town where I'd bought the fish." The tilapia were still alive when she got to her condo. "I had no clue how to properly kill a fish." So she did what any sensible person would do: she watched YouTube videos. No help there. One video featured a guy demonstrating how to kill a fish by stabbing it through the eye with a sharp knife. Still the tilapia flopped and sloshed in Lauren's Rubbermaid tub. "My friend who was in town for a visit was horrified."

Lauren and her friend went to a local market and asked a man at the butcher counter for help in humanely killing the fish. He sternly shook his head and cited the health codes that would be violated. "I totally pleaded," Lauren says. She and her friend wore their disappointment on their faces. The butcher sighed and said beneath his breath to meet him out back. On a table behind the store, he demonstrated how to kill and fillet one of the fish, sending Lauren home with the rest of the flopping tilapia to dispatch in her kitchen.

Lauren shakes her head and laughs. "A week later I found out that the Whole Foods in my neighborhood stocked local tilapia raised by inmates at a prison in Cañon City. And they cost less than live ones."

OLIVE TREES DON'T GROW in Colorado's climate. Lauren says, "I imagined a hermit hidden somewhere in the mountains who had mastered the art of growing olives in a greenhouse and hand-pressing small batches of oil—along with growing bushes of cacao and coffee." She failed to locate this mythical mother lode. The quest for oil continued.

Colorado is chock-full of sunflowers but they are exported outside the state; Lauren couldn't find locally sourced sunflower oil. Nor could she find local butter. In true pioneer fashion, she either learned to do without things or found substitutes by searching the Internet and watching YouTube videos. To solve her oil-less cooking conundrum, she figured out how to make her own butter, along with ghee—a clarified butter common in Indian cooking.

And sometimes, because she is not a fanatic, Lauren tweaked her methodology. Case in point: salt. She found she could source salt from Utah but not Colorado. Lauren, her hair falling into her face as she leans across the table and laughs, says, "There's probably a secret salt mine somewhere in Colorado too—maybe being harvested by the same hermit growing olive trees and coffee and cocoa bushes in a greenhouse. I never did find it."

She settled for commercially produced Utah salt. Baking soda and baking powder formed two more exceptions, completing a baking trifecta from beyond the state's borders. "Baking is something I've always loved doing," Lauren says. She figured these were small ingredients that would allow her to indulge her passion for making fluffy muffins and tasty bread. Sugar, too, was tricky.

Sugar beets are grown in Colorado. So far, so good. She was assured by someone in a local food store that the twenty-five-pound bag of sugar she ordered was local. "But I found out later that the sugar beets grown in Colorado are pooled with sugar beets from other states and processed together." Lauren was stuck with twenty-five pounds of a product not purely of Colorado provenance; but she used it anyway to bake delicious sugar cookies.

I gather from our conversation that eating locally doesn't mean a person has to eat gruel. (Gruel, actually, would be difficult to source locally.) Lauren's first dinner during her year-of-living-as-a-locavore was inspired by some aged goat cheddar from Basalt, Colorado, bought by her brother. After a trip to In Season Local Market, she hatched a plan to use the goat cheddar in a frittata, along with some smoked Gouda, Colorado asparagus, red onion, mustard greens, spinach, and herbs. Thanks to a nonstick pan, she managed to cook the frittata without oil or butter, which she didn't figure out how to make until day two.

What about eating at restaurants? "Eating out became a special occasion, in part because most of the super-local restaurants like Root Down, Table 6, and Potager are pretty expensive. I always called ahead to discuss my needs. In some cases, especially with Root Down, they went out of their way to prepare a special 100-percent-local dish. I had one of the most amazing, all-local meals at Root Down ever—tempura-battered squash blossoms stuffed with goat cheese, a salad, and a pork entrée."

I finally ask the question that's been nagging me ever since I first met Lauren. The most important question of all.

Beer?

"Colorado Native," says Lauren, who is herself a Colorado native.

Colorado, often called the Napa Valley of beer, hosts the Great American Beer Festival in Denver each October. Colorado also produces more beer than any other state. But Coloradans who want to drink beer made solely from locally sourced ingredients have to skip many mouthwatering microbrews. Brewers rely on dried hops for most of their recipes. In Colorado there is no pelletizer to preserve the hops, so most brewers can only use locally grown hops fresh from the field. This results in a tasty fresh-hop style of beer, but the supply is seasonal and limited. AC Golden Brewing Company (a subsidiary of MillerCoors) buys locally grown hops and trucks them up to the Pacific Northwest to be pelletized for use in Colorado Native, an amber lager made with 100 percent Colorado ingredients.

Lauren and I share a laugh over the MillerCoors juggernaut offering the only commercial brew widely available for a committed Colorado locavore. Then we get serious. I want to know what this is all about. I'm intrigued with the logistics of Lauren's enterprise, and I admire her fortitude, but I still don't get it. An expedition to Antarctica would have taken less preparation and planning. What's the point? There is, of course, the vexing issue of our foodshed being the size of the planet. But just how local should a foodshed be? Do I need to give up my microwave burritos to be a responsible citizen of the world?

Lauren assures me there will be plenty of indulging in three days' time when she concludes her year of eating locally. "But I'll never again take food for granted," she says. "Fresh kale in winter seems almost like a miracle." Items often overlooked and underappreciated, such as salad dressing and condiments, have earned Lauren's abiding respect. "I feel more connected to my food and more aware of where it comes from. My project gave me an appreciation for how much work goes into feeding a human being."

From talking with Lauren, I gather that to challenge oneself to eat locally is to eat contemplatively. Olive oil, coffee, and salt become more than objects consumed by voracious appetites, more than tokens of desire and satisfaction. They become substances to be cherished, foods to be celebrated. And food becomes stories.

"I have great memories of shelling peas at Telluride Bluegrass Festival," Lauren says. "I ran out of time to shell them at home before the festival began, so I took them with me. My little sister, my college roommate, and a bunch of other friends helped me haul a heavy cooler full of peas around the festival grounds. We shelled an entire bushel, about thirty pounds, while we listened to Tim O'Brien, Bela Fleck, and some other great musicians. Then I took the peas to a friend's house in Telluride and blanched them and froze them there."

Lauren is quick to admit that her year of eating locally was not an exercise in purity and perfection. As an experiment, it probed her own psychology as much as it examined the nation's food systems. Her conscience and cravings came under as much scrutiny as industrial food processing. "The bakery where I worked was a chocolaty pit of temptation," Lauren says. "But for every time I gave in to my craving, there were ten times when I didn't. I feel like it makes me a better person to not be so hooked into every spontaneous want that I have. I realized that sometimes food can be a source of pleasure, and sometimes it serves as nourishment. Food doesn't have to be this spectacular perfect event every time. You know, sometimes I'd come home at the end of a long day and thaw some homemade soup and feel satisfied."

Lauren began her yearlong experiment in order to make a statement. She quit the globalized food system to point out its insidious effects on natural resources and communities. Now, at the end of her year, she speaks of simplicity in eating not as a form of deprivation in service of a larger cause but as a means to achieve personal empowerment. She says, "I realized you can live a good life without getting everything you want when you want it."

What at first struck me as some kind of extreme stunt now seems more of a meditation on the meaning of food. What I learned from Lauren is this: When we make our own experiment in eating—whether we choose to eat locally for a year, or to forego meat for a month, or to not order something on a menu we know would taste good but would do some harm in the world that we cannot stomach—we rise above our whims and desires. We become more than the sum of our cravings. To pay attention to what we put on our plate is to shake ourselves from the stupor of consumerism. And in pushing back against consumerism, we begin to appreciate food for what it is, and people for who they are.

After my meeting with Lauren, I take some time to walk the city streets, wandering through the forest of fast-food franchises along Colfax Avenue. As I thread my way through cars parked outside a Popeyes, the scent of fried chicken makes my stomach gurgle with hunger. I remember a point Lauren made: Our ancestors lived happily before superstores and fast food satisfied their appetites. And many people around the world now live lives of abundance and joy without stuffing their bellies with every substance under the sun.

Posters in the windows of a Taco Bell draw me inside for a burrito. As I sit in a plastic booth, limp shreds of lettuce fall onto my tray, and I think about Lauren telling me she'll never again take food for granted. "Fresh kale in winter seems almost like a miracle" rings in my ears as I bite into the burrito.

I've always subscribed to the culinary philosophy that with enough hot sauce or maple syrup, pretty much anything tastes good. I got hooked on Taco Bell mainly because it was the only place open in the late hours when the munchies set in during a year in college I'd rather forget. In truth, the burrito I'm eating tastes pretty good. But the word *miracle* is not on my lips. Instant gratification can be terribly ungratifying.

I doubt I'll ever reach the level of appreciation for food that Lauren has achieved—and I don't really feel like I need to. I don't harbor the slightest desire to eat locally for a year. I do, however, want some of what she has: I want eating to seem more like a deliberate act that I control, rather than a reaction to whatever ploys marketing companies decide to use to tempt the dollars from my pocket. I want to be more than a consumer who responds reflexively to a poster in a fast-food franchise window.

So I enjoy the last few bites of my burrito, slide the waxed paper and plastic hot sauce packets on my tray into a trashcan, and I walk outside telling myself that I won't eat fast food...for a while. I don't really have a plan in place—certainly nothing as ambitious as what Lauren did. But inspired by her example, I will take a break from Taco Bell burritos and all other forms of fast food. The time I save avoiding fast food I can invest in learning how to cook meals with my wife after harvesting the plants we grow in our garden. This is a small act in the grand scheme of things, of course. But it means something to me.

WHILE I HAVE BEEN WANDERING the city in search of farming stories, my wife has been growing a bounty of food in our backyard. I'm all thumbs in the garden and none of them are green. Amy is the expert gardener in our home; I'm little more than labor. She shows me where to dig; I dig. She tells me when to water; I water. Her clever hands coax life from our narrow strip of backyard, from planters perched on a cramped balcony, from pots stacked on our tiny porch. The scent of basil swirls through our home. Bees buzz, hummingbirds hover. Branches sag beneath the weight of tomatoes, and vines twine their way up trellises. Some mornings I stand stunned in the dawn, staring at this abundance in small spaces, reveling in my good fortune to have married such a gifted gardener—and cook. Working in a kitchen smaller than a boat galley, she fills our condo on a regular basis with aromas from treats like homemade marinara sauce and made-from-scratch biscuits.

Thanks to Amy's initiative, family and friends who attend our backyard barbeques have been talking about the fat tomatoes and the lip-smacking lemon basil we've cultivated. I've grown addicted to the sorcery of turning black soil to green herb and red tomato. I'm perfecting my recipe for cakey, clean-smelling compost, grown from coffee grounds, banana peels, eggshells, every kitchen scrap I can get my hands on, shredded newspaper, and my secret ingredient—worms dug from a strangely fertile streambed behind our home. My work in our garden turning the soil and helping edible life thrive in small spaces has plastered a permagrin across my face. Each misshapen vegetable that makes its way from our yard to our table seems perfect to me because we have grown it. Tearing up sod amid a landscape of lawns and replacing this boringness with edible plants that spring from the soil strikes me as slightly subversive—like graffiti for a middle-aged guy. I have been fantasizing about moving my rebellion to the next level by battling my condo homeowners' association over backyard chickens and bees.

After I meet with Lauren, I read up on consumerism and come across a telling study. Something is rotten not in the state of Denmark but in the United States. Denmark is not a wealthy nation compared to the economic powerhouse of the United States. Yet according to the 2013 United Nations World Happiness Report—a 156-nation survey that provides an alternative to the economic measure of gross domestic product (GDP) by ranking countries around the globe based on the well-being of their citizens—Denmark is number one. Mexico, ranked sixteenth, topped the United States, which took the seventeenth spot. We have achieved the highest material standard of living in the history of human civilization, but Denmark, with its dreary Scandinavian skies, and Mexico, with its paltry per capita income and plague of murders, outrank us in happiness?

To figure out what is causing this malaise, I read *Affluenza: The All-Consuming Epidemic.* According to coauthors David Wann, John de Graaf, and Thomas Naylor, affluenza is "a painful, contagious, socially transmitted condition of overload, debt, anxiety and waste resulting from the dogged pursuit of more." By reading the book and searching Internet sites, I learn that the percentage of Americans describing themselves as "very happy" peaked in the 1950s and has remained stagnant ever since. Even though we consume twice as much as we did in the 1950s, even though our per capita income and our GDP have skyrocketed, even though our garages are the sizes of the houses our grandparents grew up in, even though we have iPads and many more cars than the generation before us did, we are no more happy now than when we lived with much less.

Rates of stress, anxiety, substance abuse, and depression are on the rise. According to the World Health Organization, by the year 2020, depression will become the second most widespread illness in the world after heart disease. Psychologist Oliver James argues that the rising rates of mental disorders in rich countries are caused by the relentless pursuit of consumption. He asserts that materialism is to mental illness what smoking is to lung cancer.

Deprivation is awful—this is obvious. No one wants to starve; no wants to be denied life-saving medicine or a roof overhead or a comfortable table to gather around with family and friends. But is gluttony just as awful?

I REACH OUT TO DAVE WANN, a coauthor of *Affluenza*, and he invites me to his home in Golden, Colorado, a city at the edge of the Denver metropolitan area along the foot of the Rockies. Dave strikes me as the absent-minded-professor kind of person who needs to find his glasses in order to see well enough to find his glasses. (I know the type too well: That I managed to find his address without getting lost is a major achievement.) We meet at Dave's townhouse in the cohousing community he helped design. The cohousing concept originated in Denmark, Dave explains as he smoothes his mussed hair and offers me herbal tea.

Bucking the American trend toward isolated living, Dave and the other residents of Harmony Village created their community so that neighbors would meet face-to-face, a striking notion in a world beset by intercoms through which we place food orders from our cars. In a common-use building at Harmony, residents gather to share meals. These communal repasts require cooperation to plan and cook, and they lead to the kind of conversations that don't normally happen in subdivisions where interacting with one's neighbors often consists of little more than a quick wave before we drive into the garage and close the door. Doors at Harmony open onto common space. In the common space is a community garden.

As Dave walks me around Harmony Village, I ask him why on earth we work so hard to accumulate possessions that don't make us happy.

"Well, we're bombarded by thousands of ads every day. That's a big part of it."

I see what he's getting at: Sex is sold in liquor ads, freedom is shilled in commercials for trucks perched on mountaintops, and we find ourselves worrying about which brand of deodorant will bolster our confidence to face the grinding world.

As we walk along a winding brick pathway beneath a canopy of trees, Dave tells me, "Our society, instead of focusing on health and wellness, has created wealth and hellness."

In 1997, as an antidote to the fast pace and lack of meaning in modern life, Dave started the slow work of building the community garden. The hardscrabble earth was almost impenetrable when he began. After countless bags of leaves and buckets of compost nourished the earth, Dave watched the dirt deepen and darken. He says, "I want the garden to be my legacy. A hundred years from now people won't know who did it. But that's not the point. It's the idea that people will think, 'Let's move into this neighborhood because it has this garden.'"

He shows me a solar-powered pump that moves water from a burbling irrigation ditch to the community garden and an orchard, which together cover almost an acre. He says he sees more and more people in his community waking up to the benefits of the garden. "When they eat from the garden they feel better, they have more fun."

"So is building a community garden the cure for affluenza?"

"In our case, with twenty-seven homes, it doesn't feed us. But it certainly supplements stale supermarket junk with real food."

Sunlight glances from the green stubs of plants. As we walk, the wet ground squishes beneath our shoes. Dave says he's watched the garden's yield increase each year. Last summer Harmony Village held a dig-your-own-potatoes day in the garden. Yukon gold spuds were unearthed and put in a pot with leeks and kale to make a tasty soup. Dave grins and says, "People in the community still talk about the flavor of that soup when they pass each other on the pathways."

While he tells me about this meal, I remember the smells of the spinach, scallions, and chives that I harvested from my wife's garden and gave to Mostafa to cook in kuku, a Persian dish similar to an Italian frittata—a dish now at the center of my best memories of friendship and food. Around Mostafa's table, as plates were passed and teacups were filled, differences dissolved in a haze of saffron laughter, and Iran seemed no more distant than my hometown of St. Louis. I suppose I didn't need the coauthor of *Affluenza* to convince me that growing food and sharing it are among the most powerful tools we have to build community.

Dave and I walk to the garden's edge and stand looking out

at a golf course. Roads rumble with traffic in the distance. Dave says, "When we grow our own food, we slow down. And instead of consuming, we produce something. That's powerful."

On my drive back home I manage to get lost. Harmony Village is in the middle of a cancerous sprawl of overbuilt houses that are threatening to turn Golden, a place blessed with natural beauty and a charming main street, into a hellscape of McMansions and shopping malls. Dave's cohousing community is one neighborhood surrounded by rampant overdevelopment. It holds a single community garden amid a landscape scattered with supermarkets stocked with processed food. It's a start.

Chapter 7
So All May Eat

D ave had taught me that when we grow food together, we pause in our duty as citizens of a culture that demands we shop. Fostering life, if only for a brief time in the garden, has the power to heal more than our food system. Community gardens can help move us toward the ideal zone between starvation and overconsumption—the place of moderate living in which we realize our full potential to grow.

While spending time with Lauren and Dave, I realized that there is so much bounty available to me in my own backyard: so many tasty foods, so many fascinating people. And I thought: Why not be a literary locavore and see what stories I could gather just around Denver? But to really do the urban food movement justice, wouldn't I have to sample from cities all over the country? Or even the world? But wouldn't that use an enormous amount of fossil fuel? Moreover, wouldn't it make a mockery of what I'd learned from Ash, Lauren, and Dave about living deeply in my own backyard?

Did I need to tell the story of the urban food revolution by circling the planet? The person who helped me answer this question had spent her career, well, circling the planet. She also helped me find the community I'd been searching for.

ONE AFTERNOON AT WASTE Farmers, John-Paul plays a recording of "Sittin' on John Wayne's Grave," a song of his that he wrote and sent to a potential investor. "Raising money has been a nightmare," he tells me. As John-Paul paces the office floor with his thumbs hooked in his overalls, Matt Celesta steps into the office to tell me that his next themed year will be the Year of the Accountant. "I'll be counting beans and cooking books," he says. Then Matt leaves to supervise soil production, and John-Paul excuses himself to go pee in a bucket (there is no indoor plumbing in the trailer that houses Waste Farmers headquarters). A woman who introduces herself as Dana Miller arrives. She is talking so rapidly about a local food event she's helping organize that I wonder what exactly she's on, and where can I get some? Dana hugs me so hard I nearly lose consciousness. Then she bolts out the door on her way to her next meeting.

"What was that all about?" I ask John-Paul when he returns from doing his business in the bucket.

"Oh, that's Dana. She's Cheerleader for the Universe."

Indeed, Dana, who recently turned sixty, had been a high-school cheerleader, and she had adopted the local-food handle "Cheerleader for the Universe." I had hung around Waste Farmers long enough to stop being surprised by the characters who turned up. A cheerleader for the universe was par for the course. When John-Paul told me that Dana had helped start a nonprofit called Grow Local Colorado, I knew I needed to hear her story.

A FEW WEEKS LATER, I jump into Aron's SUV, which smells of nitrogenous soil and burning cannabis. We head to Sprout

Down, a fundraiser at Mercury Café for Sprout City Farms—the nonprofit that helped pave the way for Nick Gruber to grow food on the grounds of Denver Public Schools. Dana with her graying hair and hazel eyes is at the event hugging everyone in sight and cheerleading her way through the room as she chats with dozens of Denverites at odds with the status quo of industrial food. School fare has changed quite a lot in the quarter century since I sat at a cafeteria table. Vegetable portions consisted of a scoop of sugary applesauce and canned peas, beans, and carrots plopped onto my Styrofoam plate; today many kids in Denver are eating fresh veggies thanks to the efforts of people like Dana.

Dana introduces me to Jessica George, who left a ten-year technical writing career to focus on local food. She's working with an organization that helps veterans start urban farms. She tells me that farming not only provides veterans with gainful employment but also helps them heal. As the son of a veteran, this interests me a great deal.

My finances tell me I desperately need a real job. My gut tells me I need to put serious employment on hold and interview veterans farming in the city, and I should keep talking with Dana, who seems to know everyone connected with the local food movement in Denver.

Dana asks me to meet her in a few days at SAME Café. When I tell her I've never heard of it, she looks at me like I said I've never heard of pants.

"Is it good?" I ask.

"Is SAME Café *good*?" Dana grabs my forearm and squeezes so hard I think she might leave bruises. "You *really* haven't heard of it?"

"I really haven't."

A few minutes later I'm chatting with another woman who mentions SAME Café. "Yeah, I'm supposed to meet someone there in a few days. So where is it?"

She gives a small gasp. "You've never been there?"

WHEN I FINALLY SET FOOT inside SAME (So All May Eat) Café on East Colfax Avenue, I'm expecting trumpets to sound or crepe paper streamers to unfurl. But it seems a very ordinary café.

The line at the counter is long, so Dana and I sit down at a table for a few minutes before we order, and I finally hear her story. Dana explains that when she first discovered local food, she wasn't a foodie or a farmer. "I came to the movement solely through panic," she says. "The first time I watched Al Gore's *An Inconvenient Truth* I felt totally overwhelmed. Climate change bummed me out big time." She explains that the global crisis of fossil fuel depletion sent her spiraling toward depression. "Then I started paying attention to the elephant in the room of overpopulation, added in a big old dose of economic uncertainty, and I spent a year thinking *HOLY FUCK!*" The world's problems seemed too big for her to solve. Not only that, but given her three decades as a United Airlines flight attendant crisscrossing the planet, her carbon footprint was roughly that of, say, the entire population of Belize.

"To get out of my funk, I followed the advice of Laurie David, the producer of *An Inconvenient Truth*." When Dana had heard David speak in Denver, an audience member had asked what she could do about global climate change. Laurie David encouraged the woman to pick one problem and work on it.

"And that's when you got into food?" I ask.

"No, bags made out of shirts."

"Of course."

Dana joined up with a friend to start a triple bottom line company making reusable bags by recycling shirts. "As far as the triple bottom line, well, we did really well on the people and planet parts. We weren't so good on the profit part." But the experience of starting and running the business gave Dana a sense of purpose. "At least I was doing *something*," she says.

Saying no to nihilism felt so good that Dana started Transition Denver, part of the Global Transition Movement. This grassroots effort encourages communities to become resilient against the challenges of climate change, economic instability, and peak oil (the point when the maximum rate of petroleum extraction is reached on the planet and then falls into terminal decline). By undertaking initiatives such as reducing reliance on fossil fuels and creating community gardens, Transition communities aim for a soft landing instead of catastrophic collapse as the world's oil supply diminishes.

Dana assembled a team of volunteers who, in their turn, recruited like-minded Denverites to gather at Mercury Café for Transition Tuesdays. At these meetings they shared information about permaculture techniques, bicycle commuting, solar installation—any practical solution that could contribute to helping Denver transition to a future beyond fossil-fuel dependence, one more prosperous than the present—a future in which do-it-yourselfers help each other raise chickens and can vegetables and collect rainwater and capture the sun's energy in solar panels mounted on the roofs of self-reliant homes.

But the same people, all of whom were already committed to change, kept showing up. Dana wanted to spread solutions throughout Denver. "I knew I needed to find a specific challenge and work on it. I needed to tackle *one* cause with a big impact."

DANA REALIZED THAT the world's entire food supply is tenuous, but she could address local food security in her community. Food unites people interested in health with gardeners and gourmands, with environmentalists and advocates for sustainable living. Libby Birky, who, along with her husband, Brad, founded SAME Café, sums it up while Dana and I eat our lunch of mushroom soup, arugula salad, and feta and pesto pizza. Libby says, "What you put on your plate is the most powerful statement you will ever make."

At SAME Café, each person who eats the delicious, nourishing food pays what she can afford. Instead of a cash register, there is a donation box. If a patron doesn't have any money she can trade an hour of work for a meal. About a decade ago, Libby and Brad thought, "What if people could work in exchange for their food instead of paying for it?" When they talked with men and women at homeless shelters, they found that people who are homeless eat a lot of fast food because it is cheap and, well, fast. "But they wanted something more," Libby says. So she and Brad invested $30,000 of their own money to start SAME Café and provide everyone with healthful food—and with dignity.

"Food is all about dignity," Libby tells me. She believes that everyone, no matter their income, should not only have access to good food, they should also be treated with respect. The food we choose to purchase, prepare, and consume affects our health, of course—but Libby explains that those choices also ripple outward to affect the health of our community. "I used to say I wanted to give something back to my community. But then I realized that saying this implies I'm somehow separate from my community. Building community is really about being a part of something—being in the midst of it, day in and day out."

SAME Café centers around a simple principle: Each of us, whether we work in LoDo or push a shopping cart through the alleyways behind East Colfax, deserves to be noticed and included in conversations. Libby tells me, "I've always liked the saying, 'Beware the everyday brutality of the averted gaze.' There's a woman who comes in here who is educated—she's three credits from a master's degree. But sometimes she has to sleep in her car. People make assumptions about her—she's lazy, uneducated, an addict. Homeless people are too often invisible to us. We walk by and avert our eyes. What they need most is dignity. When we meet them face to face, see them eye to eye, really listen to them—that's how you start to build community."

For Libby, writing checks to charities isn't enough. She would like all of us to roll up our sleeves and work together to feed our community. When Libby explains what she aims to achieve with the café, I'm reminded of Dave Wann's neighborhood garden—his effort to seed community life in a culture stricken by affluenza. Libby seems to be pushing back against the kind of consumerism that allows us to purchase a signifier of compassion without engaging in the act itself.

Clearly the principle behind SAME Café is admirable. The financial model, however, at first struck me as absurdly unsustainable. But the harder I looked at the city around me, the less strange SAME Café started to seem. I began to wonder if its sliding scale is any more unsustainable than adopting an attitude of complacency when many of our neighbors don't have access to healthful food. If people are starved for nutrition, won't all of us end up paying the costs by funding hospital beds and prison cells?

In 2003 Dana concluded her career as a flight attendant and started traveling, instead, around her hometown. When she drilled down into Denver, she discovered a rich vein of artistic talent as community revitalization spread through the Mile High City. Dana became involved in the arts and theater communities, working as hard in her capacity as a volunteer as she ever had as a salaried employee.

Dana admits that she still knows little about the nuts and bolts of growing and distributing food—her forte is connecting people. She organizes gatherings that bring together people from all over Denver who are working on food; she seeds and nurtures relationships and then reaps a rich harvest. Striking up conversations with everyone she meets is second nature: She did it for almost three decades as a flight attendant, interacting with countless strangers on airplanes. Yet she tells me that traveling deeply into the city where she was born and raised has been her greatest journey—an adventure that makes a trip to the Galapagos or Nepal pale in comparison. "It's the people," she explains. "Denver is absolutely full of yummy, yummy people. They are so earnest and adorable—they want to do good. I want to help them do good."

When Dana took on the cause of locally grown food, she cofounded Grow Local Colorado, a group of volunteers with the mission to promote local food, local community, and local economy. Whatever red tape Dana encountered in her push to cultivate a food-production network in the city she managed to burst through.

Dana explains that she used to call herself "Cheerleader for the Universe." After learning about the mind-bending concept of multiple universes, she has rebranded herself "Cheerleader for the Multiverse." Her good cheer gives everyone around her in this universe a contact high. The "Growing our Urban AgriCULTURE" potluck celebrations she helps organize are legendary among Denverites who like to gather and share their love for locally grown food. And Dana has won important people over to the cause of local food, including, in 2007, then-mayor John Hickenlooper (now Colorado's governor), who declared May 14 "Grow Local Day" and authorized a demonstration garden on the grounds of Denver's Civic Center Park. Dana arranged for Returned Peace Corps Volunteers of Colorado to tend these vegetable plots in the heart of downtown Denver. The edible plants form a landscape as lovely as any ornamental garden, and the produce that's harvested goes to feed hungry people at Urban Peak, a shelter for homeless youth.

Dana and I take a break from talking as I head back to the counter to drop another donation in the box and refill my plate.

"There is so much collaboration in the urban agriculture world," Dana tells me when I sit back down and bite into another slice of pizza. "People in the movement are working toward the same goal—making sure everyone has access to healthy food. And they love to share resources and ideas."

Dana knows that she is only as good as her team. Grow Local Colorado is a partner in Produce for Pantries. This collaborative effort between more than a dozen Denver-based organizations "encourages school, community and home gardeners across Colorado to plant, grow and share garden fresh produce with their neighbors." Or, to put it more succinctly, their motto is "We plant. We grow. We share." Grow Local Colorado also partners with Denver Parks and Recreation in raising vegetables in city parks. Even the Governor's Mansion boasts an edible garden.

Whew. That's a whole lot of collaboration.

Just before I ran into Dana, I'd started thinking that if I were going to write a book about the urban food movement, I would have to gather stories in cities around the world, or at least around the country. But there is a strange tension in traveling great distances to study a movement that celebrates what's local, a movement that finds beauty and worth in the dirt beneath our feet. I have been privileged to visit urban farms in places as diverse as the favelas of Brazil and the sky-scraper canyons of Shanghai. But nowhere in the world have I met people more interesting to me than the urban farmers in my own backyard—people trying to rebuild the world one meal at a time.

And so, instead of writing a superficial survey of urban food initiatives around the planet, I chose, like Dana, to live deeply in my own community. In doing this I immersed myself in a microcosm of a movement that is transforming abandoned stockyard buildings in Chicago, rooftops in Manhattan, vacant lots in Detroit, and strips of sterile land in Los Angeles. Across our nation and our world, dead spaces in cities stir with life.

AFTER DANA HEADS OFF to her next appointment—a meeting with faith-based organizations that have a lot of land that could provide garden spaces in the city—I stay to talk with Libby, who points out that food is at the center of the world's religious traditions. It is the focus of family gatherings and is at the heart of a movement that is helping us appreciate essentials: community, health and—especially important to Libby—dignity. "Give with dignity," Libby says. "When you give a gift, imagine you're on the receiving end, and see how you feel."

Treating people as we wish to be treated ourselves, the credo of SAME Café, is connected to many of the world's venerable moral traditions, of course. But it also has solid science to back it up. The neuroscientist V. S. Ramachandran explains that mirror neurons form a system in our brains that allows us to feel what other people are feeling. If we see someone's arm being touched, the mirror neurons in our brain that correspond to our own arm are fired, allowing us to empathize—we can imagine what it's like to be touched. We don't register the actual physical sensation because receptors in our skin send signals to our brain, telling it that we aren't really being touched. However, when experimenters anaesthetize those skin receptors in the arms of experimental subjects to disable the feedback system, and then the subjects see another person's arm being touched, they experience the exact physical sensation of their own arm being touched. Remove our skin and we are one.

At SAME Café there is one menu, one donation box, one dining room.

After that initial lunch with Dana, I returned often to enjoy delicious meals made with locally grown food. I would strike up a conversation with whoever happened to be sitting next to me. A man with a flowing white beard who reeked of booze, a woman preparing for a job interview that could provide her the break she needed to finally get off the streets, a young man with his face shadowed by a hooded sweatshirt who'd run away from home: we ate the same food. I'd drop what I could afford in the donation box, and I would feel grateful for the good work that Libby and Dana do on behalf of all of us.

I have been hounded by depression since I was a teenager, and Mostafa's death triggered one of the more debilitating bouts I've experienced. Jobless, with alcohol sweating from my pores and the hood of my sweatshirt hiding my eyes, I took my place in line at SAME Café. The thin film of separateness between me and the other patrons dissolved completely for a time. The truth is I needed to be there not to research a book but to keep from losing my mind. Meeting people like Dana and Libby was a powerful antidepressant, and meals at SAME Café were the best medicine I could find.

Chapter 8
Protectors to Providers

Using food as a means to help others flourish: This started to seem to me like the beating heart of the urban food revolution. The movement is about how we interact with food, of course. But it is also about how we interact with each other.

Ever since I'd first heard mention of Veterans to Farmers, an organization that was getting former soldiers involved with growing food in greenhouses, I knew I needed to find out more. Dana and Libby had shown me how food can bring people together in community. But can growing food heal what has been broken by war?

SOME 2,500 YEARS AGO, Greek philosopher Heraclitus wrote, "War is the father of all things." This sentence is on my mind as I search in Chu Lai, Vietnam, alongside a man I hardly know, for the ruins of a landing strip—little more than scraps of cracked tarmac. The place where my father was changed forever has been reclaimed by jungle. Only a few concrete helicopter hangars remain. We stand squinting at the gray humps of them from a distance of a few hundred yards. The scream of insects is so loud it seems a kind of silence. Humidity pearls like sweat on the leaves of plants. My dad tells me he doesn't want to get any closer when I offer to walk with him toward the hangars.

As the child of a Vietnam veteran, I know this: When you help a soldier readjust to life back home, you help more than one person. You help families; you heal communities. PTSD is not just a problem of individual soldiers; it is a problem with which all of us are faced.

Buck Adams, a former Marine Corps soldier turned farming visionary, has a solution. He has solutions to several problems, in fact. He is decentralizing the industrial food system, growing healthful produce, creating jobs for veterans, and building self-reliant communities one greenhouse at a time. He's reviving the family farm—but it's like no farm I've ever seen.

Buck Adams has a square jaw that seems as strong as his superhero-like name. But it couldn't withstand the knee of a Samoan rugby player. Along with a shattered jawbone, Buck suffered several concussions while playing rugby in the Marines. In a voice that rumbles above the sound of spilling water, he says, "I don't know if it was the concussions from rugby or the percussions from explosions that gave me my head injury." He explains that surgeons opened his skullcap to remove an osteoblastoma, a kind of tumor that was growing in his brain. His halting speech pattern now makes sense to me: It is symptomatic of someone who's had head trauma. Buck seems to be searching hard for words, and occasionally he can't find them. His laughter comes in staccato bursts, like gunfire.

We sit down at a table in a greenhouse surrounded by a forest of white plastic towers eight feet tall, each one dripping water and sprouting plants. The greenhouse is located in Lake-wood just off busy Wadsworth Boulevard, but the sound of frenetic traffic outside is absent—it's so peaceful inside this growing space we could be in the wilderness surrounded by waterfalls.

Buck tells me he spent several tense months in the early 1990s locked and loaded in the Philippines as a member of the Marine Corps Security Force. Coup attempts destabilized the government and Mount Pinatubo blew apart; then a typhoon arrived, creating a lethal mix of ash and rain, spreading social chaos throughout the Philippines. Buck was tasked with maintaining order and overseeing the evacuation of civilians.

I can easily imagine Buck, who is wearing a button-down shirt and slacks, in a Marine Corps uniform. He's in his early forties but still sports the broad shoulders, thick chest, and trim waist of a jarhead. His hair is a little longer than a high and tight military cut, and it's accented with silver that shines in the bright light of the greenhouse.

"I know how hard it is to transition back to civilian life," he tells me.

Our conversation is interrupted by Buck fielding a call on his cell phone to reschedule a meeting that he's double booked. "I'm doing too many things," he admits. When Buck finishes his phone call, I ask him why it was difficult to reintegrate when his service ended.

"I had PTSD, but it's also hard just not having a routine. No structure. Your life is so regimented in the military. When I got back stateside I drifted around. Didn't know where I belonged."

Buck lived on the beach in California and worked odd jobs like bouncing in bars and modeling for Sears back in the days when Sears had a catalogue. Buck was born the same year I was, 1971. We swap memories of the catalogue—as antiquated now as a rotary phone. "I was the construction guy in the flannel shirt and jeans," Buck says, laughing.

"So how do you get from Sears model to this?" I gesture at the towers covered in plants and splashed with sun.

"I was doing some work for a geothermal heat pump company, and that's how I caught the sustainability bug." He explains that he looked into starting a company using geothermal sources to heat greenhouses, which led him into the world of controlled-environment agriculture, a method that manipulates a crop's environment to achieve optimal growing conditions. "I learned about Mexico's $1.8 billion industry exporting tomatoes to America—almost all those tomatoes come from greenhouses using hydroponics. And I learned that China was way ahead of us in building greenhouses. I realized how far we'd fallen behind the rest of the world in growing food in controlled environments. Of all industrialized nations, we're dead last in greenhouse farming. I saw a business opportunity."

In 2009 Buck joined with a friend in Colorado to start Circle Fresh Farms, specializing in hydro-organic produce. Buck had grown up on a ranch in Texas, and when he was fifteen his family moved to Arkansas, where they raised chickens on contract for Tyson Foods. Growing tomatoes hydroponically was a long way from poultry farming. But Buck borrowed the Tyson business model, creating a central company that contracted with independently owned greenhouses and then marketed the hydroponically grown organic produce to local retailers on the Front Range. When Buck talks about launching this business, which helped scale up local food production and distribution in Colorado, the serious expression on his face changes to that of a child unwrapping a present. But what he's even more excited about is Veterans to Farmers, the nonprofit he founded. And I'm starting to understand why.

A veteran-turned-urban-farmer I spoke with a few days before I tracked Buck down told me, "When I'm in a greenhouse, nothing matters as much as the plants I'm growing. That's my whole world. Soldiers are trained to blow shit up, to break things apart. Nurturing plants to grow is the opposite of everything we're taught in the military."

Buck not only wants to help veterans heal, he wants to change the way food is grown. He tells me, "I'm trying to put the family farm back into America."

Is this really a problem? Or is yearning for the return of the family farm just a form of nostalgia? The United States Department of Agriculture (USDA) says we definitely have a problem. We are facing a serious shortage of farmers in coming years: The people who grow our food are aging and retiring, and few young farmers are prepared to take their place. The USDA is calling for one hundred thousand new farmers, and Buck is heeding that call.

The tagline for Veterans to Farmers is "Turning Protectors into Providers." Buck explains that many military recruits come from either inner city or rural areas; when they return from war there aren't a lot of opportunities available to them in their communities. And for many of them, an academic environment is too overwhelming. "Veterans who are struggling to reintegrate into society don't want to be pitied," Buck says. "They want to serve—that's what they signed up for. When they return home, they want to continue to be of service. Some of them go into fields like police work and firefighting. But that's too much stress for a lot of them. They need to find other ways to serve."

Buck taps into the military training of veterans to help them achieve success as urban farmers. They are used to routines and structure; they are accustomed to being assigned tasks and given missions. Perhaps most important, they have a deeply instilled sense of commitment to a larger cause. The task Buck has given them is to redeploy the family farm. Their mission: feed America.

Buck's larger vision is to create what he calls the National Training Center Greenhouse. This initiative will provide veterans with a stable source of income and healing as they are trained to cultivate food sustainably in urban communities across America. In a sort of boot camp they will receive intensive practical training, and the goals and challenges of the mission will be made clear to them. When their preparation is complete, they'll be redeployed to a greenhouse and given the opportunity to own it. Through their work growing food and feeding the community, they will be reintegrated economically and emotionally into society. "Protectors become providers," Buck says. "It's good for everyone."

Buck points to one of the plastic pillars bursting with greenery. "Check this out." As we walk around a white structure roughly the size of a classical column on a front porch, Buck says, "There are no pesticides or herbicides in this greenhouse. It uses one-tenth the water that conventional agriculture uses. And it yields ten times more food." Forty towers transform the 1,500-square-foot greenhouse into 23,000 feet of growing space—a fifteen-fold increase.

Throughout the greenhouse, uniform towers stand in soldierly formation. The strict discipline of controlled-environment agriculture seems a world apart from the growing systems that Nick and Ash introduced me to—techniques that celebrate the diversity found in dirt. As I stick my hand through an opening in the tower and feel the water trickling inside, Buck tells me, "The best way to make urban farming commercially successful is to go vertical."

IN THE NEAR FUTURE, it's possible that the food we eat will be grown not in fields of dirt but in multistory towers with water dripping downward. From the Hanging Gardens of Babylon to the architect Le Corbusier's boldly imagined skyscraping worlds in the 1930s, vertical agriculture is nothing new. The modern incarnation of this age-old dream of maximizing food production by growing in three dimensions is sort of like the permaculture herb spiral—but on a massive dose of organic steroids. The effort is being led by Dr. Dickson Despommier, a professor of environmental health sciences and microbiology at Columbia University. As director of the Vertical Farm Project, Dr. Despommier has issued a clarion call to architects and agronomists to erect urban farms in innovative towers, forests in the sky that have a small footprint within crowded cities.

If our food were grown in urban towers, much of the land that we have disturbed and denuded by our unsustainable agricultural practices could be allowed to heal, and ecosystems could be restored, slowing our destruction of biodiversity. Instead of inundating fields only to have irrigation water evaporate or run off, carrying pesticides and other pollutants to rivers and seas, water would be recycled inside sealed farm towers—we would use a small fraction of the water required to grow crops in fields. Because the indoor environment would be tightly controlled, there would be no need for herbicides and other harmful chemicals. The hyper-efficiency of constant light and calibrated nutrients would ensure staggering yields. Extreme weather events such as droughts, floods, and hurricanes wouldn't affect the food supply. And because the food wouldn't have to be transported far and could be delivered soon after harvest while still alive, its freshness and nutrition would be enhanced. A head of lettuce travels, on average, 1,200 miles to your plate. Vertical farming advocates like Dr. Despommier contend that shrinking this transportation distance, or "food miles," would reduce energy consumption.

Not everyone is sold on vertical farming—or even on the locavore craze. Using food miles as a simple metric of sustainability has recently come under criticism. Opponents of the food-miles paradigm insist that a much larger share of carbon emissions comes from producing food than from transporting it. They also contend that obsessing about how far food has traveled distorts discussion about the most efficient methods for shrinking the carbon "foodprint." One study, for example, found that tomatoes grown in the warm and sunny fields of Spain and shipped to Sweden had a smaller carbon foodprint than tomatoes grown locally in Swedish greenhouses heated by fossil fuels.

In Colorado's indoor growing environments, ground crops like spinach and microgreens can be covered with thermal blankets to help them survive the coldest spells. But commercial greenhouses in Colorado generally need some form of supplemental heat for part of the year. Generating that heat could create a larger carbon footprint than trucking veggies in from California. Critics of vertical farming also point out that when indoor agriculture goes multistory, the natural lighting benefits of a two-dimensional growing space in a traditional greenhouse or rooftop garden are lost; artificial lighting becomes necessary to illuminate the multiple levels, consuming energy in amounts that can negate the savings of reduced transportation distances.

While experts debate the merits of food farmed in city towers, crowded Singapore has been forced to go vertical. The land-poor, technology-rich nation has emerged as a world leader in vertical farming innovation by banking on its consistently warm temperatures and abundant sunshine. Aluminum trays are rotated toward the sun in a cleverly designed system so efficient it uses only the power required to illuminate a light bulb. But few places on the planet are blessed with Singapore's year-round, 86-degree-Fahrenheit climate and perpetual flood of sunshine.

One of the world's first multistory vertical farms is planned for Jackson, Wyoming. Similar to the system used in Singapore, plants will be moved mechanically on a conveyor belt to maximize their exposure to sunlight. Smart design has reduced the energy footprint of this sophisticated greenhouse— yet it still must be heated in a climate in which winter temperatures plummet so low they freeze the fluids in cars.

Swedish company Plantagon International is building a vertical farm in the Stockholm area, and Plantagon aspires to create skyscraping spheres and soaring conical structures in cities across the planet. Inside these futuristic greenhouses, the company's patented "transportation helix," a spiral ramp designed to slowly move cultivation boxes from floor to ceiling, will allow plants to receive an even distribution of natural light, eliminating the need for artificial lighting. The multistory greenhouse in Sweden will make use of surplus energy supplies in the city and will burn biogas generated from the greenhouse's organic waste.

The largest vertical farm in the U.S. is FarmedHere, a commercial aquaponics operation sited in a windowless, formerly abandoned warehouse in a suburb of Chicago. Taking advantage of recent advances in efficient lighting technology, FarmedHere began operations in 2013. Plans are underway to use methane gas generated by composting to light and heat the building. A similar energy scheme is being implemented in another vertical farm in Chicago's abandoned stockyards district, and post-industrial buildings in cities across America are being slated for rebirth as urban farms.

Along with biogas, a greenhouse's conventional energy use can be offset by harvesting the sun's heat stored underground. While soil's surface temperature varies tremendously throughout the year, the temperature a few feet below the surface remains relatively constant. In winter, ground source heat pumps can direct this buried warmth into a greenhouse. (Ground source heat exchange is often confused with geothermal power, which taps the tremendous heat that emanates from deep within the Earth's core to generate electricity.) Ground source heat exchange, when combined with other forms of renewable energy such as solar and biogas, could conceivably liberate vertical farms from the conventional energy grid, freeing them to produce vast quantities of food with carbon-neutral methods.

Perhaps technology can keep pace with the dream of forests in the sky. For now, the farmscrapers of the future exist in exquisitely rendered architectural drawings that stir the imagination of science fiction fans. I can't look at them without thinking about self-sufficient colonies on distant worlds. Indeed, one item on Dr. Despommier's list of reasons why vertical farming is necessary is that we won't be able to survive long term in space if we can't first figure out how to grow food on a large scale in controlled environments here on Earth.

Maybe these farms that tower upward among the world's cityscapes will always be a thing of the future, and we will find ourselves forever digging in the dirt, turning the earth with our tools, giving thanks to the microbes and worms that build the soil. There is a part of me that wants my boots to be crusted with dirt and to feel the sun on my neck as I kneel to loosen the roots of weeds with my bare hands and inhale the scent of soil. There is also a part of me—the part that read a lot of Isaac Asimov when I was a kid—that dreams of life inside sterile towers with their climates controlled by sensors and dials as we feed the planet's hungry masses and prepare to journey toward the stars.

Perhaps the truth, as always, is somewhere in the middle. Maybe a combination of radically different growing systems— some referencing ancient practices to steward the world's soils, others reaching forward to create controlled indoor growing environments in cities—will allow us to feed the nine billion people predicted to fill the planet by 2050.

REGARDLESS OF WHETHER skyscrapers of food will rise in our cities, I'm fascinated with this smaller version of the vertical farm Buck is showing me. While we talk amid the measured sound of cascading water, Buck introduces me to the owner of this greenhouse, Sgt. Evan Premer.

"I had a troubled childhood," Evan tells me. He doesn't go into details about his life before the military or during his service. In response to my questions, he tells me that when he decided he wanted to change his ways as a troubled teen, he joined the Army National Guard. He volunteered to go to Iraq, where he served twelve months as a door gunner on UH-60 Blackhawk helicopters. He ran air assaults and resupply missions to outward bases. "That's all I can say about it," he tells me. But he does talk about his insomnia, the nightmares that plague his sleep.

When Evan came back from Iraq he started a small property management and custom interiors business, but it went bust when the economy crashed. He went to school to study photography. He says, "That's really what I wanted to do, but it's hard to make a business out of it." And the flashes of light triggered wartime memories. He struggled to hold down jobs.

Seven years after his service in Iraq, when Evan sees a lone helicopter flying he feels his pulse quicken. The rational part of his mind knows there are good reasons why a single helicopter might be in the air. But in Iraq, a lone helicopter always meant something was wrong. He startles when objects are dropped. The sound of a certain tone of low bass in music brings back memories of bomb blasts. Evan says, "Most civilians don't understand the experiences veterans have gone through." He knows that his behavior can seem blunt and abrasive to those who aren't familiar with war. But in combat situations, he explains, a failure to be direct can cost lives. A soldier isn't concerned about people's feelings; he's focused on receiving and issuing orders. Evan reveals that unlearning the communication skills that saved lives in combat is no easy task.

Evan applied for a job at Walmart. "They said I was overqualified." He tells me this with no show of emotion—it's hard to get a read on how painful his unemployment was for him. "We were taught to never show weakness," he says of his military training. But small cracks appear in Evan's tough demeanor, and pain pours through. He's having trouble sitting still in his chair as we talk. "I was desperate," he says, his hands fidgeting on the table. Searching for some way to fit in to society, he started Googling "jobs for veterans." That's how he found Buck.

"I was always interested in agriculture," Evan says. "But I couldn't afford to buy land." Buck invited Evan to participate in an intensive eight-month program that trained former soldiers in both the technology and business of controlled-environment agriculture. Through Buck's program, and through connections supplied by Evan's mother, Esther Premer, who volunteered at a greenhouse and worked at restaurants, Evan and his mom were able to start this greenhouse business, Aero Farm Co.

We get up from the table and walk around the greenhouse. Evan seems more at ease when moving among his plants. As I watch his practiced hands picking leaves and checking roots, the space where he does his work seems like a decompression chamber. There are no IEDs to be wary of, no insurgents lurking in the ruins of cities, no snipers on rooftops with their sights on his back. In this safe place the temperature remains constant and the gurgle of water blends with the steady hum of fans.

Evan's mother says the changes she's seen in her son since he began his urban farm business are remarkable. His anger has diminished, his edginess has eased. His time is occupied. "I think the most important thing is he has a sense of purpose," she tells me.

Evan's wife, also a member of the National Guard who served in Iraq, where the couple met, will soon start working at the family business if everything goes according to plan. Their daughter, who is four, likes being in the greenhouse so much she asked her dad if she could camp there. "She wanted to put a tent right in the greenhouse," Evan says with a chuckle, his voice softening as he speaks about his daughter. When she was born, he gave up cigarettes. "She deserved a dad who didn't smoke," he says. "I eat the greens I grow when I'm driving to help deal with road rage, and to keep me from smoking." Evan's master plan is to build an urban farm business that he can pass on to his daughter. Food isn't just helping heal this veteran: It's strengthening his family—and his community.

Though the greenhouse is tucked back from a road and can be hard to find, people seek it out, curious about their neighborhood farmers with their space-age aeroponic towers. Aeroponics is the process of growing plants in an air or mist environment, in contrast to hydroponics, the process of growing plants in a liquid medium. NASA-sponsored research aboard the Mir space station has contributed to the aeroponic growing systems now in use on Earth.

The aeroponic towers that rise in Evan's greenhouse hold net pots—shaped like flower pots but with netlike openings, like little laundry baskets. The plants are started in rock wool, a medium made from molten rock spun into fibers. Then the seedlings are transplanted to the net pots, which tilt outward to point the plants toward the sunlight that streams through the plastic skin of the greenhouse. Water infused with a nutrient blend is lifted upward from a reservoir at the tower's base by a pump similar to what you'd find in a fish tank; the liquid trickles back down inside the tower, misting the roots with all the water and nutrients the plants need to grow. The greenhouse needs to be heated part of the year, but the natural light of Colorado's Front Range, blessed with three hundred days of sunshine a year, is sufficient to grow greens in the one-story structure. The productivity is remarkable—from seed to salad bowl in less than a month. What really gets my attention, however, is the taste.

The nutrient-rich broth that is slurped up by the plants results in fresh greens so flavorful, I wander through the vertical farm sampling crackly watercress and clean arugula, pleasantly bitter chard and tender leaves of kale, savory microgreens and basil with a spicy bite. To suppress this banquet of flavors with dressing would just be wrong. I've never eaten greens that stand so solidly on their own and offer so many distinctive flavors. "It's because they're still living," Evan explains as he shows me the roots attached to a bunch of arugula he just pulled from a pot. Local chefs are eager to purchase these plants because they are still alive when they arrive in their kitchens. The 150 pounds of super-fresh greens Evan produces each week are plated at prominent restaurants in Denver's culinary scene like Linger, Root Down, and Beast + Bottle.

The greens I'm taking home with me from Evan's greenhouse will get drizzled with olive oil and sprinkled with sea salt. Maybe a few pinches of shredded Romano cheese, maybe some cracked black pepper, nothing more. I would buy these greens from Evan because he's a good guy working hard to build his business, but the truth is, I'd buy these greens no matter who was growing them—because they taste damn good.

Community members who live near Aero Farm Co. may soon be dining on the mouth-watering greens, tomatoes, and strawberries Evan grows in his greenhouse. He's creating a CSA program for the neighborhood—the first year-round CSA in the state, Evan explains. "I can grow food in the greenhouse through the winter and feed my neighbors all year long," this protector-turned-provider tells me with evident pride.

ON MY DRIVE HOME, while battling traffic and feeling my blood pressure rise, I try Evan's therapy: I munch handfuls of arugula to keep my anger in check. The fresh bite of the leaves focuses my attention on the sharpness of their flavor—and these tasty greens put a smile on my face that the idiot in the minivan who just cut me off can't erase. I wonder what my dad's life would have been like if he'd entered the controlled environment of a greenhouse after returning from the chaos of war. And I wonder what my life would have been like.

Gardening's therapeutic value is well established in the scientific literature. Though anecdotal evidence suggests farming is highly beneficial for veterans struggling with PTSD, remarkably little science has been done to evaluate its efficacy. An expert advisory panel assembled by the Institute of Medicine determined in 2014 that the efforts of government agencies to track and evaluate the effectiveness of PTSD therapies have been inadequate. Nearly one veteran an hour commits suicide. Do we have time to wait for bureaucracies to fund research that proves that working in greenhouses helps veterans grow?

ON MY TRIP TO VIETNAM with my father, we walk along a beach. The sound of the surf stirs memories of Evan's urban farm in me. The water in his controlled growing space is a stream with many branching channels. It is lifted upward by softly humming electric pumps, and gravity cascades it back down to nourish the roots of plants in a continual loop, a soothing flow. As I imagine helicopters and mortar fire, I am struck by the idea that a greenhouse is the polar opposite of war.

My dad is as tight-lipped as Evan about his war experiences. But his shaking hands belie the steadiness of his speech as we drive back to our hotel from the ruins of the base at Chu Lai where fifty years ago he'd taken shelter in a bunker. While watching my dad's unsteady hands I think about Evan inside his greenhouse, his plants an entire world that surrounds not only him but his mother, his wife, his daughter. He nourishes the greens that give him strength, and the nutrients that cycle through his greenhouse spread through his family and his community. When soldiers return to society as farmers, swords are turned into ploughshares, destroyers become creators, and all of us are healed.

WHILE SPENDING TIME IN urban farms with people traumatized by war, I thought about Mostafa and the few times he'd told me stories of serving on the front lines of the Iran-Iraq War. What role combat stress played in Mostafa overeating I will never know, though I wonder if the calming release of chemicals triggered by sugar and fat helped steady him when memories from the front lines surfaced. Like my father and Evan, Mostafa would speak to me of his war experiences in a guarded way that made me reluctant to press him for details.

Had I known about Buck's program when Mostafa was alive, and had I known that Mostafa was struggling with his health and with the trauma of war, I would have taken him into a greenhouse. But the truth is, as much as Mostafa had enriched my life, I had paid little attention to how deeply wounded he was, whether by PTSD or by the culture shock of severing himself from his Persian traditions. I had let myself be lulled by Mostafa's stories and his saffron tea into believing that my friend was fine—and then, after he died, I was angry with him for not having been honest with me about his health. But maybe I hadn't looked carefully enough at what was going on beneath his surface. Maybe I had wanted to be charmed by his persistent cheer so that I wouldn't have to do the hard work of helping my friend find his way toward true health—instead of simply badgering him to shed some extra pounds.

One afternoon while I sat inside a greenhouse watching a former soldier grow, I was struck by the thought, as I had been in Dave Wann's community garden at Harmony Village, that what killed Mostafa might have less to do with our food system than with our culture. I had consumed Mostafa's tea and stories while giving him little of substance in return. My efforts to cajole him into exercising were perfunctory at best. That I hadn't understood the degree of his sickness was not his fault but mine. If we can't bring ourselves to take care of our closest friends in our community, how can we expect to feed the world? In the overstocked aisles of the supermarkets around my home lurked a deep poverty that I was still struggling to fill.

Chapter 9
Microchips to Crop Mobs

So many people I had met in the urban food movement were using food as a means to achieve social justice and dignity, empowerment and connection. By nurturing plants under the most improbable conditions, they were cultivating much more than kale. Soon after meeting Buck and Evan, I learned that veterans aren't the only ones who fill their need for meaningful work by growing food in the city.

When a crop mob in Denver had to be cancelled, dozens of people were disappointed because they had been looking forward to a day of backbreaking labor without pay. I needed to work for free like I needed a hole in the head, but I wanted to know what these people were up to.

THE CROP MOB MOVEMENT began in North Carolina in 2008 when local growers came together to harvest sweet potatoes. Now more than fifty crop mob groups have spread across the country. The people who participate range from professional farmers to curious city dwellers who have heard rumors that food comes from the ground. Members of a crop mob combine their skills and labor to do whatever jobs need doing, from building raised beds to removing rocks from fields, from prying apart scrap pallets to erecting greenhouses. The work is not easy, especially for people used to sitting in office chairs. Soft hands blister. Faces get sunburned. Shoulders get sore.

Petroleum powers industrial farming; sweat powers sustainable agriculture. Finding the labor to support sustainable ag is a challenge. For small farmers, a crop mob is an obvious boon: projects that would take the owners of the farm and their few farmhands months to complete are constructed in a single afternoon with the sweat of a mob. For the people who do the work, the benefit is less obvious.

ONE CRISP SATURDAY MORNING in April, an army of volunteers heads to Waste Farmers. With hammers, shovels, and the strength of their backs, they will build gardens, and their compensation will be burritos and camaraderie. When John-Paul mentions the mob to me, I head to Waste Farmers to figure out why these people are working for free.

After picking up a shovel, I enter the cheerful pandemonium of the crop mob. A two-year-old toddles between her father's legs. An eight-year-old tells me about the PowerPoint presentation on lightning she just put together, and she lets me know that a bolt heats the air to fifty thousand degrees, a temperature hotter than the surface of the sun. Her name is Flora. She goes to Denver Green School and loves Meg, the farmer who grows food on the school grounds. I watch her father wield a machete with the skill of a jungle guide. A young woman in overalls oversees the building of a garden bed. Men and women in their sixties push boulders and lift logs. A dog dodges through human traffic to fetch tossed sticks. A grandmother who is an expert urban forager points out that I'm standing in hemlock, which looks a lot like parsley or carrot tops, but if I tasted it I'd be dead. Good to know. She finds some wild rocket and we nibble pleasantly bitter leaves while meadowlarks call from the bushes. A young soldier just discharged from active duty kneels before a water cooler and puts his mouth beneath the spout. "Jesus didn't have a cup," he says as he stands and wipes his lips with the back of his hand. "At least, I think he didn't." He tells me he joined the military so he could see the world but was sent to Kentucky for seven years. I wander over to a man with a deeply tanned face smoking a hand-rolled cigarette. He's a serial entrepreneur, and his latest business venture consists of building permaculture gardens. He's a committed mycophile, and for several minutes he speaks the strange language of mushrooms and mycelium. Fungi spores are in the air all around me, he explains, waving his hands like a magician setting the stage for a trick.

After I help move a pile of logs, a man with a snow-white goatee and a do-rag, who looks like a Harley rider but with the eyes of a Buddhist saint, hugs me. Not a guys-slapping-each-other-on-the-back kind of hug. This guy squeezes me like he really means it. "He's a hugger," someone tells me as I wander off to pick up rocks. I'm having more fun than I ever had working in sales and marketing, back when I ironed my pants each evening and wondered where my life had gone terribly wrong.

A Bobcat buzzes around and people hitch rides on the forks, winging their arms for balance as they surf the bumps and divots in the dirt. One man reclines in the elevated bucket of a Caterpillar front-loader, its tires nearly as tall as the people standing beside the machine.

And then there's Oz. Sporting dark sunglasses and California surfer hair, he's fifty but could pass for thirty-five. He doesn't look like a farmer. Someone mentions that Oz organized this mob, so I strike up a conversation with him. I want to know who he is and how he got all these people to work without paying them.

Oz tells me that in Silicon Valley he scarfed Big Macs on the go so he could program around the clock. "I worked a hundred hours a week and ate Twinkies for dinner," he says. Now he brings people together to scatter seeds, building small clusters of community. An engineer who helped increase the speed of the modern world now promotes the "slow food" philosophy, an international movement that encourages alternatives to fast food. This approach to growing and eating food emerged from grassroots opposition to the opening of a McDonald's in Rome in 1986. To push back against the industrial logic that threatens to displace regional dishes on tables across the world with a homogeneous feeding trough for humanity, Slow Food promotes the farming of plants, seeds, and livestock that evolved in native ecosystems. Today, the movement spans the globe, including projects and participants in 160 countries.

I had heard of the Slow Food movement before, but Oz gets me up to speed. He also helps me understand why, despite society's efforts to liberate people from physical farm work, they now flee their cubicles to work in the soil for free. Similar to how slow food opposes fast food, crop mobs push back against consumerism: Oz lays it out for me at a coffee shop when we meet a few weeks after the mob.

While gulping chai before his yoga class, Oz tells me he teaches adult gymnastics—which seems an apt physical expression of the athletic leaps and tumbles of his thoughts. He was born James Osborn but went by Ozzy Osborn to set himself apart from his father, a Southern Baptist preacher; he dropped the *zy* when the show "The Osbournes" revealed an aging, sad-sack rocker rather than the badass who'd once fronted Black Sabbath.

Oz began his professional life as an auto mechanic; then he went to college to study electrical engineering with a focus on semiconductor device physics. He landed in Silicon Valley in 1996. This was a time when, as Oz explains it, startups were the new religion and Steve Jobs, Steve Wozniak, and Bill Gates were the high priests. Tech innovators from across the planet converged on the Santa Clara Valley, chanting strings of code and focusing like monks assembling mandalas on shrinking the size of transistors on silicon wafers. Oz explains that the mantra of these worshippers of speed was Moore's law, which postulates that the number of transistors on integrated circuits doubles approximately every two years, leading to an exponential increase in computing power. "As you decrease geometries, as you get down into nanometers, you start running into all kinds of bizarre effects."

Uh huh. I nod like I know what this means. I'm as far out of my depth as when I interviewed Ietef about hip-hop.

Basically, Oz helped develop the software that enabled Intel and its ilk to build smaller and faster integrated circuits, accelerating the pace of the modern world.

But that didn't satisfy him.

"Science used to be about serving the greater good. Take Jonas Salk, for example. He didn't patent the polio vaccine he discovered." When Oz began his career, the scientists and engineers in Silicon Valley certainly weren't as selfless as Jonas Salk, but Oz insists that there was a sense among them, these men and women who were pushing forward the power of computing, that they were part of something larger than themselves. He says, "They were members of an intellectual corps supporting a nation based on science and engineering."

But the cerebral stimulation of this endeavor offered only a mild buzz compared to the intoxication of quick wealth. According to Oz, the *esprit de corps* that once existed among the programmers in Silicon Valley disappeared, replaced with stock options and deals brokered by bankers. "It became all about business," says Oz. "And I got bored. The 2008 financial crisis was a blessing for me."

He accepted a severance package from his downsizing company, Cadence Design Systems, sold almost all his possessions, and bought a sixteen-foot trailer. He says, "It was sort of a traveling monk's cell." He headed to Spirit Rock to study Vipassana meditation in the hills outside of Santa Rosa. He explains that a broken relationship had "cracked him wide open" and he was receptive to new ideas about the world and about himself. While at Spirit Rock he volunteered in capacities ranging from running a sound system during spiritual teachers' presentations to building a children's garden, and he thought about his eighteen-year-old son, Jakob, and what kind of future he'd have.

"Throughout my life," Oz says, "I had adhered to the belief that no problem is unsolvable given sufficient analysis and engineering. But when I thought about where we've come from and where we're going, I came to the conclusion that the past performance of technological solutions is no indication of their future success."

Whew. Oz's affinity for slow and simple food doesn't stop him from delivering complicated sentences quickly. I say, "So just because we've solved problems with technology in the past, there's no guarantee technology will solve our problems in the future?"

"Exactly." Oz thumps the table, adding an exclamation point.

Like so many others in the urban food movement, Oz is focused on the fact that modern agriculture depends on fossil fuels to grow, harvest, process, and transport food. Oil powers machinery from irrigation pumps to slaughterhouse assembly lines. According to Michael Pollan, our food system uses more fossil fuels than any other sector of the economy save cars.

Oz adds, "As petroleum production peaks and then wanes, the world will find itself running low on cheap fossil fuels, and industrial farming will be faced with crisis. The technological solution of adding ammonium nitrate fertilizer to the soil has left us with the metaproblem of how to feed nine billion-plus people when the natural gas runs out."

Contrary to Oz's assertions, some economists and technology optimists say that limits are for other species—our human brains have the creative capacity to surmount every barrier that seems to stand in our way. "There is always more," is their belief. They point out that, at one time, virtually every agricultural expert on the planet agreed that there was an upper boundary to how much food we could grow. The limit had to do with nitrogen fixation. Nature, through its slow work of lightning and legumes, could only turn a limited amount of atmospheric nitrogen into molecules necessary for plant growth. Then along came the Haber-Bosch process.

An ingenious industrial procedure, Haber-Bosch breaks the tight bonds of atmospheric nitrogen, turning it into ammonia available for plants to use. An unlimited supply of fertilizer was suddenly ours, neatly removing nature's nitrogen limit. The ten-thousand-year-old challenge of how to cycle nitrogen back into the soil was solved, rendering practices that had sustained civilizations for millennia, such as crop rotation and fertilizing fields with manure, as antiquated as Atari. The industrial-scale farming that followed resulted in an unprecedented bounty of food, allowing people to fill the planet in ever-growing numbers. Now, one third of the human population is sustained by synthetic nitrogen fertilizer. In the bible of modern life it is written: Break the bonds of nitrogen and ye shall multiply across the Earth.

But the natural gas that serves as a source of hydrogen in the Haber-Bosch process is finite: there is only so much natural gas on the planet. Will further innovation free us from this constraint?

Originally, hydrogen for the Haber-Bosch process was provided by the electrolysis of water (using electric current to split water molecules into oxygen and hydrogen). In theory, renewable energy could power the electrolysis of water to supply hydrogen for the Haber-Bosch process—leading to a supply of nitrogen fertilizer limited only by the lifespan of the sun and the amount of water on this planet.

Or will we finally bump up against a limit that not even our drive to make money and our big creative brains can surmount? Sunny economists and technology optimists say "Don't worry. We'll figure it out. We always do." Many supporters of sustainable agriculture like Oz say, "Worry for all you're worth—we're fucked."

Oz started to obsess about the overarching challenge of limits. He finally concluded that no amount of what he calls "techno magic" could help us escape the finite quantities of water and soil.

His point is intriguing. Even Moore's law, for all its accuracy at demonstrating the exponential growth of computing power, eventually bumps up against a limit: there is a fixed amount of space on a silicon chip, and you can only cram so many transistors, however small you might be able to engineer them, onto that surface. You can't put an infinite amount of something into a finite space. As with silicon chips, so with farming. "You can't grow an endless supply of food with finite resources," Oz explains. "At some point you encounter limits. There are bounds to our resources that even the greatest engineers on the planet can never transcend."

I ask him if he still does any work as an engineer. He replies, "I mainly consider myself a permaculturist at this point, more than an engineer. Permaculture is really a form of ecological engineering. But the permaculture set of ethics—earth care, people care, and fair share—and the permaculture design principles, like stacking functions, provide a framework that I can operate within. In my old engineering days, I lacked that kind of comprehensive structure. In Silicon Valley I was only valued for my ability to solve specific problems."

Oz mentions that he went through a vegetarian phase but now he's back on meat. But this time he isn't gobbling factory farmed beef; he's dining on bison from South Dakota. Oz points out that cattle didn't evolve on the American plains but are descended from the now-extinct aurochs native to Europe, Asia, and North Africa. Poor grazing practices have desertified vast swathes of prairie where once the grass rose higher than a horse's stirrups and the soil was deep and black in the bottomlands. Bison evolved in the shortgrass prairie ecosystem of the American plains and thus live in balance with the plants and the earth beneath their hooves. When bison are allowed to roam as they have for millennia, they heal the land. When this keystone species returns to the prairie, so do grasses and insects and birds. So do bears and wolves and healthy human communities. Oz says, "*Buffalo for the Broken Heart* by Dan O'Brien convinced me that by eating bison I'm participating in the ecological restoration of the Great Plains."

Oz adds, "I'm convinced that complex problems can't be solved with simple, one-size-fits-all solutions imposed from above. The federal government is not the answer. Building resilient communities has to begin at a grassroots level."

He would like for everyone to have easy access to nutritious, affordable food, but he stops short of calling this a *right*. "Food justice isn't something I want to force on the world," he says. "I just show up in communities and organize crop mobs. Nature does the rest."

Organizing a mob is, of course, something of an oxymoron. "The growth I'm going for is organic—it begins with people, not policies." Oz would have me believe that when neighbors gather in mobs wielding pitchforks to turn the soil in their community gardens, seeds of revolution are sown. But can volunteers gardening without pay really change the world?

Many people who work in sustainable farming find they have little time to socialize because their hours are filled with grueling labor. But when I worked in an office I felt faced with an equally grueling task: maintaining my sanity while the minutes of my life ticked away. As Peter says in *Office Space*, "We don't have a lot of time on this earth! We weren't meant to spend it this way. Human beings were not meant to sit in little cubicles staring at computer screens all day, filling out useless forms and listening to eight different bosses drone on about mission statements."

Crop mobs bring individuals together, whether they labor in a greenhouse or toil in a cubicle, to do even more work—but to do the deeply satisfying human work of creating community, which is built, according to farmer-philosopher Wendell Berry, out of the shared stories, shared meals, shared burdens, and shared sense of place that emerge from such endeavors. A crop mob recreates a barn-raising vibe in the city. If a farmer's barn burns down, neighbors often pitch in to help rebuild it because all it takes is a few weeks of dry weather and an errant spark and their own barn could face a similar fate. To grow food is to realize how tenuous life is—nature never tires of doling out disasters. It seemed to me like the crop mobbers might be building the kind of community that comes together both to celebrate harvests and to provide support when crops fail.

Many of the people from the crop mob at Waste Farmers showed up at seed swaps, where heirloom seeds pass between the hands of people who treat them like precious stones, and friendship, too, is exchanged. They also went to potlucks organized by Michael Anderson, the kind-eyed hugger I'd met at the mob. While sharing food, people at these communal meals continued the conversations they'd started while working together in the dirt.

At a meal at Waste Farmers, I stood talking with a man I'd built a garden bed with, and together we ate caprese made with fresh tomato and basil harvested from his farm. As I listened to his story about growing the tomatoes, I remembered the feel of a tomato from my own garden as I tugged it from the grip of a vine, and I recalled the sharp green scent of its leaves. I had sliced into its ruby plumpness on a counter in Mostafa's kitchen while he simmered a stew and spun tales from Iran.

Crop mobs and potlucks helped me find some of the connection I'd lost when Mostafa's saffron tea and stories vanished from my life. This new community helped file down the sharp edge of loss attached to those memories, and grief was supplanted by gratitude for unanticipated friendships.

"THE PEOPLE WHO SHOW up at crop mobs are searching for a sense of purpose," says Oz before we wrap up our meeting at the coffee shop on Colfax. "They're looking for something more fulfilling than buying and selling stuff."

"And that's why they work for free?"

"They're hungry for meaning. For connection. We live in an atomized world." Oz explains that military drafts for the World Wars ripped young people from small towns; urban renewal in the 1960s flattened the cores of cities; and highways that were bulldozed and paved through the poorest, community-rich sections of urban and rural landscapes allowed us the convenience of traveling vast distances while cocooned in anonymity, ensconced in shells of steel. We exist separate from each other and from nature. Our neighbors are strangers, our food is alien to us. We see people next door and don't know their names. Meals appear on our plates and we have no idea where they came from.

It all seems so grim, and I say so.

"But when people are confronted with complex problems such as peak oil, they can be paralyzed and give up, or they can choose to act." I'm reminded of Dana's experience feeling overwhelmed for a year but then deciding to help build local food systems as an antidote to her despair. Oz explains that Victor Frankl, the Holocaust survivor who developed a school of existential psychotherapy, claimed that the one thing that can never be taken from us is our choice of how to react to situations. Frankl believed we're motivated by a "will to meaning." According to Oz, it is not enough to fill our bellies with empty calories and our minds with TV. He says, "Our deepest need as human beings is to participate in something larger than ourselves."

At the crop mob at Waste Farmers, as the sun simmered over the Rockies in the west, we stretched our backs and rubbed our sore muscles. Working together, our spontaneous community had turned a scruffy patch of ground into a handsome garden. I could have purchased a gym pass and run by myself on a treadmill; I could have lifted weights with music blasting through my earbuds. But I wouldn't have found the kind of bliss that doesn't have a barcode—the sense of connection that comes from building something as part of a community.

Oz IS PROGNOSTICATING A bleak future. But he sees promise in falling off the cliff sooner rather than later. "Maybe we should all chant 'Drill, baby, drill' and drive our Hummers as fast as we can toward that cliff," he says in a sincere tone. "When faced with total collapse, we'll finally be forced to relearn how to work together. We'll realize we need each other, just like we needed each other when we lived in farm communities before oil flowed from the ground."

Perhaps Oz is right, and when the structures we have built with petroleum finally fall, green shoots will sprout from the exhausted earth. Maybe the rivers will flush the last of the ammonium nitrate fertilizer away to the sea, and people will gather in gardens, and mobs will form to plant seeds. And perhaps those mobs will merge into a movement that builds a new way of being from the ground up by paying careful attention to the limits of soil and water and of the human heart, which can only stand so much separation.

Chapter 10
Petroleum Geology and
Homegrown Tomatoes

One of the most interesting people I met at a crop mob was a quiet guy named Tim whose baseball cap was pulled low over his eyes as he built raised beds. He was reciprocating for the help he'd received from a crop mob that had spread soil in his organic garden where he grows herbs and greens, tomatoes and beans.

After glancing over his shoulder to make sure no one was listening, Tim confided in me that he was "part of the evil empire." He took another look around. Then, under his breath, in the same way a person might let slip at church that he works in the porn industry, he told me what business he's in.

When folks at urban farming events ask Tim Engel what he does, he tells them he raises vegetables. Which is true. What Tim doesn't tell them is that in order to grow organic food and share it with others, he drills for oil.

A FEW WEEKS AFTER THE crop mob I meet Tim at The Infinite Monkey Theorem, an urban winery just north of downtown Denver in the trendy River North, or RiNo, Art District. No vineyard amid rolling hills for this winery. No tasting room gleaming with granite and marble. The Infinite Monkey Theorem's owners bring grapes into a back alley of the city to make batches of wine, and tastings are done in a space as understated as a Soho loft.

The overalls and boots Tim wore at the crop mob have been replaced by jeans and running shoes. "I was a fat kid," he says. "I could never seem to lose weight." Given his lean runner's physique, this admission causes some cognitive dissonance. He explains that when he began growing his own food and cooking it, he slimmed down. A compound fracture shattered his leg, but three surgeries and a near-fatal blood clot in his lungs later, he started running longer and longer distances. He grew bored with marathons and began training for the legendary Leadville 100. This former fat kid ran one hundred miles through mountainous terrain in one of the most demanding endurance races on Earth.

"So what's an oil guy doing spreading organic food through the city?" I ask when we sit down and rest our elbows on the scuffed wood of the wine bar.

Tim grew up south of Buffalo, New York, in a small town where his parents owned a feed mill and hardware store. When he wasn't putting in time at the family business, he was milking cows and throwing hay at nearby farms. "My first farm chore was cleaning out a barn knee deep in shit," he says. "I had to shovel for a week before I saw the floor."

He studied agriculture when he started college, but a geology class got him hooked on rocks. "You can get more stories out of a baseball-sized rock than you can out of most people's lives these days," Tim tells me. It takes him a couple of glasses of wine to really start talking. He lives as a bachelor with his dog, Gonzo. Mesmerized by the millions of years of history in each grain of every stone, he was astounded by the information a rock could reveal when he took the time to really look at it and study it, to figure out its origins. After taking some advanced geology classes, he realized he had a knack for geophysics. Interpretation of seismology data is a science, but it is also, Tim notes, "a lot of art and a little bit of wackiness." He could look at the wiggles of lines produced by vibrations deep below the earth's surface and reconstruct the story of unseen layers. Sometimes those stories spoke of oil. Now, when Tim finds a promising area, he buys the mineral rights and sinks a well. Some wells produce, many do not.

High stakes gambling: That's how my great-uncle Lee Grace, a wildcatter in Wyoming, once explained the oil business to me.

I GOT TO KNOW UNCLE Lee when I was living in Jackson Hole, Wyoming, an absurdly beautiful place where I went for a summer to guide rafts on the Snake River, decided to stay for a ski season, and left six years later after glutting myself on daily doses of rock climbing, mountain biking, snowboarding, paragliding, and any other sport I could try. The mountains were my church and I worshiped every day. The thought of these places being desecrated by oil and gas development sent me into spasms of outrage. I considered oil companies demonic. That I was using an awful lot of refined oil driving my car to ski and climb didn't lessen my loathing for Exxon and Shell. And so, when I sat down for dinner one night with Uncle Lee as he was passing through Jackson Hole, I was fully prepared to give him an earful about the damage he was doing to the planet. Instead, he filled my ears with stories so interesting they shut me up completely.

Long before Tom Cruise played Maverick Mitchell in *Top Gun*, Uncle Lee was training fighter pilots to prepare for battle. When he returned to the States after World War II, he escaped the family sign manufacturing business in St. Louis and headed west, where geologists hired him to fly them over Wyoming. From the windows of the plane Uncle Lee piloted, the geologists searched the ground below for domes and anticlines and telltale outcrops, landscape features that hinted at a treasure of oil. There were no satellite photos, no sophisticated seismic surveys. Uncle Lee navigated the plane through the heaving winds above Wyoming, and the geologists used their training and instincts to make guesses about places that might produce. Uncle Lee and the geologists formed a company that purchased mineral rights, and then they drilled.

"Sometimes I was up," Uncle Lee told me, "sometimes I was down." He shrugged his shoulders and continued pointing his ice-blue eyes straight ahead as he drove with both hands on the wheel of his car. Many of the wells were dry; the ones that were not enabled him to buy his own plane with a pressurized cabin. On powder days, Uncle Lee would wake up his wife and kids in Casper in the dark of morning, fly the family to Jackson Hole to ski for the day, and then have them back home in the evening. My jaw dropped when he told me this, as Jackson Hole was my mecca.

Every year for several decades Uncle Lee went on backpacking trips with a group of friends in Wyoming's Wind River Wilderness. I realized we had backpacked many of the same places, and we shared an addiction to skiing and running, and had felt suffocated by the humidity and provincialism of St. Louis. I had never really known the man when I was growing up—he was just some old guy with a firm handshake and blue eyes who said hello to me at Christmas parties and whose flying exploits trickled down to me in breathless stories told at the family gatherings in St. Louis he seldom attended. It seemed some similar genetic program had sent us west.

When I finally sat down with Uncle Lee and heard his stories of breaking into the oil business when the West was still raw, before interstate highways and the Internet, in the days before Denver was paved with suburban shopping malls and Wyoming seemed an untapped frontier as wild as the Yukon, I was envious. I realized that had I returned from a war with the skills of a pilot, and had I been afforded the opportunity to be a wildcatter flying geologists above the red hills of Wyoming, if I could have made a good living sinking wells to siphon from the earth a fluid that every single one of us uses, I would have leapt at the opportunity and never looked back.

The modern age didn't begin with the automobile or the airplane; it began in 1901 with a gusher on a mound of Texas prairie named Spindeltop. The sudden realization of the sheer amount of oil available beneath our feet spurred the human imagination to put this black bounty to use. Before Spindletop spewed petroleum, gasoline was used as a cheap solvent, and people put oil in their hair and used it to soften their skin. Petroleum's main use had been as kerosene to replace the whale oil burned in lamps. It had made John Rockefeller a fortune and had prevented the whales of the world from being slaughtered for the blubber to light our homes. Before Greenpeace, oil was responsible for saving the whales.

When the gusher on Spindletop erupted, and after a drill bit invented by Howard Hughes, Sr., the father of the famous tycoon, opened our eyes to the volume of oil stashed in Stygian depths, we scrambled to make use of this energy-dense fluid. The automobile, once a novelty that rattled around on rutted dirt roads, was soon being mass-produced on the assembly lines of Henry Ford. We laid ribbons of asphalt, a byproduct of petroleum; and King Coal was deposed from his throne by liquid fuel as ships and trains converted to oil. Airplane engines dragged contrails across the sky, and a few decades later Dustin Hoffman heard one word: "plastics."

Now we're hard pressed to find a single item in our lives that is not somehow derived from, powered by, or transported with, petroleum. Next to me on my desk as I type sits a fossil of a fern I found while hiking. If I eliminated all the food I consume that is transported with oil, I wouldn't have had the caloric energy to pick up the fossil and carry it home. And there would be no desk on which to place the fossil, nor any house to hold the desk. Get rid of everything you own that has a petroleum footprint and you will be left standing naked in a field.

I once had a neighbor who assembled a team of friends to help him move all of his belongings by bike from one apartment to another a few miles away. The spectacle of a flat-screen

TV, a kitchen table, and stacks of boxes strapped to bike trailers parading through town brought out a newspaper reporter and photographer to document this drama of human-powered transport. The man who was moving everything by bike told me he wasn't a Luddite—he loved having a flat-screen TV to watch sports on. He wasn't anti-oil or opposed to automobiles. He just wanted to demonstrate how much energy is stored in one gallon of gasoline—the energy equivalent of five hundred hours of human work. He wanted all of us to think about energy—where it comes from, how much we use, how dependent we are on it, how our lives would come to a screeching halt if its flow were to abruptly stop.

From my porch I watched this strange procession play out through the morning and afternoon. A dozen bike riders with trailers and cam straps moved furniture with the strength of their legs. Several years later I still think about this spectacle. It is staggering how much power can be produced from a gallon of liquid hydrocarbons, the remains of life that once flourished in the world's swamps and seas. Had that life not filled the oceans of earlier eras, and had it not been transformed by unimaginable spans of time and unthinkable amounts of pressure, our built environment would be a very different place today, and our lives would be so altered as to be unrecognizable. And not just our physical lives. In a monastery of Tibet I felt the pages of an ancient text pass between my fingers as I studied Buddhism—thanks to jet fuel, and thanks to the people who pull petroleum from the ground and process it in refineries.

This isn't to say I have made my peace with oil. It's not to say I don't seethe with anger when I drive through Pinedale, Wyoming, my holy land where once I found myself when I was lost, where I went to the mountains when I was young and hurting and their pristine snowfields healed me. Now the Upper Green River Basin has some of the worst air quality in the United States. Worse than the urban smog over Los Angeles. Air so dangerous that seniors and children are sequestered inside due to emissions from the natural gas wells, the steel steeples of which spread into the sullied distance as far as I dare look. Along with watery eyes, a bloody nose, and burning lungs, I feel outrage when I gaze through the smog at plastic-lined ponds of polluted water, the endless derricks and pipelines, the vast industrial zone where trucks rumble down roads day and night in a place where antelope once squeezed through the occasional barbwire fence during their annual migration.

But when I drive through the industrial wasteland around Pinedale, Wyoming, and fume about the desecration that has sullied one of the planet's special places for a few years' worth of natural gas, I am angry at myself, because I understand that I use oil and gas. And I don't know how to stop. When I go backpacking in the Wind River Range, I use Coleman fuel to cook my freeze-dried food. My boots and sunscreen and backpack, my tent and shirt and cookware, my compass and sleeping bag and plastic-coated maps: all of my wilderness gear began with petroleum. According to Michael Pollan, it takes ten calories of fossil fuel energy to produce one calorie of supermarket food. I wear oil. I live in oil. I eat oil.

I ride the bus when I can; I pedal my bike around town; I walk the streets of cities so I can look at people instead of traffic. But I still consume plenty of oil, and the water in my home is heated with natural gas. I like to linger in hot showers for much longer than it takes to get clean. Energy is required to heat the shower, and that energy doesn't come from magic—it is extracted from the ground. I have been known to pilot my Subaru into the mountains in winter, driving five hours round trip to plough with my snowboard a fresh harvest of powder. When I stare at the sickening layer of haze obscuring the Wind River Range, those gorgeous peaks of snow where rivers are born, I know that I have done this. We have all done this. Uncle Lee and Tim are to blame—but no more so than the rest of us. Each of us has oil and gas on our hands—and in our cars, and in our clothes, and in our computers, and in the fertilizer that grows our food and the trucks that transport it to farmers' markets.

TIM WENT ORGANIC AFTER reading Michael Pollan's *The Omnivore's Dilemma*. Pollan used his considerable talent as an investigative journalist to show the public where their food comes from. An awful lot of it comes from that monoculture of corn known as the state of Iowa. Strange-sounding ingredients like maltodextrin and ascorbic acid owe their provenance to corn, and so many of the packaged items on supermarket shelves and in convenience stores and in greasy bags collected for a few dollars from fast-food franchises have been engineered from the starch of the corn kernel.

Clever, yes, but there are costs. Corn craves nitrogen; agribusinesses provide it to the plants in the form of massive amounts of ammonium nitrate fertilizers made from natural gas. And vast quantities of fuel are required to power the machinery that tills the soil, harvests the corn, and distributes it to the processing plants that transform it into corn syrup and corn starch and dozens of other substances that form the basis for engineered food. "Cows did not evolve to eat corn," Tim explains. "When they're forced to eat corn instead of grass, they are constantly sick." The pharmaceutical industry supports modern agribusiness by supplying the antibiotics that keep cows alive while their rumens slosh with *E. coli* and their hide is slathered in shit. Unfortunately, strains of bacteria are evolving resistance to the antibiotics and can escape feedlots via farmworkers or meat into the general population. The more we flood factory farms with antibiotics to help create cheap meat, the more we risk rendering ineffective one of our most powerful tools to reduce human suffering.

After Tim read *The Omnivore's Dilemma* and had his epiphany about the damage industrial food is doing to our bodies and the body of the world, a job in the oil industry drew him to Denver, where he found himself missing the flavor of fresh corn. As soon as he had a home with a backyard, he turned the entire space into a mini farm that held three hundred corn plants. Within his private corn patch, he cleared a spot where he could sit surrounded by the silence of the stalks. Each

August he gorged himself for an entire month on fresh ears peeled of their husks and silk to reveal sweet cobs. After establishing his garden, he refused to eat corn unless he could pick it from the stalk himself.

"Good food for me has always been important," says Tim. His mother had canned peaches, tomatoes, and pears; she had made pickles, jams, and jellies. He revered his mom's sweet chili sauce, a blend of vine-ripened tomatoes, onions, sweet peppers, allspice, cinnamon, and sugar. He's tweaked the recipe himself by adding roasted chilies and jalapeños to form a tasty condiment that he uses as a pork chop relish. He had been growing his own vegetables for many years, ever since he got tired of bland store-bought lasagna sauce and tried to reproduce his mother's tangy recipe by raising his own tomatoes. He doused his garden with chemical fertilizer—until Michael Pollan opened his mind and Joel Salatin's teachings inspired him.

Salatin, a Virginia-based farmer who's become a celebrity in sustainable agriculture circles, grows healthy grass, which nourishes his chickens and cattle—which help maintain the health of the grass. Salatin's example of savvy farm management that mimics nature's design opened Tim's mind to the possibilities for improving the products of his garden by working with nature instead of waging chemical war against it.

Tim stopped dousing his garden with chemical fertilizers and pesticides and started cooking everything from scratch. "Nothing on my plate at home comes from a box," he says.

Tim tells me he grows all of his own vegetables—except for an occasional purchase of Brussels sprouts at the store. "I might pick up some Sriracha sauce while I'm there, maybe a few other condiments that I can't make at home. But my basket never has enough items in it to stop me from going through the express checkout lane." He makes his own bread. He only buys grass-fed, hormone-free, antibiotic-free beef from a ranch owned by a childhood friend. Tim helps to brand the cows each year during a community branding day when volunteers don old clothes and share in the hard work and are rewarded with food, stories, and beer—a sort of forerunner of crop mobs.

While talking with Tim, I have the same feeling I had after my conversation with my great-uncle Lee. Given a few tweaks of circumstance, I could have ended up happily working in the oil business instead of becoming an environmentalist who rails against it.

THE INFINITE MONKEY THEOREM winery, where Tim and I have been talking for an hour straight, makes some seriously good wine. Saying the name of the winery is a challenge; after a few glasses of Syrah, saying it correctly serves as evidence of sobriety. A guy behind the wine bar tells me that Infinite Monkey is trying to make wine-drinking greener by encouraging restaurants to switch from serving diners bottles of wine to selling them glasses of keg wine. He makes an interesting point. How many bottles of vino have been emptied by people conversing about the sorry state of the environment? Even if those bottles stay out of landfills and are recycled, it takes energy to repurpose them. And that energy has to come from somewhere.

When I met Tim at the crop mob and he told me his dirty secret about working in the oil industry, I had mentioned my wildcatting great-uncle Lee. Tim had nodded, pointed at a Bobcat, and said, "That thing doesn't run on rainbows and kittens." We'd agreed that it takes the miracle of oil to run the machinery that makes building large gardens practical. The Bobcat had just moved a massive pile of wood in the span of a few minutes; it would take a dozen workers with strong backs several hours to transport the same amount of material.

In order to put gas in the Bobcat and build gardens quickly, oil has to come out of the ground. And for the oil to come out of the ground, guys like Tim have to learn how to use calculus and read the squiggles on seismographs. And they have to risk massive amounts of investment in order to fund the extraction. No matter how expert their engineering skills, a degree of uncertainty always remains as to whether a well will produce.

Tim's outrage at people's anger toward him faded long ago. He has resigned himself to being the target of disdain directed at him by people who are blind to the fact that what he does allows them to use a Bobcat to build an organic garden. When people rail against oil, they have in mind corporations that rake in hundreds of billions in annual profit, goliaths such as ExxonMobil. But according to Tim, the vast majority of oil production in America is from independent companies, like the one he owns. (According to PolitiFact, 72 percent of domestic onshore oil and gas production is from independent companies.) Tim's Platte Valley Resources, which he owns with two partners, is no ExxonMobil. This organic gardener sporting running kicks operates his oil prospect-generation company out of his living room.

Tim points out that the food industry, by using clever marketing and branding with images of farmers in overalls, red barns, and cows grazing contentedly in rolling fields, has successfully convinced consumers that what they are eating came from small family farms, when nothing could be further from the truth. The vast majority of what we purchase at supermarkets, including organic food, comes from agribusiness giants. The oil industry, on the other hand, has done a terrible job of helping people understand that the majority of oil and gas comes from independent companies, not from the Big Oil behemoths with their brands on gas station pumps. Locally developed energy just doesn't have the same cachet as locally grown food. Selling locally extracted and refined oil and gas as "small-batch, artisanal energy" would make for provocative performance art.

Tim insists that many oil companies are finding ways to extract oil and gas with minimal disruption to the environment. He concedes that some oil companies don't care about the environment—but isn't that true of any industry, or really, of any human endeavor? "Greed is everywhere," Tim says as he stares into his glass of wine. "Sure, oil is all about money. But so is every other business. And everyone uses oil."

Hating companies that mine gold by turning mountains inside out, poisoning pristine streams, and chiding the people who wear the gleaming products of destruction; or hating furriers who peddle the pelts of lynx, and belittling the clueless buffoons who wear them at Vail; or hating the butchers aboard motorized fleets that slice the fins off sharks and let them slip bleeding back into the sea, and chastising the people who sip the soup of this slaughter—all of this make sense. It is rational and entirely warranted. But is hating the companies that produce the substance that lubricates the workings of the modern world warranted?

Oil. We drink deeply of its stored energy every day of our lives, from the time that hands covered in gloves made from petroleum molecules deliver us into this world to the time we are placed in caskets treated with petroleum products, or we are burned to ash in fires fueled with natural gas.

Just build a bunch of wind turbines, the guy in *Gasland* says as he strums his banjo and puts on his gasmask for effect beneath the poisoned skies of Wyoming. But wind turbines, aside from the obvious disruption they cause to natural landscapes, and their butchery of birds, require the use of copper in the generators that convert the mechanical energy of the spinning blades into the electrical energy that powers our iPads. Copper must be mined. The largest proposed copper mine on the planet, Alaska's Pebble Mine, has the potential to poison one of planet's last great salmon fisheries. Photovoltaic panels that harvest the energy of the sun are spread across desert landscapes where they disrupt fragile crusts of soil, and the panels must be manufactured in a process that produces hazardous waste, which has to be trucked away for disposal, creating a carbon footprint. When it comes to energy, there is no free lunch: there are consequences to every effort to power our human world. This isn't to say that renewable energy is a farce. It is just to say that, as with anything else, if it sounds too good to be true, it probably is.

Electric cars! If we all drove electric cars our problems would be solved. Except for the problem of how to produce the power to charge the batteries that run the cars. Electric cars don't run on magic, and none of us ride flying carpets to the sustainability meetings we attend. If we take public buses powered by clean natural gas to those meetings, the people of Pinedale, Wyoming, wheeze on ozone caused by the extraction of that gas, and leaked methane forces the atmosphere to warm. If we pedal our bikes to the meetings, those bikes still required petroleum to be manufactured and shipped, and the human fuel it takes to pedal them comes from food, which can usually be traced back to oil at some point in the process of growing and distributing the caloric energy that allows for clean pedal power. I stopped eating meat so I could cut my carbon footprint in half! But did I grow and harvest the soybeans for my tofu? Or did I pull the package made from petroleum from the shelves of Whole Foods after it was delivered on a truck? None of us are innocent.

IF YOU DON'T FIND TIM in his backyard garden, you might find him on a plot of land next to The Infinite Monkey Theorem winery. The owner has let Tim build a garden on this previously unutilized ground. Tim is nourishing the soil with wine pith—the waste product of the winemaking process, mixing spent skins and seeds with other organic matter to create a rich compost. This compost helps grow the radishes and zucchini he raises for Old Major, a restaurant that serves locally sourced food. Utilizing the wine pith as an organic input is a learning process, explains Tim. "I'm always experimenting to figure out what I have to do to the soil to make it happy."

The leftovers from the wine Tim and I are drinking were put back into the soil to grow the zucchini blossoms on the plates of diners at Old Major. But those happy eaters will have a hard time finding Tim to thank him. He'll be in the garden, or out in the field scouting a well site, or up in the mountains running trails. "I'm just being who I am," says Tim.

Like my great-uncle Lee, Tim has made a living at

high-stakes oil gambling, and he both accepts enormous loss-
es and reaps rewards that balance the books. He never knows
what his future will hold, and right now he's pushing the limits on his credit cards to get through some dry months. If his
prospects don't produce, he won't be able to afford to keep
growing the organic food that's plated at a restaurant where
the health-conscious dine.

It's a complicated world, and putting a solar panel on a
roof doesn't excuse us from the consequences of consuming
too much of the world's limited resources. A person who eats
homegrown produce and owns a Hummer could have a smaller
carbon footprint than someone who dines on factory-farmed
meat and drives a Prius. Eating healthful meals made from
ingredients purchased from Whole Foods is better than eating
fast-food fare, to be sure. But while talking with Tim, I begin
to suspect that it's merely a more sophisticated form of consumerism—it isn't the final answer. To grow our own heirloom
tomatoes like Tim does is a step beyond picking them from a
bin at a supermarket. When we stop berating Tim for making
his living drilling for oil, he'll be happy to show us how.

Tim seems reluctant to tell other people how they should
live. He explains that when he goes to a friend's house and
he's served a meal of mac and cheese from a box, he eats it
and doesn't complain. When that friend comes to Tim's house,
they get a meal made from scratch. If they are curious where
the ingredients came from, Tim shows them his garden. If
they decide they want a garden of their own, Tim turns up in
overalls with a shovel in hand to help make it happen.

If you get Tim talking, he'll tell you in his quiet, steady voice
that if everyone grew at least some of his or her own food, it
would make a big difference. "When we eat from our gardens
we don't have to drive to the store. We use less oil—which is
fine with me." Tim explains that if each of us voted with our
food dollars against Big Ag and industrial food, the world
would look more like France, where the produce of local growers is sold on street corners and meals are made from scratch

according to recipes handed down from mothers to sons.

Tim shoots ducks and geese and eats them. People who call hunting cruel but buy meat wrapped in cellophane from supermarket shelves don't so much annoy Tim as make him sad at how sorely they are lacking in education, how disconnected they are from their food. A report by the Food and Agriculture Organization of the United Nations in 2006 identified livestock production as one of the major causes of the planet's most pressing environmental problems, including climate change, air and water pollution, land degradation, and loss of biodiversity. The report fingered livestock production as the culprit in 18 percent of global greenhouse gas emissions, a larger share than that of transportation. And aside from their environmental impacts, concentrated animal feeding operations (CAFOs) have come to embody institutionalized cruelty.

These assembly lines of suffering are hidden from our cities, revealed only by their stench. People who manage to get through security and glimpse inside these sprawling, windowless warehouses of misery find themselves scarred by the scenes within. Lifelong hunters and carnivores cringe at the cruelty. It's hard to believe that any sane society would manufacture meat this way—as if it were a commodity like corn and didn't come from sentient creatures. Each time we purchase meat without understanding its origin we run the risk of being complicit in atrocities that will, in all likelihood, make future generations shudder. To lift a shotgun toward the sky and end a duck's life in one clean blast of steel pellets is to put animal protein on a plate honestly and by inflicting a minimal amount of suffering. To eat factory-farmed animals fed grain derived from draining and contaminating wetlands that had once sheltered ducks is a more subtle form of cruelty too seldom discussed.

"People complain about oil but few of them want to spend the effort to grow their own food," Tim says, shaking his head. Every day he encounters oil-users who hate oil companies, but rarely does he meet an individual who grows his own vegetables and cans them. "If you really want to make a difference in the world," he says, "invest in what you eat. Everybody wants everything easier and quicker. Slow down and make a statement about what's important to you. Grow your own food. Get to know your neighbors, learn to help each other. Be the change you want to see in the world," he quotes from Gandhi. Tim puts on overalls in the garden and an apron in the kitchen and cultivates a kind of sustainable lifestyle that most people—myself included—just talk about. Tim is the change that *I* want to be in the world. And his job in the oil business seems no more relevant to who he is than the gig of a waiter working in a restaurant to pay the bills while he pursues his passion for acting.

After Tim devoured *The Omnivore's Dilemma*, he thought a lot about his family's business selling feed to farms. He remembered adding bonemeal and bloodmeal to feed mixes when he was a boy, and he thought of how the massive amount of corn fed to cows distresses their rumen, designed to digest grass but not grain. He started discussing these issues with his father, who at first scoffed at "that organic farming hippie crap." But recently Tim's dad has started stocking organic grain and servicing some organic farms. "Every little bit counts," says Tim. "Any time you can influence someone to make a better and healthier decision, then you're doing that much better for your community and for everyone involved."

I know a guy who lives in a house so large it could shelter a village. His yard is the size of a nine-hole golf course. The carriage house above the garage is larger than my condo. His horse barn was built with a whole forest of wood. He sits on the boards of environmental organizations and is a regular at their silent auctions, where he bids generously on items he doesn't need in order to provide money for their causes.

Another friend of mine is a sustainability expert with an MBA degree who has worked with companies like Starbucks to help them improve their environmental performance. One evening as we sat discussing his job in his backyard, a breeze stirring the air, his air conditioner kicked on. I uncapped a chilled bottle of beer and told my buddy he didn't seem like a friend of the environment. My teasing ignited a tirade that began with him explaining that he liked his condo to stay cool and finished with him justifying his behavior by emphatically stating that he had devoted his career to helping companies be greener, so it didn't matter what he did with his air conditioner. I told him that Al Gore would agree.

A while back, I drank on Friday afternoons with a Navy Seal. Whenever he wasn't parachuting into warzones or snorkeling his way to shore wearing night vision goggles on missions so secret not even the third glass of wine would loosen his tongue, we'd tip a few back. What exactly he did in Yemen and Somalia and Afghanistan he never said, but when someone dropped a wine opener behind him, I saw his muscles instantly tense. This guy had nothing nice to say about environmentalists when the topic came up one afternoon. Two thoughts went through my head: one, he had certainly earned a right to an opinion; and two, he could kill me a dozen different ways. But before I could expand on these thoughts, I heard him chide his fiancé for throwing a beer bottle in the trash. He said to her, "Honey, reduce, reuse, recycle."

Is an environmentalist a rich person who consumes an obscene amount of resources but donates to worthy causes? Is an environmentalist someone who is paid to help companies clean up their act? Is an environmentalist someone so committed to encouraging everyone around him to reduce, reuse, and recycle that he'd risk the rolling eyes of his fiancé to make his point? Is an environmentalist someone who grows his own food? Has the meaning been so cored out of the term *environmentalist* that it is now a hollow shell that should be discarded? (In a proper receptacle, of course.)

To dismiss Tim by placing him in the category of "evil oil guy" oversimplifies the tangled wilderness of human nature. It diminishes the capacity of people to straddle multiple worlds and inhabit countless ways of being. It reduces someone to a stale series of *likes* and bumptious blog posts. Our relationship to the energy we consume is complex; but this complexity pales in comparison to the difficult jumble of a person's heart. To unapologetically drill for oil while promoting organic food is not paradoxical, or even ironic. It is frankly and refreshingly human.

Chapter 11
Gangster to Gardener

After I finished meeting with Tim, I realized that The Infinite Monkey Theorem winery is about a dozen blocks from where I had met with Ietef and Neambe in Five Points. I headed out on foot from the winery toward Five Points to get the lay of the land. As I explored streets lined with dilapidated buildings yet to be colonized by loft dwellers and creative businesses, I remembered Ietef and Neambe warning about gentrification pricing lifelong residents out of their neighborhoods; they are forced to settle on the economic fringe where the fast-food industry thrives. The tempting scent of French fries followed me down an avenue bright with the light of a Burger King sign. In an upscale enclave I ducked into a couple of restaurants to check out menus showing meals that cost more than a fast-food employee makes in a week. I started to wonder if locally grown food wasn't just a toy for the rich.

Tim had grown up in a fairly affluent family and now talks about chasing elusive flavors by growing fresh ingredients in

his garden—like a lot of other people in the urban food movement I had met. While Tim was surely one of the most interesting growers in Denver, I was starting to worry that I'd
strayed a bit from the edginess that had initially drawn me
to the movement. Sipping Syrah in the RiNo Art District is a
long way from riding on Big Bertha through alleys with Waste
Farmers. I wanted to get back to the rawness of Ietef's food
justice raps and the radical compassion of SAME Café.

When Shane Wright of Groundwork Denver told me about
an urban farmer he works with whose family emigrated from
El Salvador, I knew I needed to hear this young man's story.
Similar to Tim, Alex Sanchez had been a fat kid and is now as
lean as a marathoner. But dodging bullets, not farm work, had
preoccupied Alex when he was a boy.

IN LOS ANGELES, WHEN Alex wasn't throwing himself on the
floor of his home to avoid bullets fired through the living room
window, he listened to his mother tell stories of her family's
farm in El Salvador. She told Alex of trees in the orchard that
hung heavy with fruit and clear streams that threaded the
landscape. The family was self-sufficient. Everything they grew
was by necessity organic—chemical fertilizers and pesticides
weren't available. The entire farming process was integrated:
Dung from the animals replenished the soil that nourished the
plants that provided livestock with forage. The family never
had to worry where their food would come from. They were
blessed with abundance. There was time to talk with neighbors, time to play games with children, time for taking long
walks under the mango trees and through fields of coffee
bushes bright with ruby beans.

This is the pastoral picture Alex describes to me as we walk
beneath the Interstate 70 viaduct amid Elyria-Swansea's tangle of train tracks and intersecting streets. This neighborhood
in northeast Denver was designed as an industrial center.
Sprawling buildings and heavily trafficked roads dominate;
residential areas seem an afterthought. Homes are marooned

in a sea of concrete. A chemical tang from the Suncor petroleum refinery competes with the putrid odor of the Purina dog food plant. Hard to say which of these dueling stenches is winning, but it's no fun being in the middle. Although Denver is ranked one of the healthiest cities in the United States, none of the farmers' markets, hip farm-to-table eateries, and upscale groceries that serve the city's affluent can be found in Elyria-Swansea. And gardening here can be dangerous—the soil is contaminated with heavy metals and other pollutants. Residents who want to grow food outdoors have to build raised garden beds and truck in clean dirt.

Alex leads me out of the shadow of the viaduct toward The GrowHaus, a nonprofit urban farm, education center, and food distribution hub. When seen from outside, The GrowHaus blends with industrial warehouses. Yet within its walls, a powerful hum of human activity leads to a thousand heads of lettuce being harvested each week. Alex is short and slim. He wears his black hair neatly trimmed. A faint goatee. I wouldn't notice him if I passed him on the street. But his dark eyes dart without stopping when he speaks.

Inside The GrowHaus, the thunder of traffic from the surrounding streets is replaced by the sound of circulating water, and soft forests of lettuce supplant the city's sharp edges. As we wander down pathways through five thousand square feet of leafy greens grown hydroponically with nutrient-rich liquid, Alex tells me stories from the countryside of El Salvador. He has found a simulacrum of that paradisiacal, perhaps mythical, place here in one of the hardest parts of the city.

ALEX EXPLAINS THAT THE Salvadoran Civil War that broke out in 1979 forced his mother's family off their farm. Neither remorse nor anger surfaces in his voice as he recounts the repercussions of the chaos. His mother had to flee from the farm with her family on foot. Death squads roamed the land, hunting civilians. Fierce competition for food put the refugees moving across the countryside at odds with each other.

"My parents saw horrible violence," says Alex. "Their religion helped them get through the toughest times." Alex says that he's not religious but he understands why faith means so much to his mother. She once told him that if he didn't pray he'd die like her brother—who had one day neglected to kneel in the jungle, bow his head, and clasp his hands in prayer. A few seconds later he stepped on a landmine. Alex's mother managed to make her way into Mexico and then cross the border into California. Alex's father also found his way to California, and there they met and were married.

Alex, born in 1993, was a little boy during the peak of gang violence in South Central L.A. Bloods, Crips, and MS-13 clashed in the streets, creating a war zone not unlike the one Alex's parents had fled in El Salvador. Drive-by shootings occurred daily. Alex wondered why his parents dragged him to the floor as he wandered around the house listening to loud sounds. The family crouched together as bullets pocked the outside walls and sent glass splintering through the living room.

Alex explains that his father, in an attempt to flee gang warfare, eventually moved the family out of L.A. to Denver where he worked two low-paying jobs at Dominos and Pizza Hut. He struggled to feed Alex, his two older brothers, one younger brother, and their mother. The family settled in Montbello, a neighborhood not immune to gang violence.

"I remember our house being robbed on a regular basis when I was growing up," Alex tells me. "I had to sleep in the basement because my parents were afraid I'd get hurt during a robbery." His parents warned him not to cross the street because a gang house stood on the other side. But being a curious kid, he wandered over to take a look and gang members invited him inside. "They started showing me pipes and were trying to get me to smoke, but my dad stormed into the house and dragged my ass back home." Alex says that his father had soured on human nature. "He tried to make me believe that everyone is out to get ahead. He told me not to trust anyone. He said that every person in the world outside our home would try to beat me and cheat me and no one would ever be my friend."

Alex leads me away from the indoor lettuce farm to show me another section of The GrowHaus. He scoops his hand into one of the vermicomposting boxes he built. "Worm composting," he says when I ask about vermicomposting. "It's the shit." Literally. The castings from the worms are as dark as coffee grounds, and a fecund aroma wafts from the box. I remember Aron's stories about the worms he raised in Guatemala to help replenish the soil.

Alex puts his handful of worms back into the dark box. He closes the lid and tells me that he became paranoid as a child. "I was an absolute mute at school." He shakes his head. "I couldn't focus on my studies because I was too agitated." During a spelling test, the only thing he didn't spell wrong was *pizza*. He was put in a special education class. One day a couple of boys sat down next to him in the cafeteria and started talking about a "retarded kid." Alex scanned rows of other kids sitting in the cafeteria as he tried to spot the target of their ridicule. Before long the whole table of middle-schoolers stared at him and laughed. "This abuse started happening on a regular basis," Alex says. "I was the fat retarded kid that no one wanted to talk to."

When Alex was getting picked on, he'd come home sobbing. But he learned to keep his grief to himself. "I couldn't disturb my dad. He was exhausted from working a lot of jobs." Alex had no TV, no video games, no friends. He'd lie sprawled on the floor and try not to cry. "My dad's solution was to buy me cheeseburgers." Alex's mother also worked more than one job to make ends meet and rarely had time to cook. Alex says he ate fast food at least five days a week through grade school, middle school, and most of high school. "I felt like my dad's favorite child because he'd let me eat my brother's fries."

Those salty golden-brown fries, that cheese that drapes its melting corners over the burger patty, that sweet ketchup and tangy mustard that ooze out when you bite down on the toasted bun: Alex's adolescent emotions were coded in fast food.

He devoured a sense of belonging. He gobbled savory bites of self-esteem. Alex is five feet four inches tall. At one point in middle school he stepped on a scale and saw that he weighed 290 pounds.

"I'm only a few pounds over my ideal weight right now," he says, punching his flat stomach. "If I can stick to eating healthy, I'll have a six-pack soon."

Alex and I head toward the inner sanctum of The Grow-Haus—known as the "GrowAsis." Bright light pours through a translucent roof. Beams of sun illuminate rabbit hutches and compost bins and reflect from pools of water. As we make our way into the central sunken space surrounded by permaculture gardens, I recall that Ietef's mother, Ashara Ekundayo, was one of the founders of The GrowHaus. Dana Miller helped cheerlead it into existence by making crucial introductions among her team of food-focused friends. Adam Brock, advisor of strategic planning at The GrowHaus, has trained many of Denver's permaculturists, including Oz. "All things are connected" is, of course, a cliché to be avoided like the plague, but it's hard to avoid the truth of it when exploring the interconnected ecosystem of Denver's urban food culture.

I ask Alex to keep walking me through his life; he seems eager to continue. In middle school he was surrounded by gangs, and he noticed that the Crips looked like they were having a lot of fun. Joining a gang seemed like a way he could finally make some friends. When gang members invited him to a local park to get initiated, he eagerly accepted. Alex claims that fifteen kids circled around him and started hitting and kicking him. He liked that he was a part of a group—he appreciated the attention. He swears he didn't flinch, didn't cry. "The kids who initiated me thought I was a real badass for taking that beating with a smile. I started acting like a badass."

He continues, "There was this kid who was weaker than I was, like a cripple, and I kicked his ass because I was hard. It gives you a high." He says this with little emotion—in as straightforward a manner as when he told me about getting picked on for being fat and slow. He tells me that kids cheered him on as he beat the weaker boy. "I got respect for being ruthless. Other kids started to look to me like I was a leader. I felt so powerful. I went from being nobody to being a boss. It was a huge mental shift. I was on top of the world."

But Alex was only powerful when he was protected by his crew. If he walked outside alone, he risked getting jumped by rival gang members. He had to always be in a pack with at least five people. One time he broke this rule and was caught out on the streets by himself, surrounded by members of the El Sereno gang. They kicked his feet out from under him and knocked him to the ground. He remembers fists crashing into his face. "When they were finished with me my nose was messed up," he says, pointing at its crooked bridge.

Alex claims he became an expert at robbing houses in seventh grade. "I went pro," he says. He explains that not only did he steal stuff when he broke into a house, he made himself at home—brewing coffee in the kitchen, clipping his toenails while sitting on the homeowner's bed. He'd turn the stove on before he left because he thought it would be funny if the house burned down. He filled his gang lair with loot: iPods, gold chains, DJ equipment. "I was a hustler and I had it all. I had like thirty grand in cash and I wasn't even fifteen yet. I could have bought my own car. I had my own safe house. I was a boss. Or I thought I was."

When some of his friends got busted during a botched robbery, they ratted Alex out. After being confined to his home with a monitor shackled to his ankle, people stopped calling him. "My homies weren't hitting me up. My homegirls weren't coming around. All of the sudden everyone was gone and I was alone. I realized my dad might have been right. I really didn't have any friends. And I decided that materialistic goods are all bullshit."

Alex shakes his head and gazes away from me, into a green forest of plants. "I didn't want to get shot. And I didn't want my parents to disown me. They thought I was on my way to becoming a murderer. I wanted to be a better version of myself." But he wasn't sure how to go about changing the track he was on.

One day a letter came in the mail from Denver School of Science and Technology (DSST). Alex explains that this charter school had been founded on the principle that any person from any background could be intelligent and a contributing member of society. The school encouraged students like Alex to enroll in its programs and achieve success. When Alex had been hanging with his homies at middle school and thinking he'd go to Montbello High, he'd seen the recruitment effort for DSST and had applied. "When that letter arrived, I knew I could show my parents I wasn't a murderer. I could prove to them—and to myself—that I was a good person." He found out that DSST had chosen his name at random but it didn't matter: this was the break he needed.

He studied every day. "It was hard," he says. "But I started to see results." He earned praise for his schoolwork—something he'd never experienced before. "I started to believe I could be someone who could contribute to society."

When he took his first physics class, quantum mechanics blew his imagination wide open. Schrödinger's cat, mind-bending double-slit experiments: "That's some badass science," says Alex. "When I started learning about string theory and the multiverse, I knew I wanted to be a quantum physicist." During his second year at DSST he took advanced physics courses. He'd go in to school at 8:00 in the morning and leave at 10:00 at night. His studies were on track; his social life was not.

Alex could solve equations to calculate the trajectory of a rocket but he had no idea how to make small talk with kids his age who hadn't been in gangs, who hadn't beat people up and robbed houses for fun. "When I heard someone say something like, 'Let's go get some wheatgrass, Jake,' I'd turn around and walk away." This was a strange new world—a multiverse of values and language and social norms that baffled Alex. For all his former thuggery, Alex was still a painfully shy kid. He says, "I was embarrassed by what I used to be. I didn't make a single friend at DSST."

After a trip to El Salvador with his parents, Alex came back to Denver seriously sick. Parasites were running riot in his gut, but he couldn't go to the doctor because his family had no health insurance. "I was so sick I almost died. The only reason I survived was because I was so overweight. I lost almost 150 pounds."

How did he end up at The GrowHaus? Alex explains that when he attended DSST every student served an internship. Working for an urban farm seemed to Alex more interesting than working as the secretary to a dentist—one of the other options available. "I liked the idea of growing plants and selling them," Alex says. "And I thought maybe I'd learn how to grow my own pot and, you know, cultivate some killer weed. And I was learning about environmental issues at DSST. I wanted some skills to help me survive when the world runs out of water and food. What I learned here at The GrowHaus—it completely blew me away. Did you know that we have more prisoners than farmers in the United States?"

At The GrowHaus Alex saw a flourishing greenhouse growing bright heads of lettuce. The aquaponics system looked to him like a science fiction film set. He was fascinated by the interconnectedness of the processes—how the fish poop was used as fertilizer for plants, how the castings produced by worms could be added to soil to boost its fertility. He saw chard with scarlet stems and giant, red-veined leaves. "The plants reminded me of the stories about El Salvador my mom used to tell me." Alex started to make essential connections. Food was linked to his health and to the health of the planet. The GrowHaus offered him an opportunity to become part of the solution to global problems. "I liked working with soil. I liked watching food grow—and I liked eating it." He started adding the chard and other vegetables he grew to his meals; their nutrients began building up his health. He kept off all the weight he'd shed during his illness.

Alex is quick to admit that his eating habits aren't perfect. "My friend's a manager at McDonald's and can hook me up with free fries. That's a problem." Because he had gorged on processed food for most of his life, his neural pathways remember how cheeseburgers once soothed him when he felt small and powerless, when he was being picked on at school, when his father felt sorry for him and used the Golden Arches as a symbol of his love.

To bolster his willpower to resist processed food, Alex has put himself on an eating regimen. He consumes calories every two hours by eating small servings of beans and salad throughout the day—instead of going many hours without eating, feeling pangs of hunger, and then gobbling a cheeseburger and fries. While we talk, he eats a kale salad that he brought with him, and he explains that it's easy to eat healthy during the day; the problems come late at night. "Dude, you can't get a salad at night. And when you get out of the club at two in the morning, forget it—you just want some high-fructose corn syrup in your system."

ALEX IS APPRENTICING AT The GrowHaus in their Farmer in Training program. He has started raising edible plants commercially in a space inside The GrowHaus. He named his nursery "GrowUp." He explains that Latina women living in Elyria-Swansea do most of the shopping, and they have to take buses at least twenty minutes in each direction, sometimes much longer, to buy healthful food. Alternatively, they can purchase seedlings from Alex on a sliding scale. They transplant them to their gardens and nurture the plants into sources of nutritious food. "I feel powerful in the greenhouse running my own business," Alex tells me. "It's like that feeling of being a boss in a gang."

Alex is also teaching classes in Spanish on food justice and gardening to members of the local community. "I want to see people become self-sufficient by growing their own edible gardens," he says. "And I'm cultivating values and developing skills for myself." He's also working with Groundwork Denver as a member of their Green Team building trails and planting trees.

Alex talks about urban farming to the gang members he used to hang with, other people in his neighborhood, even strangers on buses. "A lot of people don't get it. They think I'm just growing lettuce and it's no big deal. But when you grow food, you help the health of your body, and you help the health of your community."

Alex would like to move to the Elyria-Swansea neighborhood near The GrowHaus. He wants to create a self-sustaining home with his cousins—a place where he can supply his own organic vegetables, eggs, and meat while he carefully stewards the water he uses and captures energy from the sun. "I can see taking care of myself and my family on an urban homestead. I can totally see that."

Alex's plan for his future is always in flux, and I've heard several versions of it, but he says he holds fast to these guiding principles: have fun, cultivate value, become a better person.

"I DON'T KNOW IF I want to be a scientist anymore," Alex tells me when I see him a few weeks after our conversation at The GrowHaus. He is helping build permaculture gardens on the grounds of Waste Farmers. He spears his shovel into the soil and rests his gloved hands atop its handle. "We already have technology that gives us abundance and speed. What we do with the technology—that's what matters. If I become a quantum physicist and invent something like teleportation, we'll just use it to mess up the Earth in some way. We have to learn how to live, right here, right now."

As Alex resumes scooping the soil with his shovel, he speaks to me of El Salvador. His parents risked their lives to escape the country, but he sees himself settling there some day on a farm much like the one his mother describes in her stories. "My dream is to apply the knowledge that I got at The GrowHaus to start my own farm in El Salvador and be one-hundred-percent self-sufficient. I want to grow everything organically—fruits, vegetables, beef, goats, chicken, fish—*everything.* And I want to help my neighbors relearn what they forgot because of the war. Hardly anyone knows how to farm anymore in El Salvador."

Alex kneels in the dirt to place bricks along the edge of a

spiral herb garden. As he works, he explains that he wants to spread his knowledge of nutrient cycles and connectivity, of organic inputs and permaculture principles, to help heal the soil of El Salvador. Farmers there are finding ways to get hold of synthetic fertilizer because marketers have convinced them that their crops will grow better if they drench the soil with chemicals. "But all the fertilizer they'll ever need is in their horses," Alex says. "The war wiped out in twelve years so much of the agricultural and food knowledge that used to be passed down from parents to children. Now people in El Salvador go to McDonald's and they don't understand why they're sick."

When I ask Alex if he plans to go to college after he graduates high school, he tells me, "College is just another game in society. It's one I don't want to play." He sees a student loan bubble on the horizon and is determined to not be part of it. He is predicting numerous problems in our future—peak oil, peak water, catastrophic climate change—and he wants to be ready as we smack up against them. He wants to be self-sufficient. And he wants to help other people become self-sufficient, too. "I see a storm coming," he says. "I want to show people that the storm is all in our heads and we can live a life of value and abundance."

Chapter 12
Eating Weeds

After talking with Alex, I met a woman at a potluck at Waste Farmers who told me that a neglected abundance surrounds us in the city. She said she forages for edible plants in parks and along sidewalks and streets. I wondered if she had lost her mind. Or could she see something hidden from most of us in plain sight? Is our food system really so broken that we need to eat the weeds we step on? There was only one way to find out. I signed up to go on one of Kate Armstrong's foraging walks.

IN HER CHACO SANDALS, cargo shorts, and faded red tank top, her arms and legs bronzed from working outdoors, Kate could pass for a seasoned rafting guide in Moab—which is actually one of the few jobs she hasn't had. Though she is nearing seventy, Kate looks as fit as a forty-year-old.

On this Saturday morning in May, she is leading a group

of a half dozen walkers curious about edible plants through Denver's Sunnyside neighborhood around 44th and Vallejo. I focus on the weedy edges of the sidewalk. When we cross the street, I have to remind myself to look up and check for traffic so I don't get flattened. This is urban foraging, and the rural soundtrack of streams tumbling over stones and wind whistling through trees is replaced by the thumping bass of low-rider trucks and the chesty growls of Rottweilers crouched behind chain-link fences.

We shuffle down the block, leaning forward with our backs slightly hunched and our faces pointed toward the ground. Sometimes we stumble as we make our way along the sidewalk. Urban foragers can look like extras in a zombie apocalypse film. Kate, her white hair cascading in curly profusion, stoops down next to a sidewalk. She plucks a green leaf that looks like one of the weeds my parents used to make me pull, and pops it into her mouth. Few topics spark curious questions in the public spaces of a city like people munching mouthfuls of greens they've picked from cracks in the pavement. As Kate leads our foraging group down sidewalks and across streets, residents come out of their houses to watch this procession of people with coffee cups in hand on a Saturday morning snacking on plants by the side of the road. Strangers stop on the street to ask Kate questions.

"How do I get rid of goathead weeds?" a woman in heavy makeup wonders aloud as she wobbles by on heels. Kate coaches her in the use of an old blanket to capture the spiky seeds and explains that a mixture of boiling water, vinegar, and salt will decimate most weeds.

"Just please don't use chemicals," Kate implores the woman, who agrees to stay away from dangerous sprays that would contaminate the plants in her yard and put her pets—and urban foragers—at risk.

"People will love you and kiss your feet if you come and pick their weeds," Kate says. She volunteers to remove weeds from people's gardens. While using her pair of stout scissors to uproot the plants, she sees that what people thought were worthless weeds are really violets and mint, clover and chives, all of which can be tossed in a tasty salad.

As Kate walks and talks to our group of urban foragers inching our way through a mixed residential and commercial neighborhood, the information just keeps coming. There is so much to see and to think about in the span of a few city blocks. I'm taking notes as fast as I can.

Kate explains that if you have lambsquarters growing in your lawn, this means you have good dirt. If prickly lettuce is spreading, you have a problem with your soil fertility. The edible plants in urban surroundings offer a treasure trove of potential nutrition and medical applications. Kate reads the weeds in a yard like lines in a book. Each plant she sees has lore attached to it that she loves to share.

She plucks a leaf of wild rocket, lifts it up for us to view, and then holds forth. Salads became common at the beginning of a meal because the bitterness of some greens stimulates the gall bladder, putting bile in the stomach, starting the digestive process. "There's wisdom in our meals," she says. And insanity. Kate recounts that she recently tried to eat a piece of Kentucky Fried Chicken but had to spit it out. She trusts that her impulse of disgust was keeping her safe. "I only eat meat if I know where it came from," she tells the group.

Kate is as worried about the provenance of the pork she purchases as I am with the safety of the wild rocket I gather. But the more time I spend learning about toxic pesticides and feces in meat products and other costs of the industrial food system, the more dangerous the supermarket seems. And a salad of foraged plants grown from soil and sun in the city begins to strike me as much safer than a fast-food burger.

I pause to look at a plant Kate shows the group called cranesbill. When I stoop down and scrutinize its design, I am delighted to see a miniature bird's head repeated a hundred times. This wonder is rooted in a thin wedge of dirt in a seam of concrete. Crowds hurry past it each day, but no one stops to smell the dirt, which is a shame, because mixed with the microbes that break down plants and give dirt its distinctive smell is an organism that passes from the soil into our nose, Kate explains. When we smell dirt, we inhale a bacterium known as *M. vaccae* that releases serotonin from nerve cells in our brain, the same cells targeted by Prozac. In essence, this microorganism causes changes in our neurochemistry that lift our mood; our brain sends us back to play in the soil because it craves more of the serotonin that our little friend *M. vaccae* boosts inside us.

LATER IN THE DAY, KATE and I sit and chat at Sunnyside Farm, located on the site of a former parking lot at 44th and Vallejo. A piece of city pavement has been turned into an urban farm. Sunnyside Farm has managed to invert the Joni Mitchell lyrics: "They paved paradise / And put up a parking lot."

Kate and I had discussed urban foraging at a crop mob and at a potluck, but until now I hadn't heard her whole story. She tells me that her father, after growing disillusioned with the rat race of Manhattan, moved the family to a sheep farm in rural New York. And so began what Kate and her brother and sister dubbed the "Great Farm Experiment." Kate says, "We went back to the land before 'back to the land' had a name."

It was a classic 1950s farm. A lot of chickens, a couple of pigs, and a few head of beef cattle roamed around; the family used the manure from these animals to fertilize their one-acre garden. The farm was organic before organic was cool—not from some forward-thinking principle but out of necessity. The family ate seasonal food: other than the produce they canned and preserved, they dined on greens in the spring and squash in the fall. What they didn't grow or gather, and with the exception of a few staples bought at a local store, they didn't eat. Kate says, "We were locavores before *locavore* was a word."

The family canned 150 quarts of tomatoes to supply them until the next year's harvest. They put a ladder on their truck and drove to the Hudson Valley, harvesting as many as six bushels of apples, peaches, or pears; then they froze the fruit, dried it, or preserved it in jellies and jams. Their basement shelves held seasonal bounty that lasted through the winter. "The amount you have to put up for a family of five to get through the winter is astonishing," Kate says, shaking her head.

Kate's mother had spent a year in Paris in the 1930s studying at the Sorbonne and taking cooking classes at Le Cordon Bleu. Through trial and error—a lot of error—the family figured out how to smoke their own hams and cure their own bacon. Kate learned how to bake bread from scratch by watching her mother in the kitchen. In the spring, the family grazed on wild greens and made dandelion tea to cleanse them of "winter funk" caused by subsisting on canned food, salted meat, and wrinkly apples and shriveled potatoes from the root cellar.

Kate and her siblings provided the only labor on the farm. "If you're seven years old and there's a thirty-five-foot row of green beans you're supposed to weed before lunch, it's not fun." She learned how to do repetitive tasks—how to go into a sort of meditative trance as she powered through the same motions that lasted for long hours in the summer. This might explain her diligence when searching for edible plants. The group foraging walk lasted two hours. After about twenty minutes of inspecting the ground, I found my mind wandering to the TED Talk about 3D printing I'd watched the night before. But Kate, it seems, could search the city for edible plants all day.

Life on the family farm wasn't all monotonous labor, Kate tells me. "The freedom!" she shouts, eyes twinkling behind her thick glasses. "That was the best possible kind of education. The farm was my classroom, and my parents encouraged my curiosity." She would climb atop the pig house at birthing time. When she asked her mother where eggs came from, the next time her mother cut open chickens she showed Kate the different stages of egg formation inside the hens. Kate learned to stanch the bleeding in her cuts with a spider web. "It was normal to be a competent kid," she says. "I know how to do almost everything from scratch. On the farm, we didn't waste a thing. When we bought a tablecloth, we used it until it had holes, and then we cut it into napkins. When the napkins wore out, we used them as rags. When the rags fell apart, we put them in the compost. The weeds we pulled in the garden were used as mulch. We only went to the dump every couple of months. In the fall, we turned the pigs loose in the garden so they could root it up, fertilize it, and fatten themselves. And I know how to use every part of a pig so that the only thing you waste is the squeal."

On their farm, the chickens had ranged freely, eating insect pests and pooping nitrogen, phosphorous, and potassium into the soil. When Kate's father ended the birds' lives, he hung them by their legs; when they were suspended upside down, they stopped struggling. With a sharpened penknife he nicked their necks, severing their jugular veins. There is little panic and pain in bleeding to death. Kate says, "There is an art to killing animals. We've forgotten that art."

Toward the end of the 1950s, Kate's father saw the writing on the wall. Actually, he read it in the *Wall Street Journal*. You can take the man out of the city, but you can't take his newspaper away. All signs in *WSJ* pointed toward a collapse of the chicken business for small farmers. Industrial farming was rising, and its shadow was starting to fall across family farms. Kate's father warned his neighbors to sell their chickens as fast as they could. But most of them ignored this former city slicker with his fancy newspaper talk. He sold his poultry just in time. Kate explains that a few family farms with four thousand free-roaming chickens were replaced by a megafarm with fifty thousand birds packed into crates. The era of the factory farm, arguably one of the great environmental, human health, and community catastrophes in American history, had begun. Earl Butz, the brusque and bumbling Secretary of Agriculture in the Nixon administration, advised farmers: "Get big or get out." And he urged them to plant commodity crops "from fencerow to fencerow."

Before "progress" shut down Kate's family farm, the pigs shared a half-acre pen. Within this sprawling pig estate, they found the lowest place in the pen and did their business there. Each generation of pigs went to that corner, and only that corner, keeping the rest of the pen as clean as a pigsty. "That's what pigs, given enough space, do," Kate explains. Her dad harvested their manure and spread it on the fields. When he heard fertilizer salesmen hawking their miracle products, ammonium nitrate fertilizers made from natural gas, he refused to listen. They had piles of perfectly good pig poop to make their fields fertile.

"I saw bluebirds disappear in the countryside around our farm," Kate tells me after I mention chemical inputs in agriculture. When her mother had read Rachel Carson's *Silent Spring* and explained Carson's philosophy to Kate, her young mind began to appreciate how connected everything is, and how dangerous it is to think we can outwit nature with chemicals. "I cried when I saw the first bluebird in New York after they'd been gone for so many years," she says. Which reminds me: I've been meaning to ask her about the risk posed by ingesting chemicals on foraged weeds. But first I need to know how she ended up in Denver.

"I'VE BEEN YANKED AROUND by life," Kate tells me. She had married a man who worked for IBM, but one day when she was in the garden, she felt like she was suffocating; she left her first marriage, taking her three children with her. She started a wallpaper company. She worked as a lifeguard at public pools and became a professional organizer. She pumped gas. She served drinks at a bowling alley where she learned that on men's league night she should never wear a skirt. She taught guitar.

After fleeing the cold climate of New Hampshire with five children and her second husband, she landed in Tucson, where her second marriage ended. In order to feed her kids, she honed her skills as an urban forager, "shopping" behind supermarkets, salvaging edible food that the stores left out for whoever needed it. She was a freegan before freeganism (reclaiming and eating food that has been discarded) was a movement practiced by people committed to anti-consumerism. "I had very little money," Kate says. "But my children ate well and we never felt poor."

With her third husband, Kate moved to Thunder Bay, Ontario. There she earned an undergraduate psychology degree and a master's degree in clinical psychology. She worked with clients who had challenges from traumatic brain injuries. She explored the boreal forest of the far north and competed as a sailor. She smiles when she talks about photos of her on a foredeck putting up the spinnaker. "But one day when I was about to go to work, I burst into tears and realized I was burnt out on psychology." Fleeing the isolation and frigid temperatures of Ontario, she headed back to Tucson where one of her daughters lived. Surrounded by the strange plants of the Sonoran Desert—the cereus cacti that bloom in the night, the century plant that flowers but once at the end of its life—Kate envisioned a new life.

When two of Kate's daughters in Denver convinced her to leave the desert and move to the Mile High City, Kate did what she has always done after arriving in a new environment: she studied the lay of the land and learned what she could eat beneath her feet. Friends started asking her questions about edible plants. Strangers sought her out to pick her brain about fruit trees and greens. And soon she was leading walks through Denver to teach people about edible plants in the urban landscape. "The community recruited me as a teacher," she says.

Kate's sage advice about making the best use of the bounty that spills from city lawns and verges soon turned her into something of a celebrity among the city's locavores. What could be more in line with eating local than grazing on the greens growing next to your sidewalk?

"But how do you figure out what's safe to eat and what's deadly?" I ask. "Surely we can't encourage kids to eat weeds growing around their yards, right?"

"Oh, yes we can," insists Kate. And to prove her point she introduces me to Gia, one of her eight grandchildren.

WHEN KATE, GIA, AND I visit the backyard of the house where Kate lived until a recent move, Gia remembers the yard well. At age three, Gia was tagging along with her Nini on foraging walks around the yard. She once said to Kate, "Nini, I'm going to go outside and get some mint because my tummy hurts."

She'll be five soon, she tells me as she clings shyly to her Nini's leg. A crown perches atop Gia's head, and her frilly dress with pastel shapes like jelly beans, leggings emblazoned with bright diamond outlines, and sequined sandals, remind me of Kate's own colorful shirts and skirts.

Gia points out the mint plants to me. She tastes their leaves and tells me which one is peppermint and which one is catmint. Then she races through the grass, ricocheting between dandelions as if hunting Easter eggs. "I like every flower," she shouts as she twists back and forth, twirling her dress. "Purple is the best. And pink. And yellow is the best, too." Kate watches from a corner of the yard like a fairy godmother that spreads the magic of plants across the generations.

Kate's daughter and Gia's mother, Sarah Marcogliese, became a professional gardener. The organic apple didn't fall far from the tree. Sarah's company, Native Earth Landscape, provides custom garden maintenance for some very pricey private gardens: many cost a million dollars or more to create; Sarah has worked on three gardens with price tags of $2 million-plus, she tells me. Sarah and her husband, Pete, are committed to organic gardening—even when their clients aren't. This leads to "subversive organic." Owners of gardens who believe organic is hippie nonsense can walk paths through their thriving plants nurtured with natural alfalfa meal. They can admire the bountiful blooms and robust leaves of plants that have had their pests zapped with Spinosad, a natural product derived from bacteria. As long as Sarah and Pete deliver gorgeous gardens, whatever method they choose to use is fine with the garden owners.

As Sarah and I talk, Gia runs around the spacious yard of the urban homestead Sarah and Pete are establishing in Lakewood, a short drive from downtown Denver. They just bought a one-acre property with valuable water rights and plenty of room for vegetable gardens, chickens, ducks, and beehives. The family's long-term plans include planting every type of fruit tree that can survive in the climate and someday building a greenhouse where Sarah can grow citrus, mangoes, and avocadoes, making the family totally produce-independent. Pete hunts deer and elk to fill the freezer with meat, and sometimes the family purchases a quarter of beef from a local rancher. Sarah and Pete's urban farm echoes Kate's family farm in rural New York before agribusiness crushed her father's agrarian dream.

While I tour the grounds of the Marcogliese homestead, Gia pulls on her tiny gardening gloves and jumps in the trailer behind the tractor Pete is driving around the yard. On her lips are petals from a flower that Kate told her is safe to eat. "She's been taught to never put plants in her mouth unless she's been given permission," Kate explains. Without prompting, Gia grabs a hose and begins watering the flowers in plastic trays her mother is storing on the driveway to be planted in clients' gardens. Sarah tells me that her mother raised her to live lightly on the Earth and to eat fresh, locally sourced organic food. But when Sarah left home as a teenager, like all young people she craved a taste of the forbidden fruit. "After binging on Hamburger Helper and other junk I decided I didn't feel well. I went back to eating real food instead of processed stuff that made me sick."

When Gia kept coming home from school with stomachaches, Sarah suspected the cause was the food Gia was eating there, instead of eating the food that Sarah sent with her. "The school food tastes better than your food," Gia said. Sarah tried to explain how chemicals are used to make things taste so good they become addictive, and we keep eating them even if they are bad for us. "I don't understand," said Gia to her mom. "Why do they feed us food that makes us sick? I love my teachers." Sarah told Gia it wasn't the teachers' fault. But how do you explain the industrial food system to a five-year-old?

Urban foraging is about being tuned in to our environment—it's also about being tuned in to what is happening in our bodies, according to Kate. "I can tell what's going on in my body by what I'm drawn to forage. If I find myself foraging for a lot of dandelion, which isn't one of my favorite foods, I know my alimentary canal needs help." This does make sense from an evolutionary standpoint: our ancestors who ate the foods their bodies needed were able to survive and pass on their genes. Perhaps buried somewhere deep in the primitive structures of our brains are neural pathways that direct us toward the foods with the nutrients we lack, and our conscious mind goes along for the ride. Our cravings for the macronutrients of fats, carbohydrates, and protein—cravings that served us well in the lean environments in which our ancestors foraged— have to be curbed in this modern world of over-rich food. But Kate thinks we would do well to heed our cravings for micronutrients—the minerals and vitamins that we need in order to thrive. If you find your hand reaching for a leafy green, it may be a sign that your body needs beta-carotene.

Evolution has also equipped us with exquisitely tuned senses to help us avoid toxins. During a foraging walk, Kate demonstrates to the group how she approaches unfamiliar plants. She plucks a small leaf and holds it beneath her nose. She touches it to her lips. If she detects any strange smell or taste, she stops. If her senses trigger no alarms she takes the tiniest nibble, just denting the leaf with her two front teeth and touching it with the tip of her tongue, bringing into her mouth a bit of fluid. She waits a moment to gauge the reaction on her lips and tongue. If there is no bitterness or stinging, no astringency or tingling, she takes the smallest possible bite, chews it, and then spits it out. And again, she waits. She closely monitors her body for signals.

Kate explains that toxic plants will sicken you; poisonous plants will kill you. One category that she insists everyone steer clear of is parsley lookalikes. "Don't go there," Kate says, laughing. "Stay away from that." She points at lacy green leaves growing close to the ground and tells us they are harmless, as are the feathery leaves of carrots, parsnips, Queen Anne's lace, and young mustard plants—but these are difficult to distinguish from hemlock. "Think Socrates and suicide. Eating a rhubarb leaf will make you puke. Hemlock will kill you." Kate tells us she stays away from teaching about edible mushrooms, leaving that to professional mycologists. The consequences of making a mistake with mushroom identification, easy to do for the neophyte, can be lethal.

Some plants are better left alone not because they are toxic or poisonous but because they could aggravate a person's medical condition, Kate explains. Wood sorrel, for example, while giving salads a lemony lift, could worsen the symptoms of an individual with kidney stones, gall stones, or gout because it contains a lot of oxalic acid, as does spinach and Swiss chard. Some people in the group nod their appreciation of this knowledge; others take notes.

Kate tells the group that along with providing a garden of food, wild plants growing in the city offer a stocked pharmacy. Plantain grows low to the ground, allowing it to survive in mowed lawns; it can be used as a salve to soothe stings, scrapes, and burns. You chew the plantain leaves into what Kate calls a "spit bolus"—this process, unsurprisingly, amuses kids to no end. Kate says, "I love that word: *bolus*." The green, mucilaginous mass can be smeared onto sore skin: nature's Bactine in your backyard. Mullein's velvety leaves can be lit on fire and left to smolder in a "smudge," the smoke of which relieves the symptoms of asthma—something I learned from Kate, and also from Cattail Bob Seebeck, a legendary forager of plants. I also learned that mullein, because of its velvety softness, is known as "cowboy toilet paper."

Dandelion, a diuretic, also contains potassium. Doctors who prescribe diuretics to patients also prescribe supplements to replace the potassium that is flushed from their systems. The dandelion plant offers two prescriptions in one. Few plants provide the forager as much pleasure as the dandelion. According to Kate, who picks a yellow bloom from a scraggly patch of grass and holds it up for our group to see, this bane

of tended lawns was brought from the Old World on the May-
flower. "When the Pilgrims set sail from Europe they weren't
sure if they'd find any edible plants. They brought their dandelions with them." Kate explains that dandelion greens can
be boiled in salted water for three minutes to remove the bitterness, making them sweet as spinach. Every part of the plant
is edible. The dandelion can be made into medicine, food,
wine, cordial, and a dark coffee-like drink, yet we think the
dandelion is ugly in our lawns. *Maybe this says more about
our lawns than it does about the dandelion*, I think as I stoop
down to take a close look at this untapped food source I've
been trampling on my entire life.

Lawns provide soft places in the hard city where children
can play. In the parched West, our determination to grow
green grass in this semi-arid land that is, by nature's design,
the color tan (with the exception of a few lush months in the
spring and early summer) accounts for roughly half of our urban water use. Our obsession with the uniformity of lawns is
a holdover from rainier places in Europe where the greenest
and shortest grass was a sign of wealth and culture. As the
aristocracy dined on the whitest bread baked from processed
grains to demonstrate their wealth, so their clipped lawns became an emblem of the heights to which the civilized aspired.
Nature's diversity can be downright frightening when you
wander as a naked ape through the wilderness. Fanged snakes
coiled among tangled plants, insects in our food: danger once
lurked in every dark and weedy crevice, in every patch of vine-
wrapped shadow. To bleach our bread and subdue wild grass
was, at one point in our development, a reasonable response to
nature's deadly variety: It allowed us to exercise some control
over a world that could kill us in so many ways. The white
loaves and green lawns of Europe have become the Wonder
Bread and monoculture grass of American suburbia.

"Nature hates a monoculture," Kate explains when her audience peppers her with questions about how she identifies
plants that are safe to eat. She patiently explains that if she sees
plants she wants to eat growing in a public park, she finds out

if the city has sprayed chemicals on the gardens and grass. If she can't determine with certainty the spraying history of a place, she makes educated guesses. For example, if she spots a peach tree surrounded by weeds instead of a uniform lawn, she concludes that there has probably been no pesticide use, and she picks the peaches. If she sees a patch of identical plants, she suspects that chemicals are at work and she steers clear. If she sees only grass, she turns and heads the other way. If plants' leaves are shriveled or have what Kate calls a "crunkly look," she passes them by. She uses her nose, testing the air for the scent of pesticide.

Kate notes that plants growing near a propane gas tank are fine, but the area around a gasoline tank is no good for grazing because the liquid leaks into the ground. She seeks out plants that don't grow close to busy streets so they aren't saturated with auto exhaust, and she encourages foragers to rinse the greens they gather. And dog pee? Just sniff. Your nose knows. "Watch the neighborhood so you can note the dog-walking routes," says Kate.

Toxic sites in cities should always be avoided, of course. Kate encourages foragers in industrial zones to look up the city's Superfund sites online to make sure they are steering clear of areas contaminated with cadmium, lead, mercury and other heavy metals, or carcinogenic chemicals such as benzene and TCE. At first this all sounds horribly off-putting and makes me hesitant to try my hand (and palate) at urban foraging. But the more time I spend talking with Kate, and the more effort I invest in reading about what the ingredients in processed food do to our bodies, the less clear I am about what's more dangerous: a foraged dandelion from the city or Red Dye #40.

Kate's encyclopedic plant knowledge continues to astound me. She explains that the common mallow has leaves you can roll up like lettuce wraps and fill with guacamole or egg salad. While I nibble on the leaf of the common mallow plant plucked from the side of a street, Kate explains that Native Americans harvested a marshmallow for its sticky white substance that they dried and made into the original marshmallows—which are now made not from a plant but from concoctions of chemicals and corn syrup. Everyone in our foraging group murmurs our appreciation of this fact we just gleaned from Kate. The mallow tale concludes with a tirade delivered by Kate against the food-like substances that fill supermarkets. "That isn't food. That's poison." Kate's class of six rapt foragers nods vigorously in agreement.

In a nearby yard stands an apple tree. As we walk toward it, Kate explains that gleaning traditionally meant to gather crops after a harvest—picking grain the reapers missed, for example. Farmers would deliberately leave some grain and fruit in the field to be gleaned by those who were hungry but couldn't afford to purchase food, a practice codified in the Old Testament. Some farmers carry forward this ancient tradition by inviting community members to glean leftover crops from their harvested fields. But urbanites generally use *glean* to mean gathering food that isn't completely wild. Kate forages greens from a vacant lot but gleans apples from a homeowner's tree. When she sees a fruit tree in a private yard, she knocks on the owner's door and asks if she can harvest the fruit. She offers to leave some behind and to bring back jellies and preserves. "I almost always receive permission," she says. If no one is home, she leaves a sticky note and her card with her contact information and her tag line: Gleaner, Gardener, Grandmother.

Kate has developed an impressive following. Like dandelion seeds in a breeze, word has spread across the city of her prowess identifying plants. Citizens of Denver seek her out, asking Kate to come to their yards and let them know if a mystery weed is edible. "People who pay a fortune for elderberry tonics in a health food store to boost their immune systems might have elderberries growing in their own backyards." Plantain, the previously mentioned plant that makes a soothing salve, produces the psyllium seeds that are all the rage these days in gluten-free baking. Kate helps urbanites understand that a whole micro-universe of tasty and nutritious food lies beneath our feet: nature's plenty at the edges of overgrown sidewalks, a salad bar sprouting from every crack.

ONE MORNING WHEN I go outside, I decide to do some foraging in the field behind my house. I spot a clutch of wood sorrel and lick my lips as I sample the lemony leaves. The shape of the leaves resembles clover—wood sorrel, like clover, is a legume that fixes nitrogen in the soil. Kate taught me that the seed pods are known as sour pickles and taste scrumptious in salads. Next to the wood sorrel I find lambsquarters, which makes a tasty pesto. I spot some purslane, which has more omega-3 fatty acids than any other leafy green—more than some fish oils.

As I walk to my neighborhood coffee shop, I snag a few stalks of rye grass growing next to the curb and stick them in my mouth. I remember from Kate's class that the term *hayseed* comes from farmers chewing grass stems, which are rich in chlorophyll and provide a boost of energy to get farmers—and urbanites—through the workday. When I come home in the evening, I pluck some leaves of dock from an empty lot and make dolmas for dinner. I dip the leaves in boiling water to wilt them; then I wrap them like grape leaves around rice. The stems of dock form spears that look like asparagus and taste delicious when gently steamed, splashed with lemon, drizzled with butter, and sprinkled with sea salt.

How about some freshly gleaned fruit for dessert? In the old neighborhoods of many cities grow trees, bushes, and vines laden with unused produce. Early residents of cities sowed the seeds of this abundance a century ago or more as part of their food source. Now this bounty is available for the taking. In dead-end alleys cluttered with trashcans I find grapevines and berry bushes that fill my nylon sack to bursting. In abandoned lots I pick peaches and gather crisp apples from the ground.

"THE URBAN FORAGING I teach in Denver has completed my circle of life," says Kate. From an organic farm she came; to the world of wild food she has returned, after a middle time of going to college, raising children, and finding work.

As Kate and I sit and talk at Sunnyside Farm inside a hoop house covered in high-tech bubble wrap to protect plants from temperature extremes, I wonder if urban foraging is just a quirky hobby. Does it address big-picture problems?

"I can't stand the thought of food being wasted," says Kate. That Americans throw away 40 percent of their food upsets her. An organization in Denver called We Don't Waste gathers leftover food from restaurants and caterers in the city and then distributes it to community-based nonprofits that help feed the hungry. Some of Kate's friends go dumpster diving to harvest discarded edibles. Kate teaches people to make use of the bounty that is all around them.

Like so many other participants in the urban food movement, Kate offers her educational services on a sliding scale. She charges full price to participants who can afford her class, but she will teach anyone who wants to learn, no matter their income. "I want to help the homeless understand that they are surrounded by food," Kate says. "If people are looking for a way to eat healthy food, I'll find a way to help them." I'm reminded of the donation box at SAME Café, Alex's edible plants business in Elyria-Swansea, and Gabrielle's Garden farmstand, which I recently discovered.

Inspired by SAME Café, Candice and Jon Orlando, founders of UrbiCulture Community Farms, began selling some of the food they grew at Gabrielle's Garden on a sliding scale. Their farmstand in Denver's Santa Fe district posts a suggested donation price for each item of produce based on what it would cost in a commercial marketplace. The farmstand is located where neighborhoods with diverse income levels come together, where destitution meets gentrification. The generosity of patrons with the means to pay more than the suggested donation cancels out the deficits caused by residents who cannot afford to pay market value—the finances tend to balance out.

The edible garden has become a symbol of the urban food movement. But the sliding scale is just as emblematic of the movement, which is about empathy, as much as nutrition.

Sign up for one of Kate's urban foraging classes soon. She has never stayed in one place for long, and the ocean is calling. Kate tells me she loves the time she has spent in Denver teaching urban foraging to people in the city, but she misses the sea, and she thinks she might crew on a sailboat in exchange for room and board. It puts a smile on my face to know that wherever Kate Armstrong is in the world she'll be making the best use of the bounty around her, living lightly on the land and sea, teaching others to do the same, and making sure everyone has enough good food to eat.

Chapter 13
Eating Cactus

While tagging along with Kate on urban foraging walks, I learned that harvesting wild greens and feral fruit is a way of finding food in the city that doesn't require a lot of resources to produce and transport—hyper-locavorism. When I heard talk of Denverites eating prickly pear pads, I wondered if I had stumbled onto a strange form of masochistic dining: Was this the culinary equivalent of self-flagellation? Or was it a solution to the locavore's dilemma in Denver, a land of little water?

The prickly pear produces a sweet red fruit that I had picked on desert hikes and munched like a pear. But eating the spiky pads? The thought of devouring cactus was, however, easier to stomach for most people than dining on insects. Just after foraging with Kate, I had met some urbanites obsessed with eating crickets and other insects as a solution to our environmental woes. Word on the street was that mealworms were scrumptious toasted in the oven and sprinkled on soup. Insect eaters pointed out that some of the little creatures that squish beneath our shoes offer superb sources of protein. Whereas cows require vast acreage to thrive, mealworms and crickets can be raised in a box under the bed. But it's difficult to argue logically with the impulse of disgust buried deep in our brain, which was pretty well summed up by Jules in *Pulp Fiction*: "Hey, sewer rat may taste like pumpkin pie, but I'd never know 'cause I wouldn't eat the filthy motherfucker."

When John-Paul of Waste Farmers first mentioned his business idea of selling edibles made from cricket flour, I dismissed it as bizarre. Then a few months later when I was traveling in the Amazon Basin some of my Brazilian friends fed me roasted crickets and fried ants. We snacked on them like popcorn and peanuts and washed them down with beer. Not bad. Not bad at all. And I appreciated their protein when I went for long runs in the rainforest. Back in the States, I saw energy bars made from crickets on sale at Whole Foods. Twice the protein of beef and more iron than spinach! Were insects becoming cool? Had that boat already sailed? I figured I better get ahead of the curve and skip right to eating cactus.

AFTER HEARING FROM ARON of Kelly Grummons's skill at cultivating cacti, I meet Kelly at Timberline Gardens. He co-founded and co-owns this nursery in Arvada, a twenty-minute drive from downtown Denver. A customer from Nebraska arrived just before I did; he had driven more than three hundred miles to purchase some of Kelly's renowned giant yuccas. This seems less surprising to me after spending time with Kelly and learning that he is regarded as a legendary nurseryman in the West. Kelly is an impressively large man, and given a different temperament he might have ended up as a linebacker in the NFL. But in his growing space on Colorado's Front Range, his lumberjack size is scaled down by his impossibly tall plants. An agave with striped leaves at least six feet long catches my attention. Kelly explains that when he removed the gargantuan plant from its former pot with the help of a forklift, freeing the parent plant from its offshoots ("its babies," Kelly calls them) that were sucking it dry, the agave soon doubled in size. Kelly tells me that some agave species, such as *Agave parryi*, known as "Parry's agave" or "mescal agave," native to Arizona, New Mexico, and northern Mexico, flourish on Colorado's Front Range. Could I ingest a steady diet of tequila and agave sweetener and call myself a water-wise locavore?

The prickly pears Kelly is famous for cultivating yield fruit that is turned into a delicious jelly and a juice as sweet as strawberries, which is used by local chefs to flavor foods as diverse as barbeque sauce and sorbet. The fruit of the prickly pear, sometimes called a "cactus apple," also forms the basis of nutritious beverages sipped by locavores looking to reconnect with a plant that has served as a staple of indigenous people's diets for thousands of years. These foods are well within my comfort zone—what I really want to do is sink my teeth into a cactus's fleshy, paddle-shaped pads.

Timberline Gardens is located just a stone's throw from Waste Farmers headquarters—so while watching Kelly cultivate prickly pear, I can stack functions by learning about permaculture from Ash, listening to John-Paul's latest song and business plan, and getting a whiff of soil shamanism from Matt Celesta. What I've done to deserve such a rich mix of friends is beyond me, but it's an unexpected gift I celebrate.

On the grounds around the greenhouses Kelly tends is a building that looks like a one-room schoolhouse. Kelly teaches classes in gardening topics from composting to cultivating vegetables. He is always teaching, whether in the crowded classroom of the schoolhouse or while wandering the nursery to chat with customers and answer questions. His nursery is more than a place to buy plants—it's an educational center, a community resource where people gather and learn how to grow. When a man so tall he could play for the Nuggets asks Kelly which kind of carrot seeds he should buy, Kelly doesn't just point out a packet. He tells the man that to cultivate a long and slender carrot requires patience and planning. "If the soil is compacted the carrot will grow in contorted shapes," Kelly explains. "You have to loosen the dirt and dig down deep. To do it right, you want to build a raised bed above to give that long taproot plenty of room to grow."

The man leans forward, listening.

"Cover the seeds lightly with pulverized soil," Kelly continues. He moves his hands through the air, smoothing an imagined surface. "Then place a thin cloth over that layer so the seeds don't dry out, so they can germinate."

The man nods his appreciation of Kelly's craftsmanship.

"Oh, and to make the carrot sweet, you have to add phosphorous to the soil."

This person who came to the nursery to purchase a package of seeds has received an impromptu vegetable-growing lesson from a master horticulturalist, who as a child had experimented for endless hours in his family's garden until he learned how to grow the perfect carrot. Kelly's enthusiasm is contagious. I confess to not having previously rated nurseries high on my list of must-visit venues. But when Kelly is working at Timberline Gardens, try to pull me away.

Kelly talks to me as he waters cacti. He pauses to study the stream and then touches the soil's moist surface with the tip of a finger, a look of meditative calm crossing his broad face. He leans forward to inspect the flower of a prickly pear cactus. He says, "When I was a little boy, I watched my family drag metal chains across the ground with trucks to pull up prickly pear. It was so painful to see all those pretty blooms ruined."

Kelly was raised on the hardscrabble high plains of Wyoming. The family's property straddled the Wyoming-South Dakota border eighty miles from Rapid City. His father worked as a mechanic and clocked hours in oil refineries to make ends meet. As a boy, Kelly's father had been known for his talent breaking mustangs. As a man he was valued for his ability to manipulate machinery. The city boys at Kelly's high school played football; the country boys were into rodeo. The Cowboy State doesn't place a high value on Kelly's lifelong passion, the cultivation of flowers.

Kelly's love of horticulture did, however, have a practical

application. He helped his family boost the productivity of their food garden. His success raising championship plants with the local 4-H club led to a trophy being named after him when he left for college. "I never attended the Wyoming State Fair," Kelly says. "My family didn't have the money to send me. Neighbors would drive off with my carrots and turnips and come back with ribbons."

In seventh grade Kelly developed a science project by slicing the heads off cacti and grafting them to different bodies. His fascination with cultivating succulents in arid and semi-arid environments has carried forward to this day. He has traveled throughout the American West to study and collect native populations of cacti. "Most of my prickly pears are ornamental," Kelly says. "But I'm working on developing strains for edibility. *Opuntia humilis* is quite winter hardy. I'm planning to hybridize it with the Mexican nopal, *Opuntia ficus-indica*, which is sub-tropical. I'm hoping that the offspring will be more cold-hardy and larger than the *Opuntia humilis*, which is quite small."

If you want to eat locally grown food, it makes sense to know what thrives in the local climate. And it's a smart move to become friends with someone like Kelly who really knows how to grow.

"I KNEW I WAS GAY from the time I was born," Kelly tells me. "But I didn't have a name for it." Nor did he have anyone he could talk to about who he was. When he tried to speak to people, his voice caught in his throat. His heart hammered in his chest and his palms dripped with sweat. He was overwhelmed by the need to flee. He surrounded himself not with people but with paintings and plants.

In the town florist, Kelly found a role model. Kelly's mother told the florist about her son's love of plants; he agreed to let Kelly work for him as an apprentice. A gardening club scholarship provided Kelly the opportunity to leave the ranch and attend the University of Wyoming in Laramie. Then a student exchange program sent him to Colorado State University in Fort Collins, where Kelly earned degrees in horticulture, the science of growing plants, and floriculture, the science of growing flowers. When he was studying at CSU in the early 1980s, Colorado was considered the cut-flower capital of the world. A special variety of carnation that had been developed in the state was shipped all over the globe, but when graduates of CSU figured out that they could do it cheaper in Bogotá, the cut-flower industry shifted from Colorado to Colombia. The knowledge Kelly accumulated at CSU, this Harvard of horticulture, helped transform his passion for plants into technical mastery of all aspects of propagation and cultivation.

When Kelly finished college in Fort Collins and landed a job at a commercial greenhouse in Denver, heavy pesticide use was standard. He would don a spacesuit and breathing apparatus. Then, following the instructions given to him by his boss, he would blast away, blanketing all twenty acres of the nursery with Temik, a toxic pesticide, nuking all insect life. Among the legions of lifeless insects he would find dead birds, their beaks agape as they lay on flightless wings. "I was horrified," says Kelly. "But the greenhouse was one of the best in Denver, and that's just the way things were done."

When Kelly felt a lump on the left side of his chest, a mammogram revealed that he had a tumor. A surgeon removed the mass without complications and Kelly remained healthy. "But I couldn't get the tumor out of my mind," he tells me. "I had never known anyone in my family who had cancer before." It was impossible to prove that his exposure to pesticides had caused the tumor, but Kelly's suspicion was ever present. "I started to worry about all of the damage the chemicals were causing not just for me but other people. The workers at the nursery who handled the plants after I sprayed them in my suit and respirator got a lot more exposure than I did. And the customers who bought the plants—they were exposed to the chemicals, too."

The silent toll those pesticides were taking on the environment kept Kelly up at night. Not only were they damaging ecosystems, they were spawning insects that evolved resistance to the chemicals, forcing nurseries to use even stronger toxic concoctions. "I knew there had to be a better way," Kelly says.

As a boy on the ranch in Wyoming he had ordered organic gardening books from Rodale Press and used them to guide him through experiments. One of his first forays into organic pest control involved grinding up potato bugs (Colorado potato beetle) in his mother's blender to use as a natural insecticide. The experiment was a success: Kelly's creation repelled live potato bugs, a pest to the family's crop of spuds.

Folks in Wyoming say that if the wind ever stopped, the cows would fall over because they're so used to leaning into its push. The Siberian elm was imported from the frozen steppes of Central Asia to form living fences around homesteads on the high plains, anchoring topsoil from wind erosion and helping Wyomingites maintain a modicum of sanity amid the constant scream of prairie gusts. When these living windbreaks were put in jeopardy by an infestation of elm leaf beetles, citizens of the high plains scrambled for solutions. Word of Kelly's precocious genius with plants reached the ear of an elderly matriarch concerned about the plight of the trees, and young Kelly found himself explaining to the woman that dish soap effectively repels insects—that's what Kelly's grandmother had taught him. "She don't use no tabacca?" the incredulous woman asked. She shook her ancient head and showed Kelly a washtub filled with cigarette butts that she had brewed into a foul tea—a spray of this concoction could kill whole armies of insects. Kelly would later learn in college that chemicals similar to nicotine form the basis of some of the most widely used insecticides.

When Kelly started Timberline Gardens, he committed himself to avoid using chemicals. "I decided that if I couldn't grow it naturally, I just wouldn't grow it." In college Kelly had studied the use of predatory insects to control harmful pests, but he didn't know anyone who had put that knowledge into practice on a large scale. In his greenhouses at Timberline Gardens he observed tiny wasps that preyed on aphids. He would see aphids swell up; then a circular hatch would open on their backs. "It was like the lid of a tin can peeling open. Then a wasp would pop out." He began introducing more of the native wasps into the nursery to control aphids. He also started using nematodes, tiny roundworms that occur naturally in soil, to control the western flower thrips, an insect that gorges on fruits and vegetables in gardens. Kelly now purchases beneficial nematodes by the billions, which he applies to plants using a low-pressure sprayer so not to damage these minuscule creatures suspended in liquid. The nematodes disperse in the film of water sprayed on the leaves of plants to devour thrips.

Ladybugs, though efficient aphid predators, aren't used for pest control by Kelly, in part because they soon fly away but mainly because they are harvested from the wild instead of being cultivated in captivity. Kelly's condemnation of this practice caught my attention: I have a history of ladybug harvesting. While running mountain trails I would fill the mesh pockets of my shorts with live ladybugs I gathered from summits, where the glossy insects covered slabs of rock in bright ruby mats. When I ran back down to town, I would release the ladybugs in our garden, hoping they would deposit eggs before they moved on. With luck, their nymphs, which look like tiny black and orange alligators and are voracious predators of other insects, would devour the aphids that disfigured the plants. But my days of ladybug gathering are over: Kelly has convinced me to change my ways. Now when I stumble upon the startling abundance of a summit boulder covered in ladybugs, like some strange form of collage and each carapace a tiny jewel, I stop to admire these diminutive creatures that gather by the millions in high places. And when I return to the plains below, I kneel in the garden and spray the plants with a mist of dish soap while the ladybugs on the mountaintops remain untouched.

In part because of the time I've spent with Kelly, I have grown fascinated with insects, especially beetles. Beetles comprise a shocking one-quarter of all animal species on this planet. The armored bodies of beetles with their myriad defenses and elaborate designs seem part works of art, part miniature machines. Some are decomposers that break down our flesh after death and return it to the soil, reducing our bodies to polished bones.

Kelly explains that another natural substance effective at deterring insects is neem oil. It was discovered by serendipity in the wake of the world's worst industrial disaster. A Union Carbide plant in Bhopal, India (now owned by Dow Chemical Company) that manufactured pesticide exploded in 1984, exposing over half a million residents of shantytowns to toxic gas and chemicals, killing between fifteen thousand and thirty thousand people. When westerners went to India to mitigate the damage, one of them noticed that the Indian women on the train he was riding had healthy hair free of lice, while the heads of newcomers swarmed with the pests. An Indian on the train explained that to repel lice local women used oil from the seeds of the neem tree, a species native to the Indian subcontinent, in their hair. From this chance discovery in the wake of the world's worst chemical plant catastrophe, word of neem oil's efficacy as an organic insecticide spread. Nurseries like Timberline Gardens started using it as an alternative to toxic chemicals. Kelly says, "I have fewer insects now than when I used to put on a spacesuit and spray chemicals onto the plants so thick it was like powdered sugar on donuts."

KELLY, IT SEEMS, IS incapable of growing an ugly plant. He molds each cactus into a piece of plant art. When we take a look at his prickly pear gardens outside, I feel like all the plants he's shown me in the greenhouses were a prelude to this finale of color, this fireworks display he has coaxed from the dry flesh of the earth.

He tells me that on his family's ranch, after the tenacious cacti were decapitated with chains dragged by trucks, their roots remained intact. Each summer, when the yellow and red flowers of the prickly pear brightened dusty fields, he would squat down to watch bees work their way into the cupped beauty of the flowers. Now, as a seasoned horticulturalist, Kelly propagates over one hundred varieties of prickly pear, including many hybrids of his own creation, some of which he has bred to bloom multiple times throughout the year. Their flowers glow in the sunlight with a striking palette—bleeding scarlet and bold yellow, sassy bronze and flamboyant tangerine. And their pads look delicious.

I had read that right after a rain, the prickly pear pads, known in Mexico as nopales, are plump, juicy, and packed with nutrients. After my visit to Timberline Gardens I took a page out of Kelly's book and combined it with Kate's. I knew exactly where to forage for nopales—I had stepped into a patch of prickly pear while wearing flip-flops in a field next to my home and listening to one of Mostafa's stories. Mostafa and I had drunk copious quantities of saffron tea in his condo, a few doors down from mine; then we had taken my pale Labrador, Boo Radley, for a walk in the field.

As we walked, Mostafa told me he'd met a pretty young woman in a library. They exchanged glances and smiles, and Mostafa struck up a conversation. "She was a beautiful girl and I thought she was the one I had been looking for. I couldn't believe how lucky I was." He asked her if she wanted to drink wine but she said she didn't drink alcohol. "I told her I could make her saffron tea but she didn't drink tea." No coffee, either. What kind of person was this? "I asked her if she drank water. She said she would come to my home to drink water and she would bring machinery. I was studying mechanical engineering, so I thought of cogs and pumps. I thought maybe this girl was very strange." On the day she was supposed to meet Mostafa at his apartment, three men in suits showed up. "I learned a new word. *Missionary.* And I knew that this woman didn't want to go on dates with Mostafa. She wanted me to go to church and be a machinery too."

I had laughed my way off the path and into a patch of prickly pear. The long, stiff thorns I had easily pulled from my skin, but the tiny, hairlike prickles required tweezers to remove. After that, I had given the spiky bastards a wide berth. But one wet afternoon after visiting Timberline Gardens, those prickly pears started to look particularly plump. I watched a couple of YouTube videos at home and then donned a pair of leather gardening gloves and went out to the field. I gripped the nopales with barbeque tongs, severed them with a pocketknife, and carried home my prize in a nylon stuff sack. After using a kitchen knife to shave off the spikes bristling from the pads, I trimmed their tough outer edges, sliced them into strips, gave them a bath in egg batter, and rolled them in breadcrumbs. I browned the strips in a pan bubbling with olive oil and then wrapped them in tortillas garnished with tomatoes and avocado.

At my backyard table I feasted on fried cactus paddles that had traveled some three hundred yards from harvest to pan. They were as tasty as anything I've ever cooked. Faint praise, perhaps, given my track record in the kitchen. But beneath the oily crispness was a bright-green flavor reminiscent of garden-fresh string beans or bell peppers. Now, when I'm walking in the fields around my house, I stay close to the places I used to avoid to study the nopales, searching for sustenance beneath their spines.

KELLY'S SUCCULENT GARDENS taste succulent indeed. What ranchers saw as a threat and ripped from the earth of this nurseryman's childhood now offers us a way to eat in the West that exacts a faint environmental footprint. As climate change accelerates and the rivers that supply the western United States with water continue to dry up, Kelly's reservoir of knowledge about how to cultivate plants in dry environments becomes an increasingly critical resource in the region.

The heirloom tomato, that charming symbol of the food movement, is a water hog that evolved in moister climes and arguably has no place on the parched high plains, where sparse precipitation creates an environment more suited to cultivating cactus than tomatoes. In the place where gold-seekers settled in Colorado, the indigenous Arapaho and Cheyenne had pitched their tepees among sheltering cottonwoods that grew along stream banks. But these first Coloradans always moved on, following the shifting resources of the piedmont and plains as the seasons cycled. They knew better than to try to establish a permanent civilization in a land of little rain.

If those of us who have chosen to live in areas not naturally conducive to growing large quantities of food are to be honest about sustainability, then we need to dramatically alter our diets to include mostly drought-tolerant, seasonally grown foods. Otherwise, we are going to have to pack up our Subarus and head to the strip of lush land in the Pacific Northwest, or east of the 100th meridian, where rain falls with enough regularity to sustain crops without large-scale irrigation systems. We have wrapped the arid West in a Rube Goldberg scheme of pipework and dams, replumbing the region on a scale that has altered the very tilt and rotational speed of the planet. Our rivers have been reduced to tenuous trickles. To grow all of our own food locally on the Front Range, we will be forced to divert even more water from the Western Slope of the Rockies, requiring more dams and diversions, taming and draining the last of our wild rivers to fulfill our locavore's dream.

Switching from growing water-guzzling crops to drought-friendly plants in Denver and in metropolises from Phoenix to Las Vegas is a step in the right direction. Redirecting irrigation water from commodity crops shipped across the nation to nutritious foods distributed locally is a smart move. Greenhouses that recirculate water are a boon. But for large-scale commercial greenhouses in Colorado to grow food year-round, they have to be heated. In mountain towns such as Aspen and Jackson Hole, with growing seasons measured in weeks, not months, we must face the fact that enormous quantities of food will always have to be grown elsewhere and trucked in to feed the local population. Or we will have to rely on heated greenhouses perched high in frigid valleys and on the frozen slopes of mountains.

"We always condemn most in others...that which we most fear in ourselves," wrote Robert Pirsig in *Zen and the Art of*

Motorcycle Maintenance. I loved the years I spent in ski towns living on imported food. And it is easy to start an irrigated garden in a western metropolis and then rail against the rest of the world for its unsustainable ways—a trap I fell into as I became involved with the urban food movement. But as I thought about Kelly's prickly pear I realized that by choosing to make a life for myself in a western city, where precipitation, the most indispensable of all agricultural inputs, is in scarce supply, I have signed off on an inherently unsustainable lifestyle. Those of us who live in heated greenhouses should not throw stones.

Kelly's prickly pear strikes me as a more appropriate symbol for locavores in the arid West than the heirloom tomato. Just be careful of its spines when you forage for it beneath the cloudless sky.

ON MOTHER'S DAY KELLY and I sit on a stone bench at Timberline Gardens. Business has finally slowed down at the nursery after the sunny weather brought in a steady stream of people purchasing plants and seeking advice. One of the highlights of the day for Kelly was when he watched a woman smile and heard her say, "I like it in here. It doesn't smell like chemicals."

As we sit and talk, long rays of the late-afternoon sun illuminate the greenhouse. Kelly says, "This is the perfect place for me. I couldn't stand living in Brooklyn." As a boy he had walked everywhere, and he was always on the lookout for plants, for pops of color in the tan and olive land. The emerald lushness of the East Coast was overrated, he decided. The Rocky Mountain region is a hotbed of horticultural innovation, its crisp air and flood of brilliant light perfect for cultivating plants from the mountain and plateau regions that make up much of the planet's land surface. "I couldn't wait to get back West."

And thank goodness he returned. We need his talent raising edible plants suited to the local environment, his devotion to spreading organic techniques among urban farmers, and his commitment to cultivating beauty.

"The Lakota say their goodbyes to each other with 'walk in beauty,'" Kelly explains. "It means to walk in harmony with all living things." Each evening, after everyone else has left the nursery and only Kelly remains, he walks among the many rows of plants he has grown, this sprawling acreage free of toxins. "As long as I can maintain this," Kelly tells me, gesturing with his large hands at the life around him, "I will walk in beauty. If I can keep sharing this with people, I will keep moving forward toward my goals."

Chapter 14
Guerrilla Gardener

The next person I tracked down was as committed as Kelly to spreading beauty. But instead of cultivating plants inside greenhouses, Jimmy Bacon built illegal gardens and bombed the city with seeds.

I STAND WITH JIMMY AT the edge of a raised bed, sprigged with weeds and tangled with irrigation lines that vandals have ripped from the ground. A year ago, Jimmy fired up community members about this garden in Denver's La Alma neighborhood, where the crime and poverty rates are higher than city and national averages. He helped organize a crew to cultivate what's known as a "hell strip": the sliver of land between sidewalk and street, a growing space notoriously hostile to plants because of heat reflected from paved surfaces, lack of water, pedestrian traffic, dog traffic, and road chemicals. Residents of La Alma joined with Jimmy to dig the soil, construct raised beds with trellises, and install a system of irrigation lines hooked up to the hose of a nearby house in the night. Did Jimmy and his collaborators have permission to build the garden? Why was the irrigation system hidden from sight and detached from its water source in the light of day? Jimmy's answers are vague. These aren't the kind of details he likes to dwell on.

"There was so much food growing here," says Jimmy. "We harvested squash and tomatoes, greens…" His voice is lost amid the din of traffic and the sound of girders clanking at a construction site across the street. Locating a garden here on this strip of land between the sidewalk and the busy road seems about as likely as selling tofu at a tractor pull. But Jimmy tends to see things as they ought to be, not as they are. He's wearing a t-shirt emblazoned with the Statue of Liberty and the phrase "No Human Being is Illegal."

Jimmy has bluish eyes and sandy hair that curls out from under his ball cap. On his hat, instead of the John Deere logo you might expect from a guy raised in farm country outside of Lincoln, Nebraska, is NGOMBE. Jimmy explains that this is the Swahili word for cow and also the name of a Kenyan farm company. After studying colonialism and racism in college classes and exploring the topics on his own, he decided he had to go to Africa. One of his professors connected him with people in Kenya so he could start tackling poverty. "When I got to Kenya I realized how complicated Africa is." Tension between tribes had led to disparities in wealth and power similar to racism. He encountered Westerners who had "parachuted in" to poor regions of the country to develop farms and schools but had soon bolted back home, raising expectations among desperate people and then failing to deliver. "It's so easy to walk away from projects," says Jimmy. "And there's too much at stake in a place like Kenya to start something and not finish it. I realized that if I was going to do any good there, I'd have to become a pro."

Jimmy understood that to become a pro he needed to commit at least two years to learning about the country's many

distinct cultures, mastering a local language, and building relationships and establishing trust with community members.
Then he would have to deliver. "I felt guilty knowing that the
fifteen hundred bucks I'd spent on airfare could put a couple
of Kenyans through college," Jimmy says. "I didn't want to be
a dabbler." He headed back home to figure out how he could
create sustainable change in his own backyard.

Drawn to Denver due to the diversity of the inner city and
the inequities he saw there, so many of which were related to
food, he settled on the city's north side and considered enroll-
ing in a Master Community Gardener program through Denver Urban Gardens (DUG). This nonprofit organization, established in 1985, has the mission to work with Denver residents
to "grow community—one urban garden at a time." And that's
exactly what they've done. Surely the city would be a much different place—and much poorer in every sense—if not for these
sustainable, food-producing neighborhood gardens, thirty of
which are based at schools.

But Jimmy was young and ravenous for change. It can take
two to three years to get a DUG garden going; Jimmy wanted to feed people in Denver's food deserts *right now*. Denver
Urban Gardens, being a serious organization that achieves serious results, has plans, protocols, and paperwork to approve
projects. Jimmy went radical and, with some friends, founded
DRUG (Denver Radical Urban Gardeners). DRUG gave Jimmy
a quick gardening fix, but its long-term effects are a matter of
some debate.

Back in his DRUG days, Jimmy lived in an old boarding-
house. Attached to the bedrooms were mini bathrooms with
sinks but no toilets; these spaces were converted into bedrooms, and Jimmy and his comrades added more rooms in the
attic. Twenty-five people lived in the house, which its residents
dubbed The Pitchfork. On a vacant lot behind the building,
against the wishes of the property owner, they began guerrilla
gardening; and amid the graffiti-covered alleyways and busy
streets they reaped a bountiful harvest of amaranth and kale.
Basketfuls of cucumbers and carrots were carried past sagging

chain-link fences and windrows of litter into The Pitchfork to feed its residents, along with a constant stream of Food Not Bombs members from out of town.

Food Not Bombs, an all-volunteer global grassroots movement, serves free vegetarian meals in public places. Members of the movement have no tolerance for hunger in the face of abundance. Much of the food they serve comes from supermarket surplus that would otherwise go to waste. Their free meal events take place out in the open so everyone can see—a subtle form of protest against corporate and government priorities that lead to poverty and war.

Eventually The Pitchfork cleared out. "We had two problems," Jimmy says. "One was bedbugs. The other problem was that half the people at the house were committed to activism but the other half were just into hanging out and partying."

The owner of the vacant lot took a lawnmower to Jimmy's first guerrilla garden, and so ended the utopian experiment of The Pitchfork. But that didn't dampen Jimmy's enthusiasm for putting neglected land to use and growing food free for the taking. He started throwing bombs.

Seed bombs are a signature tool of the guerrilla gardener. Also known as "seed balls" and "green grenades," seed bombs are designed to be tossed onto neglected earth, causing explosions of life in dead patches of ground. The classic clay-based seed ball is credited to Masanobu Fukuoka, a Japanese farmer and philosopher who has become a legendary figure in the worlds of sustainable agriculture and permaculture. His seminal book, *The One-Straw Revolution*, first published in 1975, has been translated into more than twenty languages. Fukuoka advocated an approach known as "natural farming," which makes optimal use of the local environment, avoids tilling and chemical use, and celebrates the practices of indigenous cultures. His natural farming philosophy provides a spiritual and aesthetic approach to life that is as much about cultivating human beings as it is about raising crops.

Fukuoka's seed-ball recipe of compost, clay, and seeds was borrowed from an ancient practice. Seeds were mixed with humus or compost and then rolled in clay to form balls, giving the seeds the substances to encourage germination when the balls were thrown into fields. Modern guerrilla gardeners have tweaked the recipes into various concoctions and have built bombs in several sizes and shapes (one popular design looks like a 9mm pistol). Guerrilla gardeners throw the seed bombs onto ground that is difficult to access due to physical or legal barriers.

When I ask Jimmy what books have influenced his thinking, his second answer, after *Pedagogy of the Oppressed*, surprises me: *1491*. Subtitled *New Revelations of the Americas Before Columbus*, Charles C. Mann's work chronicles human civilization in the Americas before Europeans arrived and wreaked havoc with germs. One of the central revelations of the book is how the sophisticated cultures of the Native Americans, far more populous than previously presumed, reengineered landscapes for thousands of years, mostly with fire. In essence, the "pristine" wilderness of the Americas is a western construct with little basis in reality. The Americas were more managed gardens than nature preserves before Europeans arrived.

Jimmy points out that one of the most significant changes caused by humans currently taking place across the planet is desertification. Clearing, overgrazing, and unsustainable agricultural practices on drought-prone lands leave them stripped of life. Once established, these deserts are difficult to reclaim. Guerrilla gardeners have an answer. Seeds from vanishing habitats can be rolled into balls and scattered across denuded land, slowing the march of deserts. "Seed bombing in cities to fill vacant lots with crops is empowering," Jimmy explains. "Our cities make us feel small and powerless. By scattering seeds we can exercise control over our surroundings. We can transform the landscape in a way that benefits hungry people, like human beings have been doing for ages."

During the Occupy Denver movement in 2011, Jimmy spearheaded an effort to make hundreds of seed balls, and he gave them away, encouraging armies of the outraged to carpet-bomb the city. He had big plans for an Occupy Denver guerrilla gardening event at Civic Center Park—mobs gathering in the night with pitchforks, people hauling gardening supplies in bike trailers. Farming armies didn't storm the space on the scale Jimmy had imagined, but he did manage to pull off one "flash garden" by quickly digging a bed in the park, filling it with manure, covering it with leaves and topsoil, and then planting some carrots and radishes. The fate of this illegal garden in the heart of downtown is unclear to Jimmy. He doesn't think there's anything growing there now. "It was kind of naïve," he admits. "But fun. And if it helps start a conversation about food, then that's a good thing."

Guerrilla gardens in parks and along streets prompt people to think about the purpose of public space and challenge traditional ideas of beauty in much the same way that street art does. Is it acceptable to have pretty parks filled with ornamental plants when people are hungry? Should scarce resources be used to grow grass? Should all of our public gardens be edible? One guerrilla gardener told me, "Cultivating food in plain sight in cities is performance art at its most powerful. An illegal garden is graffiti that grows."

For many of us, finding a parking spot at Safeway is the greatest challenge we face in securing our food. Before I met Jimmy, guerrilla gardening struck me as unlikely to topple the industrial food system and feed hordes of hungry people. But if guerrilla gardening challenges citizens to think about the importance of food, perhaps these acts of benevolent criminality can stimulate public discussion about how we should feed ourselves in ways that foster the health of all people, and of the planet. That's a discussion Jimmy would very much like to have, and he'll keep throwing bombs to get it started.

How does Jimmy support himself? He orchestrates some impressive hustles to make ends meet. He says, "If you're going to be a guerrilla gardener, you can't have a regular job. You've got to get creative." A buddy hooked him up selling Christmas trees in New York City, and Jimmy came back to Denver with a wad of cash. He peddles burritos at concerts with two friends from Mexico, and they make a killing. "One of them is a wizard with Craigslist," says Jimmy. "He finds ridiculous deals on old vans and school buses." They fix up the vehicles and then use them for a transportation service, shuttling partiers around to concerts and bars and selling them burritos. Jimmy explains that his friends recently purchased skiing and snowboarding gear so they can take people on adventures in the mountains—and sell them burritos.

Because Jimmy's revenue streams are intermittent trickles, he finds ways to eat for free—gleaning fruit, for example. In an effort to map the fruit trees of Denver so residents could make use of this source of unused and nutritious produce, Jimmy's friend Pippin staged a pieathlon. Jimmy explains, "The event was a cross between a scavenger hunt, an alley cat—that's a race through the city organized by bike messengers—and a pie baking contest." Pippin gave all pieathlon participants a map of the city indicating the location of fruit trees. The pieathletes had a couple of hours to go out and gather fruit and then bring it back to a central location with a kitchen. "The low-hanging fruit was picked first," Jimmy says. "Kids climbed up trees to harvest fruit up high. The teams returned with plums, cherries, apples, and peaches, and they baked up a bunch of pies." Points were awarded for verifying the existence of the fruit trees already marked on the map and for adding the locations of new fruit trees. Bonus points were given for innovative strategies like enlisting the help of neighbors. And points were awarded based on the deliciousness of the pies, of course. Each participant left with a belly full of pie and a paper map marking Denver's fruit trees. The paper pieathlon map eventually became an electronic resource that people use to this day throughout Denver, adding notes to the digital file to direct foragers toward free sources of fruit, most of which had gone to waste before Pippin and the pieathlon mapped this abundance.

In addition to competing as a pieathlete, Jimmy shoots a mean slingshot. He goes often to the Pine Ridge Indian

Reservation, home of the Oglala Sioux, a subtribe of the Lakota people, to provide food support for political demonstrations,
for activist training, and for camaraderie. "I've got a reputa-
tion there among some of the younger warriors as a rebellious
wasichu—a non-Indian. Some of them call me 'Slingshot.' I
can do things on my bike in the city with a slingshot that people on the reservation do on a horse with a bow and arrow. But
I've *never* used my slingshot for violence against people. Only
against objects." Exactly which objects he visits with violence
he doesn't specify. Jimmy uses his slingshot to launch seed
bombs. Depending on the circumstances, he scatters seeds for
beautification purposes, for native plant restoration, and for
food justice. From his many Native American friends he has
learned which native plants he should grow in Colorado. He
writes this list for me:

> Saskatoon (native and edible), Rocky Mountain Bee
> Plant (native and beautiful), Amaranth (semi-na-
> tive, edible and beautiful), Sunflower (native, edi-
> ble and beautiful), Chokecherry (native edible, and
> when in bloom, exquisitely beautiful), Currants
> (some are semi-native, edible), Wild Rose (native,
> pretty flowers, medicinal parts and edible hips),
> and Prickly Pear (native, edible fruits, and some
> people think it's pretty).

Another tool in Jimmy's guerrilla gardening arsenal is a
backpack with mesh pockets. After a rainy spell he fills the
pockets with mushrooms and rides his bike on streets and
pathways, spreading billions of spores—another way to
stealthily produce food and rewild the landscape of the city.

Jimmy pedals his bike along the Platte River and Cherry
Creek bike trails broadcasting seeds by hand, throwing seed
bombs, and slingshotting seeds: a one-man seed arsenal. Explosions of corn, beans and squash seeds; bombardments of
tomato, tomatillo, and clover: vacant lots and verges turn to
war zones when Jimmy Bacon rides. During breaks in his

bombing raids he stops to talk to homeless people about edible plants, introducing them to an abundance of free food. Part trickster, part social theorist, part soldier of seed fortune, Jimmy is an amalgam all his own.

AFTER MOVING AROUND DENVER and starting some legal gardens and several guerilla gardens, Jimmy has finally found the perfect base for his operations. The little Victorian in the Cole neighborhood that he rents was built in 1883, has caught fire twice, and was trashed by junkies who may or may not have cooked meth there. However, the elegant posts of the porch and the gingerbread trim near the roof are still intact. On the front porch sits a bench seat from a car and a chair made from a metal tractor seat welded to a giant metal can. After the junkies moved out and Jimmy moved in, the landlord granted Jimmy and his roommates some rent-free months in exchange for fixing the place up. Inside the house, fresh coats of paint cover the walls, but the vacant lot that connects to the backyard still looks sketchy.

The blackened ring of a bonfire pit is scattered with cigarette butts. I hunt through the surrounding weeds for needles or meth pipes but my search reveals a decapitated doll, candy bar wrappers, chip packages, and beer cans, along with dark stains of dubious origin that rain has not dispersed. Bungee cords seem to be holding critical pieces of a car in place. It's not clear whether the car has been abandoned or is just parked. In the lot grows a beautiful crop of wild dock, which I wouldn't eat if you held a gun to my head. This is one of three lots around the house that are at the center of Jimmy's dream. "I imagine neighborhoods without property lines where all of the available space is used to grow food," he says. "Everyone contributes to the production scheme, and so much food is produced that no one is hungry."

This is an admirable dream, to be sure. As I try to visualize rows of raised beds filling the ten thousand square feet, a quarter of an acre, I can't conceive of mustering the stamina to follow this project through to completion. But Jimmy is a pro. He's in it for the long haul. He has mapped the empty plots of land and has sought out the owners. He's been granted permission by one landlord and been politely denied by another (and started tilling anyway). He has calculated the amount of wood needed to build raised beds ("a totally astounding amount," he says), and he has added up the tonnage of soil necessary to get the gardens going. A nursery in Denver has donated soil to his garden projects in the past, but on those occasions the loaded bed of a pickup truck did the job. To make these three lots productive he will need dump trucks, not pickups.

Jimmy's mind is always on the mower that the spiteful landowner took to his first guerrilla garden. He thinks he might fill the one lot where he hasn't been able to secure permission with pickle buckets. He can get the buckets free from Home Depot and grow tomatoes in them, making his guerrilla operation mobile. With a flash farming mob he could install the pickle bucket garden at night; and if the situation got heated with the landowner, he could relocate the buckets. He won't declare victory until the lot is filled with raised beds bursting with food free for the taking. But every war requires careful strategy and compromise, and a savvy guerrilla gardener knows which battles to fight.

Jimmy cites Brazil's Landless Workers' Movement (*Movimento dos Trabalhadores Sem Terra*, or MST) as one of the main sources of inspiration for his neighborhood-style guerrilla gardening. MST is a social movement that swept across Brazil in the dying days of the nation's military dictatorship as landless farm workers united to fight for agrarian reform. MST believes that land property should fulfill a social function, and big landowners shouldn't be able to hoard huge swaths of land, which in many cases were acquired through unfair means due to social inequalities. Jimmy says, "MST has organized the most marginalized people in Brazil to epically successful proportions." He sees his rebel gardening movement in the city growing into something roughly analogous to MST.

He tells me, "One of the reasons I'm talking to you is

because I'm probably going to get sued someday. Maybe your book will provide some cover for me. Some protection." For all Jimmy's pranksterism, there are some sobering consequences to what he does: He could, conceivably, be fined and spend time in jail. According to Jimmy, the crimes he could be charged with while trying to grow food to feed hungry people include trespassing and destruction of property.

MOST RESIDENTS IN JIMMY's neighborhood are Spanish-speaking; some of his neighbors are African American. Jimmy has talked with them about his plans to develop community gardens, and he says that most of them are on board. He acknowledges that convincing neighbors to support the idea of community gardens is relatively easy. "The challenge is to develop a production scheme in which everyone in the neighborhood participates. I'm convinced that part of the answer to getting people involved is aesthetics." He's sketched some designs of the gardens with raised beds doubling as benches and clustered together to invite groups to gather.

I ask Jimmy if he runs into any resistance because he's a white guy from rural Nebraska trying to organize change in an urban neighborhood of such racial diversity.

"I've spent a lot of time studying the effects of racism. The topic is always on my mind. But when I talk with people, I just talk to them like they're people. All of us have to eat. And nothing brings us together like food."

As Jimmy and I walk the streets, I watch him greet all his neighbors, from guys who look like gang members to seniors on bikes. His earnest smile brings cordial greetings in return. Though Jimmy has yet to build the gardens he envisions in the three lots around his house, he has already begun the gratifying work of becoming part of a community. He knows people's names, where they came from, what they like to eat.

"Growing food is incredibly hard," Jimmy says, shaking his head. "And getting communities organized takes a huge amount of time." But he's willing to make that investment. He

cites as one of his guiding principles "seven-generation sustainability": a concept attributed to the Iroquois that urges
us to consider the consequences of our choices seven generations into the future, roughly 140 years. If I remember the
meetings I have scheduled next week it's a minor miracle. But
Jimmy isn't kidding. His eyes are straining toward a horizon
that few of us can see. The more time I spend with Jimmy, the
more I start to wonder which scenario appears stranger when
we train our sight into the distance of future generations: me
driving my car to the grocery store, or Jimmy riding his bike
to scatter seeds.

Urban farming has been heavily hyped recently and Jimmy worries that guerrilla gardening is becoming trendy. These
days, starting a community garden often becomes a media
event. Jimmy is looking forward to a future in which cameras
don't need to roll each time a neighborhood breaks ground in
a place where citizens will grow their food together. Being a
decent human being shouldn't merit media attention. But for
now, it does. I hope there's a day when I don't have to write a
story about Jimmy because everyone I meet is as sincere about
helping each other as he is.

Jimmy tells me, "Tom Waits says that there are three
things—fast, cheap, and good. And you can only have two."
Jimmy explains that in his neighborhood there is plenty of access to food that is fast and cheap, but the food is not good.
South Central Los Angeles's Ron Finley, arguably the greatest
guerrilla gardener since Johnny Appleseed, says, "The drive-
thrus are killing more people than the drive-bys." In the areas of gentrification creeping toward Jimmy's neighborhood,
new residents can pedal their fixie bikes to boutique grocery
stores and get good food fast, but it is not cheap, and Jimmy's
neighbors cannot afford it. What they need is good food that is
cheap—and that takes time.

Together Jimmy and I stand in a lot, gazing at the vacant
space that surrounds us, imagining what could fill it. Jimmy
grins as he populates the emptiness with gardens in his mind.
He speaks of plans to make this barren land bloom by working

angles with people who have resources—landscapers with the tools to build beds, tree trimmers who can provide material for mulch. As we talk, plastic food wrappers scuttle across the ground and stick to the weeds around our feet. When the wind shifts I can smell the funky reek of rotting manure. Jimmy has a pile of it in his backyard. He is ready to amend the soil. He is preparing to build the fertility of neglected lots, however long it takes.

Jimmy has made a promise to himself and to his community that he will see his project through to completion. No matter if his guerrilla gardens are mowed over, no matter if they are shut down by the city, no matter if they suffer from vandalism or neglect, Jimmy will carry on. He will spread life in the abused land, scattering seeds in hope of growing not just gardens but relationships—relationships resilient enough to help his neighbors believe that their homes extend beyond their front doors, beyond their fenced yards, into the alleyways and empty lots, the common spaces where they can mingle and merge as members of a community in places that are now treated as dumps, but which Jimmy is convinced hold the potential to produce bountiful food.

Jimmy is smiling. On the coffee table of his house in the hardscrabble city is *The Encyclopedia of Country Living*. Day by day, he is scattering seeds and shouting hello to his neighbors—he is happy.

And so, finally, am I.

Chapter 15
Taking Over the World

A year ago, when Mostafa died and Aron convinced me to work as wingman at Waste Farmers, I went along for the ride. The more urban pioneers I met, from a rapper rhyming about brown rice and broccoli to a grandmother gleaning by the side of the road, the better I felt. Mine has been a harvest of people, and of hope.

There is one last person I want to talk with before my journey through the urban food movement comes to a close. When Shane Wright of Groundwork Denver says he works with at-risk youth—at risk of taking over the world—a young man named Carlos Macias is who he has in mind.

"YOU SHOULD SEE THE other guy!" Carlos jokes when I ask him about a bleeding cut on his cheek. He explains that he was helping build an obstacle course for bikes in a park near his house when he decided to test out one of the ramps. His jump went well; his landing did not.

As Carlos guides me on a walk through his neighborhood of Valverde, which I have passed while commuting on I-25 countless times but have never set foot in, he points out a fenced field. As a kid, he would sneak through a break in the fence and explore the landscape. "I liked to look at insects," he says. "Especially butterflies."

He leads me toward a park near his house. To call it a "park" is a bit of a stretch. There is one basketball hoop without a net. A tiny concrete court. A narrow strip of grass. I watch a crow peck at fast-food bags scattered around the street; the bird flies away with a ketchup package dangling from its beak. From a concrete curb I pick up the bullet casing from a .45. "Gang activity isn't too bad in this neighborhood," Carlos says. But he points out a house a few blocks away where Bloods hang out and sell drugs. "Three of my cousins got involved with dealing drugs."

I ask him if he'd ever gone down that road.

"I never really felt pressured to join a gang. But if I'd wanted to, it would have been real easy."

Through a student leadership program at his school, Carlos learned about watersheds and ecosystems and global climate change. He took part in a service learning project to build trails in parks and to protect native streamside vegetation. The student leadership program led to Carlos getting involved with The Greenway Foundation, a nonprofit that has transformed the South Platte River corridor from a junkyard and cesspool into an environmentally restored resource that provides beauty and recreation to residents of the city. The Greenway Foundation provided Carlos with opportunities to work outside his neighborhood, beyond the concrete and asphalt world he'd known as a boy. "I saw that there were other neighborhoods in Denver that had paths where people could walk and parks where children could play. I started to wonder why my neighborhood wasn't like that."

As we try to find a route past buildings and fences to the South Platte River, Carlos points out a fenced park with a locked gate. It's next to a police station, which along with a brand-new animal shelter and a pregnancy crisis center form a trifecta of attractive buildings in an industrial landscape. To navigate the neighborhood on foot we have to walk along concrete drainage ditches. Each time we cross an intersection I get a jolt of adrenaline more powerful than when I dodge my mountain bike between boulders. Walking through Carlos's neighborhood is an adventure sport—but the consequences aren't the bruised ego and cracked bones from smashing your snowboard into a tree. A person could get killed by traffic here.

As we wander the never-ending streets that surround a King Soopers distribution center, which seems roughly the size of Cincinnati, the driver of an eighteen-wheeler swings his vehicle wide to make a turn. He looks right at us and then heads straight for us. We jump out of the way to avoid being hit. I entertain thoughts of dragging the driver from the cab of his truck and inflicting bodily harm. Carlos laughs. "That's just the way people drive here. If you're walking, you'd better get out of the way fast."

"What about little kids?" I ask.

"They learn to pay attention and move fast. Or else they get run over."

In the twenty or so blocks Carlos and I walk in a couple of hours, we don't see a single crosswalk or a single pedestrian. Vehicles race by on concrete and asphalt streets stretching into the distance in every direction. Besides human beings encased in buildings and cars, there seems to be little life here. The occasional scraggly tree looks like an overgrown weed.

Carlos explains that while working with Groundwork Denver, he moved mulch to gardens. "I started to wonder if I could have a garden of my own."

Re:Vision, a Denver-based nonprofit with the mission "to work with people in marginalized neighborhoods to develop resident leaders, cultivate community food systems, and grow resilient economies," helped Carlos get started. They tilled the land in his backyard, showed him how to plant seeds, and loaned him a water storage and irrigation system. Carlos bought a hand saw and dismantled an old bunk bed;

using his dad's hammer and a handful of nails and some irrigation tubing to hold the pieces of wood together, he built a fence. The fence was key—it kept his family from stomping through the plants, Carlos explains. "My family is very destructive," he says, laughing as he leads me around his house to the backyard, which is cluttered with bikes and bottles and broken boards. Past an abandoned big-screen TV, I see the fenced garden. "We grew so much," Carlos says as he leads me toward the soil. "Tomatoes, potatoes, tomatillos, cucumbers, chilies, watermelons, pumpkins, corn, lettuce. Lots of lettuce." Carlos's dark eyes sparkle as he smiles. "But the garden took a lot of commitment. I had to plant and weed and harvest."

His family appreciated the food, but what really excited Carlos was building the garden. He bought sheets of thick black plastic to spread on the ground. On Craigslist he found free particles of smashed rock, which he had used in the past to surface trails in parks. With the skills he'd acquired through Groundwork Denver, he was able to create a path. His voice speeds up as he explains the process of shaping the path and constructing a garden fence with a door.

Carlos tells me he's living with his sister and her boyfriend in the house where he grew up; his parents are now living in Mexico. Immigration officers came into their home while searching for a person without documentation who had used the family's address. They found Carlos's father instead. He was deported. Carlos's mother, even though she had documentation, accompanied him to Mexico. "I couldn't do anything about my dad getting deported," Carlos says. "But I built this door after my parents left, and I worked in the garden every day. It gave me something to focus on."

Carlos and I walk into the garden through the doorway and he leads me down the path. He tells me that along with studying and attending class, he is working as a crew leader with Groundwork Denver. Each Friday he oversees a group of young people who are helping Ash build permaculture gardens on the grounds of Waste Farmers. "I think it's important for us to take care of the Earth," he says. "We keep consuming more and more of our resources—it's mindboggling how much we consume. I guess that's just human nature. We think about the present instead of the future."

I ask him if he thinks we will change.

"We're starting to think about the future, about how all of us can live on this small Earth. I want to be a part of this paradigm shift."

"What would have happened if you hadn't discovered The Greenway Foundation and Groundwork Denver?"

He thinks for a moment, and then he says, "I'd probably be working at McDonald's."

Carlos, now twenty, is studying at the University of Colorado, Denver. He got hooked on urban planning while constructing pathways and observing how neighborhoods are designed. He wants to keep building his knowledge and eventually become a college professor. "I think it's important not just to accumulate knowledge but to also share it with others. I want to help make this neighborhood better for children. I want this neighborhood and other ones like it to have parks and pathways and gardens."

He explains that his backyard garden gave him a sense of purpose, and he was proud of the food he grew and then cooked in his home. His diet includes more fresh fruits and vegetables these days because of what he learned while working with the soil. And in his neighborhood, edible landscapes are spreading. "This garden gave other people the same idea. Three of my mom's friends started their own gardens. It was good to see that. I think more people should be able to grow their own food. We rely on monocultures of crops. And if there's a problem, like an interruption in the fuel supply that shuts down transportation, then we have a crisis."

This is something I've heard from almost every person I've met in the urban food movement. From Nick the edible-garden entrepreneur to Ash the permaculturist, from Oz the crop mobber to Alex the gangster turned gardener—all point toward our overreliance on fossil fuels for food production as an immense challenge. Yet they are powered by relentless optimism. They acknowledge the gravity of the world's problems, and then they go plant in the earth of their local gardens and farms.

Carlos would like to see more and more global citizens becoming self-reliant by planting, harvesting, and preparing their own food. "Every edible garden is one step closer to not relying on grocery stores," he tells me. His backyard garden, seeded by Re:Vision, provides his family some control over their food, their health, their income.

I look around the garden. There doesn't seem to be much growing here now.

Carlos explains that as his schedule became busy with working, volunteering, and studying, he spent less time tending to his plants, and the garden's yield decreased. "But I feel good about the food I grew for me and my family," he says. "I know I could do it again if I had to. And knowing that makes me feel strong. Do you know what I mean?"

I know exactly what he means. Recently my mind has strayed from my garden to the stars. Call it relentless curiosity, call it ADD, but my focus has shifted from studying the microbes in soil to learning about the cosmos. Physics lessons delivered by Mostafa while we were hiking and drinking tea planted a seed in me—and now it's growing into a fascination with the people who probe the far edges of space. When I lose track of time reading about the Kepler spacecraft or the Oort cloud or some such thing, I pop a frozen burrito in the microwave and call it dinner. Plans for permaculture gardens and backyard chickens are still in my imagination rather than my yard. My gardening and eating habits have always fallen short of the virtuous bar set by many people I've met in the urban food movement. Now they seem to be slipping even lower. I have made some changes, though.

For the past year I've managed to treat meat as a celebratory item for singular occasions rather than a mainstay of my meals. And I have resisted the seductive ringing of Taco Bell while driving late at night. Most important, never again will I take for granted food or the people who grow it.

I feel strengthened by the relationships I've cultivated from this movement, the stories I've gleaned. Nothing I could have purchased, not a single item bought or sold anywhere in the world, could possibly have made me feel as good as I do right now. As I set out to interview scientists obsessed with other worlds, I am heartened to know that there are so many good stewards tending the gardens of this planet. And if there does come a day when the oil runs out and the supermarket shelves are empty, I'll know what to do. I'll head to Waste Farmers to gather my friends. Together we'll work in the soil, and together we'll grow.

Carlos and I walk down the path he created and we pass through the garden door. Carlos clicks it shut. As we step past the abandoned TV in his yard, he tells me, "I helped one of my aunties start a garden at her daycare. Me and my cousin, we had to dig down a couple feet through the soil because it was so compacted. We didn't really know what we were doing. We had to figure it out."

As we head down the street to check out the gardens spreading through his neighborhood, Carlos gives a grin so enormous it stretches his cheeks. "Making that garden for my auntie was really fun because when we were digging, all the little kids at the daycare got so excited. They were jumping all around us. They used their toy shovels to help us plant seeds."

Sources
and suggestions for further reading

Chapter 1: Saffron for Laughing

Albrecht, William A. *The Albrecht Papers*. Edited by Charles Walters. Raytown, MO: Acres USA, 1975.

American Diabetes Association. www.diabetes.org.

Argo. Directed by Ben Affleck. Burbank, CA: Warner Bros., 2012.

Dalby, Andrew. *Dangerous Tastes: The Story of Spices*. Berkeley, CA: University of California Press, 2000.

Darwin, Charles. *The Formation of Vegetable Mould, through the Action of Worms, with Observations on Their Habits*. New York: D. Appleton and Company, 1896.

Edwards, C. A., and P. J. Bohlen. *Biology and Ecology of Earthworms*. London: Chapman & Hall, 2005.

Galeano, Eduardo. *The Book of Embraces*. New York: W.W. Norton and Company, 1991.

———. *Open Veins of Latin America: Five Centuries of the Pillage of a Continent*. Translated by Cedric Belfrage. New York: Monthly Review Press, 1997.

"Guatemala." *Peace Corps*. www.peacecorps.gov/volunteer/learn/wherepc/centralamerica/guatemala.

Idiocracy. Directed by Mike Judge. Los Angeles: Twentieth Century Fox Home Entertainment, 2008.

Kinzer, Stephen. *All the Shah's Men: An American Coup and the Roots of Middle East Terror.* Hoboken, NJ: J. Wiley & Sons, 2003.

Lee, K. E. *Earthworms: Their Ecology and Relationships with Soils and Land Use.* Sydney, Australia: Academic Press, 1986.

"Maya Religion." *Authentic Maya.* www.authenticmaya.com/maya_religion.htm.

"Number of Americans with Diabetes Projected to Double or Triple by 2050." Centers for Disease Control and Prevention. www.cdc.gov/media/pressrel/2010/r101022.html.

Satchell, John E. *Earthworm Ecology: From Darwin to Vermiculture.* London: Chapman and Hall, 1983.

Schlesinger, Stephen C., and Stephen Kinzer. *Bitter Fruit: The Untold Story of the American Coup in Guatemala.* Garden City, NY: Doubleday, 1982.

Shafia, Louisa. *The New Persian Kitchen.* Berkeley, CA: Ten Speed Press, 2013.

Stewart, Amy. *The Earth Moved: On the Remarkable Achievements of Earthworms.* Chapel Hill, NC: Algonquin of Chapel Hill, 2004.

Waste Farmers. www.wastefarmers.com.

Willard, Pat. *Secrets of Saffron: The Vagabond Life of the World's Most Seductive Spice.* Boston: Beacon Press, 2001.

Chapter 2: Farming Waste, Growing Soil

Berry, Wendell. *The Unsettling of America: Culture and Agriculture.* San Francisco: Sierra Club, 1986.

"Center for Agroecology and Sustainable Food Systems." *University of California Santa Cruz.* http://casfs.ucsc.edu.

The Esalen Institute. www.esalen.org.

Ferdman, Roberto A. "Americans Throw out More Food Than Plastic, Paper, Metal, and Glass." *Washington Post,* September 23, 2014.

Flores, H. C. *Food Not Lawns: How to Turn Your Yard into a Garden and Your Neighborhood into a Community.* White River Junction, VT: Chelsea Green Publishing, 2006.

Fungi Perfecti. www.fungi.com.

Grace, Stephen. *It Happened In Denver.* Guilford, CT: TwoDot, 2007.

Gunders, Dana. *Wasted: How America Is Losing Up to 40 Percent of Its Food from Farm to Fork to Landfill.* NRDC, August 2012. www.nrdc.org/food/files/wasted-food-ip.pdf.

Hāna Ranch. http://hanaranch.com.

Harner, Michael J. *The Way of the Shaman.* San Francisco: Harper & Row, 1990.

Howard, Albert. *An Agricultural Testament.* London: Oxford University Press, 1940.

———. *The Soil and Health: A Study of Organic Agriculture.* New York: Schocken Books, 1972.

———, and Yeshwant D. Wad. *The Waste Products of Agriculture: Their Utilization as Humus.* London: Humphrey Milford, Oxford University Press, 1931.

Kolbert, Elizabeth. "Turf War." *The New Yorker,* July 21, 2008.

Lindbo, David L., Deb A. Kozlowski, and Clay Robinson. *Know Soil, Know Life.* Madison, WI: Soil Science Society of America, 2012.

McMillan, Tracie. "Shift to 'Food Insecurity' Creates Startling New Picture of Hunger in America." *National Geographic,* July 16, 2014.

Montgomery, David R. *Dirt: The Erosion of Civilizations.* Berkeley, CA: University of California Press, 2007.

Ohlson, Kristin. *The Soil Will Save Us: How Scientists, Farmers, and Foodies Are Healing the Soil to Save the Planet.* Emmaus, PA: Rodale Books, 2014.

Organic Cannabis Growers Society. www.ogcannabisgrowers.com.

Soil Foodweb Inc. www.soilfoodweb.com.

Stamets, Paul. *Mycelium Running: How Mushrooms Can Help Save the World.* Berkeley, CA: Ten Speed Press, 2005.

Waste Farmers. www.wastefarmers.com.

Chapter 3: Going Green, Living Bling

Allen, Will, and Charles Wilson. *The Good Food Revolution: Growing Healthy Food, People, and Communities.* New York, NY: Gotham Books, 2012.

"Artists, KRS-One." *Rolling Stone.* www.rollingstone.com/music/artists/krs-one.

"Ashara Ekundayo." *TEDxMileHigh.* www.tedxmilehigh.com/speakers/ashara-ekundayo.

Chang, Jeff. *Can't Stop, Won't Stop: A History of the Hip-hop Generation.* New York: St. Martin's Press, 2005.

DJ Cavem. www.djcavem.com.

Gregor, Alison. "In Denver, Beat Starts to Pick Up in a Once-Thriving Hub for Jazz." *New York Times,* August 20, 2013.

Harris, Kyle. "Beverly Grant of Mo' Betta Green Marketplace Talks About Urban Food Deserts and Urban Agriculture." *Westword,* July 31, 2014.

"Ietef Hotep Vita." *TEDxMileHigh.* www.tedxmilehigh.com/speakers/ietef-hotep-vita.

KRS-One. *The Gospel of Hip Hop: First Instrument.* Brooklyn, NY: PowerHouse Books, 2009.

Leonard, Andrew. "Ietef Vita: Rapping the Righteousness of Wheatgrass Juice." *Grist,* December 23, 2011. http://grist.org/sustainable-food/2011-12-23-ietef-vita-rapping-the-righteousness-of-wheatgrass-juice.

Piskor, Ed. *Hip Hop Family Tree, Book 1: 1970s-1981.* Seattle, WA: Fantagraphics, 2013.

Siebrase, Jamie. "'The Harlem of the West': A Page Turns on Welton Street." *Confluence Denver,* July 23, 2014. www.confluence-denver.com/features/welton_street_072314.aspx.

"Speaker, Beverly Grant." *Slow Money.* www.slowmoney.org/national-gathering/2013/speakers?id=BeverlyGrant.

The Sugarhill Gang. "Rapper's Delight." www.youtube.com/watch?v=rKTUAESacQM.

Wallace, Hannah. "The Freshest Prince: A Denver Rapper with Rhymes About Kale." *Oprah,* September 23, 2013. www.oprah.com/food/DJ-Cavem-Vegan-Hip-Hop-Movement.

Weismann, Brad. "Sweet Sounds." *5280,* May 2012.

Wenzel, John. "Neambe & Ietef Vita: Food, Music, Activism and Family." *The Denver Post,* November 7, 2013.

Wolf, Stephanie. "How Five Points Came to Be the 'Harlem of the West.'" *Colorado Public Radio,* May 15, 2014. www.cpr.org/news/story/how-five-points-came-be-harlem-west.

Chapter 4: The American Way

"Blue Bear Farm." *Colorado Convention Center.* http://denverconvention.com/about-us/sustainability/blue-bear-farm.

Cockrall-King, Jennifer. *Food and the City: Urban Agriculture and the New Food Revolution.* Amherst, NY: Prometheus Books, 2012.

Colorado Farm to School. http://coloradofarmtoschool.org.

"DPS Garden, Greenhouse and Urban Farm Program." *Department of Sustainability, Denver Public Schools.* http://sustainability.dpsk12.org/stories/storyReader$98.

Feldman, Megan. "Parks and Recreation." *5280,* May 2012.

Gardens for Growing Healthy Communities. http://rafimetz.com/gghc.

"Gardens for Growing Healthy Communities." *Denver Urban Gardens.* http://dug.org/GGHC.

GreenLeaf. www.greenleafdenver.org.

Groundwork Denver. http://groundworkcolorado.org.

Grow Biointensive. http://www.growbiointensive.org.

John Jeavons. www.johnjeavons.info.

Karnik, Sameera, and Amar Kanekar. "Childhood Obesity: A Global Public Health Crisis." *International Journal of Preventative Medicine* 3, no. 1 (January 2012): 1-7.

McIvor, David W., and James Hale. "Urban Agriculture and the Prospects for Deep Democracy." *Agriculture and Human Values,* February 2015.

McKibben, Bill. "The Cuba Diet." *Harpers,* April 2005.

Mercury Café. http://mercurycafe.com.

Philpott, Tom. "From Motown to Growtown: The Greening of Detroit." *Grist,* August 25, 2010. http://grist.org/article/food-from-motown-to-growtown-the-greening-of-detroit/full.

Produce Denver. http://producedenver.com.

Slow Food Denver. http://slowfooddenver.org.

"Slow Food Movement, Colorado Farm to School, Andrew Nowak." *TEDxColoradoSprings.* http://tedxtalks.ted.com/video/Slow-Food-Movement-Colorado-Far.

Slow Food USA. www.slowfoodusa.org.

Sprout City Farms. http://sproutcityfarms.org.

"Stop Subsidizing Obesity." *U.S. PIRG.* www.uspirg.org/issues/usp/stop-subsidizing-obesity.

UrbiCulture Community Farms. www.ucfarms.org.

U.S. Environmental Protection Agency. "Source Water Protection Practices Bulletin: Managing Agricultural Fertilizer Application to Prevent Contamination of Drinking Water." August 2010. www.epa.gov/safewater/sourcewater/pubs/fs_swpp_fertilizer.pdf.

Chapter 5: Spiraling Upward

Aranya and Patrick Whitefield. *Permaculture Design: A Step-By-Step Guide.* Hampshire, England: Permanent Publications, 2012.

Bane, Peter. *The Permaculture Handbook: Garden Farming for Town and Country.* Foreword by David Holmgren. Gabriola Island, BC, Canada: New Society Publishers, 2012.

Bloom, Jessi, and David Boehnlein. *Practical Permaculture for Home Landscapes, Your Community, and the Whole Earth.* Portland, OR: Timber Press, 2015.

Brock, Adam. "Perennial Crops, Perennial Cultures: How What We Grow Becomes Who We Are." *Permaculture Activist Magazine* 95 (Spring 2015).

Denver Permaculture Guild. www.denverpermacultureguild.com.

Dr. Joel Fuhrman. www.drfuhrman.com.

Fat, Sick and Nearly Dead. Directed by Joe Cross and Kurt Engfehr. Reboot Media / Bev Pictures, 2010.

Forks Over Knives. Directed by Lee Fulkerson. Virgil Films and Entertainment, 2011.

Fuhrman, Joel. *Eat to Live: The Amazing Nutrient-rich Program for Fast and Sustained Weight Loss.* New York: Little, Brown and Company, 2011.

———. *The End of Diabetes: The Eat to Live Plan to Prevent and Reverse Diabetes.* New York: HarperOne, 2012.

———. *Super Immunity: The Essential Nutrition Guide for Boosting Your Body's Defenses to Live Longer, Stronger, and Disease Free.* New York: HarperOne, 2011.

Fukuoka, Masanobu. *The One-straw Revolution: An Introduction to Natural Farming.* Emmaus, PA: Rodale, 1978.

Hemenway, Toby. *Gaia's Garden: A Guide to Home-scale Permaculture,* 2nd ed. White River Junction, VT: Chelsea Green Publishing Company, 2009.

Holmgren, David. *Future Scenarios: How Communities Can Adapt to Peak Oil and Climate Change.* White River Junction, VT: Chelsea Green Publishing Company, 2009.

———. *Permaculture: Principles & Pathways beyond Sustainability.* Hepburn Springs, Central Victoria, Australia: Holmgren Design Services, 2002.

Holzer, Sepp. *Sepp Holzer's Permaculture: A Practical Guide for Farmers, Smallholders and Gardeners.* East Meon, Hampshire, England: Permanent Publications, 2010.

———, and Anna Sapsford-Francis. *Sepp Holzer's Permaculture: A Practical Guide to Small-scale, Integrative Farming and Gardening.* White River Junction, VT: Chelsea Green Publishing Company, 2010.

Mollison, Bill, and Reny Mia Slay. *Introduction to Permaculture.* Tyalgum, Australia: Tagari Publications, 1994.

Permaculture Activist Magazine. www.permacultureactivist.net/index.html.

"Permaculture Articles by Paul Wheaton." *Richsoil.* www.richsoil.com/paul-wheaton.jsp.

Permaculture Research Institute. http://permaculturenews.org.

Permies. www.permies.com.

Pollan, Michael. *In Defense of Food: An Eater's Manifesto.* New York: Penguin Books, 2008.

Shein, Christopher, and Julie Thompson. *The Vegetable Gardener's Guide to Permaculture: Creating an Edible Ecosystem.* Portland, OR: Timber Press, 2013.

Wilson, Edward O. *The Future of Life.* New York: Alfred A. Knopf, 2002.

Chapter 6: A Cure for Affluenza

Ackerman-Leist, Philip. *Rebuilding the Foodshed: How to Create Local, Sustainable, and Secure Food Systems.* White River Junction, VT: Chelsea Green Publishing, 2013.
"Affluenza." *PBS.* www.pbs.org/kcts/affluenza.
Colorado Brewers Guild. http://coloradobeer.org.
Colorado Native Lager. www.coloradonativelager.com.
Graaf, John De, David Wann, and Thomas H. Naylor. *Affluenza: The All-consuming Epidemic.* San Francisco, CA: Berrett-Koehler Publishers, 2005.
Great American Beer Festival. www.greatamericanbeerfestival.com.
Hamilton, Clive, and Richard Denniss. *Affluenza: When Too Much Is Never Enough.* Crows Nest, NSW, Australia: Allen & Unwin, 2005.
Harmony Village. www.harmonyvillage.org.
Helliwell, John, Richard Layard, and Jeffrey Sachs, eds. *2013 U.N. World Happiness Report.* United Nations, 2013.
James, Oliver. *Affluenza: How to Be Successful and Stay Sane.* London: Vermilion, 2007.
———. *The Selfish Capitalist: Origins of Affluenza.* London: Vermilion, 2008.
Kingsolver, Barbara, Steven L. Hopp, and Camille Kingsolver. *Animal, Vegetable, Miracle: A Year of Food Life.* New York: HarperCollins, 2007.
Koehler, Lindsey. "Fruits of Their Labor." *5280,* December 2014.
Markus, Ben. "Local Hops Can't Keep Pace with Colorado Breweries." Colorado Public Radio, October 2, 2014. www.cpr.org/news/story/local-hops-can-t-keep-pace-colorado-breweries.
Mitchell, Kirk. "Colorado Inmates Catch Useful Trade in Raising Fish for Food." *The Denver Post,* January 3, 2011.
Smith, Alisa Dawn, and J. B. MacKinnon. *The 100-mile Diet: A Year of Local Eating.* Toronto: Random House Canada, 2007.
South Metro Urban Farmers. www.southmetrourbanfarmers.com.
Wann, David. *The New Normal: An Agenda for Responsible Living.* New York: St. Martin's Griffin, 2011.
———. *Reinventing Community: Stories from the Walkways of Cohousing.* Golden, CO: Fulcrum Publishing, 2005.
———. *The Zen of Gardening in the High & Arid West: Tips, Tools, and Techniques.* Golden, CO: Fulcrum Publishing, 2003.

"World Happiness Report 2013." *Sustainable Development Solutions Network*. http://unsdsn.org/resources/publications/world-happiness-report-2013.

"World Health Report, Chapter 2: Burden of Mental and Behavioural Disorders." *World Health Organization*. http://unsdsn.org/resources/publications/world-happiness-report-2013.

Chapter 7: So All May Eat

Coal Town Reunion. "Sittin' on John Wayne's Grave." www.youtube.com/watch?v=slWDZRbzZg0.

Colorado Transition Network. http://coloradotransitionnetwork.org.

Grow Local Colorado. www.growlocalcolorado.org.

Hamm, Catharine. "In Denver, SAME Cafe May Be Ultimate Example of Sharing Economy." *Los Angeles Times*, September 1, 2014.

Hopkins, Rob. *The Transition Companion: Making Your Community More Resilient in Uncertain Times*. White River Junction, VT: Chelsea Green Publishing, 2011.

———. *The Transition Handbook: From Oil Dependency to Local Resilience*. Totnes, UK: Green Books, 2008.

An Inconvenient Truth. Directed by Davis Guggenheim. Produced by Laurie David, Lawrence Bender, and Scott Z. Burns. Paramount Pictures Corporation, 2006.

"Libby Birky." *TEDxMileHigh*. www.tedxmilehigh.com/speakers/libby-burky.

Local Food Shift. http://localfoodshift.com.

Maher, Jared Jacang. "SAME Café: The Restaurant Where You Pay What You Can." *Westword*, February 26, 2009.

Mercury Cafe. http://mercurycafe.com.

"The Neurons That Shaped Civilization." *TED*. www.ted.com/talks/vs_ramachandran_the_neurons_that_shaped_civilization?language=en.

Produce for Pantries. www.produceforpantries.com.

Ramachandran, V. S. *The Tell-tale Brain: A Neuroscientist's Quest for What Makes Us Human*. New York: W.W. Norton and Company, 2011.

———, and Sandra Blakeslee. *Phantoms in the Brain: Probing the Mysteries of the Human Mind*. New York: William Morrow and Company, 1998.

SAME Cafe. www.soallmayeat.org.

Sprout City Farms. http://sproutcityfarms.org.

Thompson, Sheri L. "SAME Cafe: Denver Couple Cooks For the

Masses." *Huffington Post*, April 1, 2011. http://www.huffingtonpost. com/2011/04/01/same-cafe-denver-couple-c_n_843855.html.

Transition Network. www.transitionnetwork.org.

Chapter 8: Protectors to Providers

Aero Farm Co. www.aerofarmco.com.

American Horticultural Therapy Association. http://ahta.org.

Brasch, Sam. "Farming a Future for Veterans." *Modern Farmer*, July 22, 2013.

Christian, Sena. "Farming Could Save Veterans, and Vice Versa." *Newsweek*, November 16, 2014.

Circle Fresh Farms. www.organic-produce.co.

Committee on the Assessment of Ongoing Efforts in the Treatment of Posttraumatic Stress Disorder, Board on the Health of Select Populations, Institute of Medicine of the National Academies. *Treatment for Posttraumatic Stress Disorder in Military and Veteran Populations*. National Academies, 2014.

Despommier, Dickson D. *The Vertical Farm: Feeding the World in the 21st Century*. New York: Thomas Dunne Books / St. Martin's Press, 2010.

Dunbar, Brian. "Progressive Plant Growing Is a Blooming Business." *NASA*, April 23, 2007. www.nasa.gov/vision/earth/technologies/ aeroponic_plants.html.

FarmedHere. http://farmedhere.com.

Farmer Veteran Coalition. www.farmvetco.org.

Jefferson, Elana Ashanti. "From Guns to Greens: Iraq Veteran Digs into Hydroponic Food Growing." *The Denver Post*, May 9, 2014.

Kavilanz, Parija. "Veterans Farm Helps Heal Vets." *CNN Money*, April 5, 2012. http://money.cnn.com/2012/04/05/smallbusiness/veterans-farm/index.htm?source=linkedin015.

"National Center for PTSD." *U.S. Department of Veterans Affairs*. www.ptsd.va.gov.

Plantagon. http://plantagon.com.

"Redeploying the Family Farm." *Future Growing LLC*. https://futuregrowing.wordpress.com/2013/05/15/aerofarmco.

Tower Garden. www.towergarden.com.

"The Tricky Truth About Food Miles." *Shrink That Footprint*. http:// shrinkthatfootprint.com/food-miles.

"A Vacant Lot in Wyoming Will Become One of the World's First Vertical Farms." *Fast Company*, February 23, 2015. www.fastcoexist. com/3042610/a-vacant-lot-in-wyoming-will-become-one-of-the-worlds-first-vertical-farms.

The Vertical Farm. www.verticalfarm.com.

Veterans to Farmers. http://veteranstofarmers.org.

Weber, Christopher L., and H. Scott Matthews. "Food-Miles and the Relative Climate Impacts of Food Choices in the United States." *Environmental Science & Technology* 42, no. 10 (2008).

Chapter 9: Microchips to Crop Mobs

Berry, Wendell. *The Art of the Commonplace: Agrarian Essays of Wendell Berry.* Edited by Norman Wirzba. Washington, DC: Counterpoint Press, 2002.

Crop Mob. http://cropmob.org.

"Denver Crop Mob." *Slow Food Denver.* http://slowfooddenver.org/community-table/denver-crop-mob.

Denver Green School. www.denvergreenschool.org.

Frankl, Viktor Emil. *Man's Search for Meaning: An Introduction to Logotherapy.* New York: Pocket, 1963.

McLaughlin, John R., Leigh Weimers, and Ward Winslow. *Silicon Valley: 110 Year Renaissance.* Palo Alto, CA: Santa Clara Valley Historical Association, 2008.

Muhlke, Christine. "Field Report: Plow Shares." *The New York Times,* February 27, 2010.

O'Brien, Dan. *Buffalo for the Broken Heart: Restoring Life to a Black Hills Ranch.* New York: Random House, 2001.

Office Space. Directed by Mike Judge. Twentieth Century Fox, 1999.

Petrini, Carlo, William McCuaig and Alice Waters. *Slow Food: The Case for Taste.* New York: Columbia University Press, 2003.

Pollan, Michael. "Farmer in Chief." *New York Times Magazine,* October 12, 2008.

Rayman, Noah. "How a McDonald's Restaurant Spawned the Slow Food Movement." *Time,* December 10, 2014.

Slow Food International. www.slowfood.com.

Slow Food USA. www.slowfoodusa.org.

Smil, Vaclav. *Enriching the Earth: Fritz Haber, Carl Bosch, and the Transformation of World Food Production.* Cambridge, MA: MIT Press, 2001.

Chapter 10: Petroleum Geology and Home-grown Tomatoes

"American Lung Association Gives Sublette County an 'F' for Ozone Pollution." *Environmental Defense Fund,* April 25, 2013.

Bass, Rick. *Oil Notes*. Boston: Houghton Mifflin, 1989.

Bleizeffer, Dustin. "Despite Ozone Spikes, More Drilling Proposed in Wyoming Community." *WyoFile*, May 17, 2011.

"Fight Cruelty." *ASPCA*. www.aspca.org/fight-cruelty/farm-animal-cruelty/what-factory-farm.

Foer, Jonathan Safran. *Eating Animals*. New York: Little, Brown and Company, 2009.

Food, Inc. Directed by Robert Kenner. Magnolia Pictures, 2008.

GasLand. Directed by Josh Fox. WOW Company, 2010.

The Graduate. Directed by Mike Nichols. Embassy Pictures, 1967.

Gruver, Mead. "Wyoming Is Beset by a Big-city Problem: Smog." *USA Today*, March 8, 2011.

"Industrial Livestock Production." *GRACE Communications Foundation*. www.sustainabletable.org/859/industrial-livestock-production.

The Infinite Monkey Theorem. http://theinfinitemonkeytheorem.com.

Jacobson, Louis. "Rep. Dan Boren Says Most Domestic Oil Is Produced by 'Small Independent' Companies." *PolitiFact*, June 3, 2011. www.politifact.com/truth-o-meter/statements/2011/may/03/dan-boren/rep-dan-boren-says-most-domestic-oil-produced-smal.

Johnson, Kirk. "In Pinedale, Wyo., Residents Adjust to Air Pollution." *The New York Times*, March 9, 2011.

"Livestock a Major Threat to Environment." *Food and Agriculture Organization of the United Nations*, November 29, 2006. www.fao.org/newsroom/en/news/2006/1000448/index.html.

McPhee, John. *Annals of the Former World*. New York: Farrar, Straus and Giroux, 1998.

Old Major. http://oldmajordenver.com.

Owen, David. *Green Metropolis: Why Living Smaller, Living Closer, and Driving Less Are the Keys to Sustainability*. New York: Riverhead Books, 2009.

Pew Commission on Industrial Farm Animal Production. www.ncifap.org.

Pollan, Michael. "Farmer in Chief." *New York Times Magazine*, October 12, 2008.

———. *The Omnivore's Dilemma: A Natural History of Four Meals*. New York: Penguin Press, 2006.

Salatin, Joel. *Everything I Want to Do Is Illegal*. Swoope, VA: Polyface, 2007.

———. *Folks, This Ain't Normal: A Farmer's Advice for Happier Hens, Healthier People, and a Better World*. New York: Center Street, 2011.

———. *The Sheer Ecstasy of Being a Lunatic Farmer*. Swoope, VA: Polyface, 2010.

Tarbell, Ida M. *The History of the Standard Oil Company.* Edited by David M. Chalmers. New York: Harper & Row, 1966.

Yergin, Daniel. *The Prize: The Epic Quest for Oil, Money and Power.* New York: Simon & Schuster, 1991.

Zaitchik, Alexander. "Big Ag's Big Lie: Factory Farms, Your Health and the New Politics of Antibiotics." *Salon*, January 12, 2014. www.salon.com/2014/01/12/big_ags_big_lie_factory_farms_your_health_and_the_new_politics_of_antibiotics.

Chapter 11: Gangster to Gardener

"Ashara Ekundayo." *TEDxMileHigh*. www.tedxmilehigh.com/speakers/ashara-ekundayo.

Byrne, Hugh. *El Salvador's Civil War: A Study of Revolution.* Boulder, CO: Lynne Rienner, 1996.

Chester, Marvin. *Primer of Quantum Mechanics.* New York: Wiley, 1987.

Cordell, Kasey. "The Grocery Store Gap: Denver's Food Deserts." *5280*, July 5, 2013.

Coulter, Lindsey. "The GrowHaus Urban Farm Oasis." *EthicalFoods.com.* May 29, 2014. http://ethicalfoods.com/growhaus-urban-farm-oasis.

Denver School of Science and Technology. http://dsstpublicschools.org.

Greene, Brian. *The Hidden Reality: Parallel Universes and the Deep Laws of the Cosmos.* New York: Alfred A. Knopf, 2011.

The GrowHaus. www.thegrowhaus.com.

Heffel, Nathan. "Globeville and Elyria-Swansea: Gentrification Wary, But Looking For Change." *KUNC*, January 24, 2014. www.kunc.org/post/globeville-and-elyria-swansea-gentrification-wary-looking-change.

Midson, Lori. "Adam Brock, Founder of The GrowHaus, on Permaculture, Food Boxes and Modern-day Agriculture." *Westword*, September 18, 2013.

———. "GrowHaus Founder Adam Brock Weighs in on Permaculture Elitism." *Westword*, September 19, 2013.

"Seventy-Five Reasons to Love the West." *Sunset.* www.sunset.com/travel/best-of-the-west/best-of-the-west_43.

Chapter 12: Eating Weeds

Carson, Rachel. *Silent Spring.* Boston: Houghton Mifflin, 1962.

"Dandelion." *A Modern Herbal.* www.botanical.com/botanical/mg-mh/d/dandel08.html.

Falling Fruit. https://fallingfruit.org.

"Farmstands and Classes." *UrbiCulture Community Farms.* www.ucfarms.org/farmstands-and-classes.html.

Freegan Info. http://freegan.info.

Gibbons, Euell. *Stalking the Wild Asparagus.* New York: D. McKay, 1962.

Glausiusz, Josie. "Is Dirt the New Prozac?" *Discover Magazine,* July 2007.

Jenkins, Virginia Scott. *The Lawn: A History of an American Obsession.* Washington, DC: Smithsonian Institution, 1994.

Kennedy, Pagan. "How to Get High on Soil." *The Atlantic,* January 31, 2012.

Kershaw, Linda. *Edible & Medicinal Plants of the Rockies.* Renton, WA: Lone Pine Publishing, 2000.

Kolbert, Elizabeth. "Turf War." *The New Yorker,* July 21, 2008.

Lerner, Rebecca. *Dandelion Hunter: Foraging the Urban Wilderness.* Guilford, CT: Lyons Press, 2013.

Moore, Michael. *Medicinal Plants of the Mountain West.* Santa Fe: Museum of New Mexico Press, 2003.

Native Earth. http://nativeearthco.com.

Of the Field. http://ofthefield.com.

Philpott, Tom. "A Reflection on the Lasting Legacy of 1970s USDA Secretary Earl Butz." *Grist,* February 8, 2008. http://grist.org/article/the-butz-stops-here.

Runyon, Linda. *The Essential Wild Food Survival Guide.* Shiloh, NJ: Wild Food Company, 2007.

Seebeck, Cattail Bob. *Best-Tasting Wild Plants of Colorado and the Rockies.* Englewood, CO: Westcliffe Publishers, 1998.

"Sunnyside Farm." *Feed Denver: Urban Farms & Markets.* www.feeddenver.com/sunnyside-farm.html.

"Superfund Sites Where You Live." *EPA.* www.epa.gov/superfund/sites.

Thayer, Samuel. *The Forager's Harvest: A Guide to Identifying, Harvesting, and Preparing Edible Wild Plants.* Ogema, WI: Forager's Harvest, 2006.

The Urban Forager. http://urbanforager.co.

Watson, Molly. "Food Gleaning." *About Food.* http://localfoods.about.com/od/localfoodsglossary/g/Food-Gleaning.htm.

We Don't Waste. www.wedontwaste.org.

What Grandmother Knew. http://whatgrandmotherknew.com.

Zachos, Ellen. *Backyard Foraging: 65 Familiar Plants You Didn't Know You Could Eat.* North Adams, MA: Storey Publishing, 2013.

Chapter 13: Eating Cactus

"Adam Brock." *TEDxMileHigh.* www.tedxmilehigh.com/speakers/adam-brock.

Agro-industrial Utilization of Cactus Pear. Food and Agriculture Organization of the United Nations: Rome, 2013.

Carr, Anna, and Miranda Smith, Linda A. Gilkeson, Joseph Smillie, and Bill Wolf. *Rodale's Chemical-free Yard & Garden: The Ultimate Authority on Successful Organic Gardening.* Emmaus, PA: Rodale, 1991.

Cold Hardy Cactus. www.coldhardycactus.com.

Denver Botanic Gardens. www.botanicgardens.org.

Evans, Arthur V., and C. L. Bellamy. *An Inordinate Fondness for Beetles.* New York: Henry Holt, 1996.

Grace, Stephen. *Dam Nation: How Water Shaped the West and Will Determine Its Future.* Guilford, CT: Globe Pequot, 2012.

———. *The Great Divide.* Guilford, CT: TwoDot, 2015.

Martin, Daniella. *Edible: An Adventure into the World of Eating Insects and the Last Great Hope to Save the Planet.* Boston: New Harvest, Houghton Mifflin Harcourt, 2014.

McQuaid, John. "The Secrets Behind Your Flowers." *Smithsonian Magazine,* February 2011.

Pirsig, Robert M. *Zen and the Art of Motorcycle Maintenance: An Inquiry into Values.* New York: William Morrow, 1974.

Pleasant, Barabar. "Organic Pest Control: What Works, What Doesn't." *Mother Earth News,* June-July 2011.

Pulp Fiction. Directed by Quentin Tarantino. Miramax, 1995.

Rodale's Organic Life. www.organicgardening.com.

Shrivastava, Paul. *Bhopal: Anatomy of a Crisis.* Cambridge, MA: Ballinger Publishing Company, 1987.

Timberline Gardens. www.timberlinegardens.com.

Tozer, Frank. *The Organic Gardeners Handbook.* Felton, CA: Green Man Publishing Company, 2008.

Chapter 14: Guerilla Gardener

Colorado Native Plant Society. www.conps.org.

Denver Urban Gardens. http://dug.org.

Emery, Carla. *The Encyclopedia of Country Living,* 10th ed. Seattle:

Sasquatch Books, 2008.

Food Not Bombs. www.foodnotbombs.net.

Freire, Paulo. *Pedagogy of the Oppressed,* translated by Myra Bergman Ramos. New York: Continuum, 2000.

Friends of the MST. www.mstbrazil.org.

Fukuoka, Masanobu. *The One-straw Revolution: An Introduction to Natural Farming.* Emmaus, PA: Rodale, 1978.

Guerrilla Gardening.org. http://guerrillagardening.org.

Howard, Catharine. "Guerrilla Gardening: A Report from the Frontline." *The Guardian,* October 10, 2014.

Kettmann, Matt. "How Guerrilla Gardening Can Save America's Food Deserts." *Smithsonian,* June 19, 2013.

Mann, Charles C. *1491: New Revelations of the Americas before Columbus.* New York: Knopf, 2005.

Reynolds, Richard. *On Guerrilla Gardening: A Handbook for Gardening without Boundaries.* New York: Bloomsbury, 2008.

Robinson, Joe. "Guerrilla Gardener Movement Takes Root in L.A. Area." *Los Angeles Times,* May 29, 2008.

Ron Finley. http://ronfinley.com.

"Ron Finley." *TED.* www.ted.com/speakers/ron_finley.

Wax, Emily. "'Guerrilla Gardeners' Spread Seeds of Social Change." *Washington Post,* April 14, 2012.

Wolford, Wendy. *This Land Is Ours Now: Social Mobilization and the Meanings of Land in Brazil.* Durham: Duke University Press, 2010.

Chapter 15: Taking Over the World

The Greenway Foundation. www.thegreenwayfoundation.org.

Groundwork Denver. http://groundworkcolorado.org.

Jacobs, Jane. *The Death and Life of Great American Cities.* New York: Vintage Books, 1992.

Re:Vision. www.revision.coop.

Acknowledgments

I f Mostafa Salehi hadn't shared his meals with me, the topic of food would never have captured my attention. I am thankful to have received the gift of Mostafa's friendship before his heart stopped beating on Quandary Peak.

I didn't set out with a clear plan to tell the story of the urban food movement in Denver. Instead, I let this book grow organically. The people profiled in these pages are a small and somewhat random sample of multitudes pushing forward a movement. For example, had serendipity led me to Andrew Nowak early in my journey, I most likely would have written his story in full rather than merely mentioning it. This large-hearted chef who for fifteen years developed an innovative gardening and "food literacy" program with Denver Public Schools deserves a book of his own. I am appreciative of all the people in this book, and beyond its pages, who are pioneering creative solutions to help repair our severed ties to the natural world and to each other.

It took a community to grow this book. I am indebted to all of the people I profiled for sharing their stories with me. Aron Rosenthal got me started by talking me into winging it with Waste Farmers. When I went completely off the rails with this book—which happened more times than I care to remember—Aron helped guide me back on track. When I needed work, John-Paul Maxfield hired me in capacities ranging from mixing soil to chronicling his company's history. His generosity is much appreciated. Matt Celesta told me stories that demanded to be written, and so began my Year of Writing a Book about the Urban Food Movement.

A mind-bending conversation with sculptor Rik Sargent in his studio provided much of the initial momentum to get me started on a book of stories rooted in local soil. Shane Wright helped ignite my interest in urban farming by introducing me to Groundwork Denver's Green Team. Shane led me to Silivere, Alex, and Carlos, three young men whose stories motivated me to keep writing when I was tempted to abandon the book and go snowboarding instead. Alysha Havey Burney's positive response to an early draft helped me maintain momentum through the long slog of rewriting. The enthusiasm of Kerri-Ann Appleton, Kathleen and Jeff Hale, Rachel Hansgen, Blair Gawthrop Miller, and Kate Beaulieu provided fuel to help me power through to the finish line. Dana Miller stoked my enthusiasm for Denver's urban agriculture scene and helped me make crucial connections. She introduced me to Michael Brownlee and Lynette Marie Hanthorn, publishers of *Local Food Shift* magazine. I sincerely appreciate their enthusiasm for the book. I am thankful to Jessica George for introducing me to the concept of veterans transitioning into farmers. And I am grateful to my father for sharing his journey back to Vietnam and providing me with the most meaningful travel experience of my life.

Thanks to the following: Jason Hanson for sharing his beer scholarship; Adam Brock for sharing his passion for permaculture; Ian Davidson for sharing his composting and soil-building expertise. Many thanks to Beverly Grant, Jon Orlando, Candice Kearns Orlando, and Larry Sweet for sharing stories that inspired me.

I am grateful to the following organizations and businesses for the good work they do: Groundwork Denver, The Greenway Foundation, SAME Café, Denver Public Schools, Slow Food Denver, Slow Food USA, Slow Money, The GrowHaus, Re:Vision, Mo' Betta Green MarketPlace, UrbiCulture Community Farms, Sprout City Farms, Veterans to Farmers, Waste Farmers, Produce Denver, Granata Farms, GreenLeaf, Urban Farmers Collaborative, LiveWell Colorado, Denver Permaculture Guild, Grow Local Colorado, The Infinite Monkey Theorem, Denver Urban Gardens, Sustainability Park, Sunnyside Farm, Aero Farm Co., We Don't Waste, Produce for Pantries, Colorado Transition Network, Mercury Café, Native Earth, Timberline Gardens, Cold Hardy Cactus, Denver Botanic Gardens, Rocky Mountain Land Library, and *Local Food Shift* magazine.

I am thankful to the following people for reading and reviewing chapters: Aron Rosenthal, John-Paul Maxfield, Matt Celesta, Nick Gruber, James Hale, Anne Wilson, Ietef Vita, Lauren Blair, Ashley Harris, Dana Miller, Esther Premer, Jessica George, Buck Adams, Oz Osborn, Timothy Engel, Alex Sanchez, Kate Armstrong, Kelly Grummons, Jimmy Bacon, Carlos Macias, Tangier Barnes, and Shane Wright.

Bob Rosenthal read an early version of the manuscript and gave me thoughtful feedback. Kate Beaulieu graciously lent a hand with editing. Courtney Oppel provided diligent and thoughtful proofreading. My cousin Ilima Loomis, a talented journalist, also happens to be a stellar editor. Her advice was invaluable; the mention of the Oort cloud in the final chapter is for her. Also crucial was the editorial input of Mary Davidson, who did three months' worth of editorial work in three weeks to help bring much-needed order to the chaos of my prose.

I am deeply grateful to Allen Morris Jones for his

enthusiasm for this project and for his hard work to bring this book into the world.

My wife, Amy, not only had to survive the tempestuous sea of my tortured metaphors as my first reader, but also she had to put up with me as I struggled my way through this book, giving up on it and then starting again—sometimes several times in a single day. For more than fifteen years she has given me a reason to grow.

About the Author

WHILE CARETAKING A HOUSE where the poet T. S. Eliot lived, Stephen Grace studied novel writing with Stratis Haviaras, founding editor of *Harvard Review*. After his first novel was published, Grace moved to a trailer park in Laramie, Wyoming, in the wake of the Matthew Shepard murder, to work with at-risk youth and research a novel. To publish a book about the historical cartography of Colorado, he collaborated with Library of Congress curators and with Vincent Virga, called "America's foremost picture editor." To research a narrative nonfiction book about China he sought out experiences as diverse as photographing skyscrapers in Shanghai and trail running in Tibet. To write *Dam Nation: How Water Shaped the West and Will Determine Its Future*, a Colorado Book Award finalist, he followed rivers west of the 100th meridian and charted currents throughout the region's history. He served as a consultant for the film *DamNation*, which has won numerous national and international awards. He is the author of *The Great Divide*, a companion book to the film of the same name, about the past, present, and future of Colorado water. *Grow* is his eighth book.

CPSIA information can be obtained at www.ICGtesting.com
Printed in the USA
BVOW05s0739180715

408913BV00010B/57/P